Critical Images
The Canonization of Don Quixote *through Illustrated Editions*
of the Eighteenth Century

How did the tall, lanky Don Quixote and the short, stout Sancho Panza become staple figures of Western iconography so well known that their silhouettes are easily recognizable in Picasso's famous work? How did the novel *Don Quixote*, a parody of the romances of knight errantry, become a paean to the long-suffering, impotent nobility of its deluded protagonist? According to Rachel Schmidt, the answers to both questions are to be found in the way in which the novel's characters and episodes were depicted in early illustrated editions. In *Critical Images* Schmidt argues that these visual images presented critical interpretations that both formed and represented the novel's historical reception.

Schmidt analyses both Spanish and English illustrations, including those by William Hogarth, John Vanderbank, Francis Hayman, José del Castillo, and Francisco de Goya y Lucientes, and explores several of the iconographic traditions present in the illustrations: the burlesque, which focuses on the work's slapstick humour; the satirical, which emphasizes Cervantes' supposed didactic, Enlightenment message; and the sentimental, which highlights Don Quixote's purity of heart and purpose. Schmidt demonstrates that the illustrations offset the neoclassical criticism contained in the same volumes and reveals an intriguing variety of historical readings, highlighting the debates, controversies, and conflicts of interest surrounding interpretations of *Don Quixote*.

Dealing with such topical issues as canon formation, visual semiotics, and the impact of visual media on public opinion, *Critical Images* will be of great value not only to literary scholars and literary historians but also to art historians and those engaged in cultural and media studies.

RACHEL SCHMIDT is associate professor of Spanish, University of Calgary.

Critical Images

The Canonization of Don Quixote *through Illustrated Editions of the Eighteenth Century*

RACHEL SCHMIDT

McGill-Queen's University Press
Montreal & Kingston • London • Ithaca

© McGill-Queen's University Press 1999
ISBN 0-7735-1754-5

Legal deposit first quarter 1999
Bibliothèque nationale du Québec

Printed in Canada on acid-free paper

This book has been published with the help of a grant from
the Humanities and Social Sciences Federation of Canada,
using funds provided by the Social Sciences and Humanities
Research Council of Canada. Publication has been made
possible, in part, by a grant from the Endowment Fund of
the University of Calgary.

McGill-Queen's University Press acknowledges the financial
support of the Government of Canada through the Book
Publishing Industry Development Program for its activities.
We also acknowledge the support of the Canada Council for
the Arts for our publishing program.

Canadian Cataloguing in Publication Data

Schmidt, Rachel, 1963–
Critical images: the canonization of Don Quixote through
illustrated editions of the eighteenth century
Includes bibliographical references and index.
ISBN 0-7735-1754-5
1. Cervantes Saavedra, Miguel de, 1547–1616. Don Quixote –
Illustrations. 2. Cervantes Saavedra, Miguel de, 1547–1616 –
Criticism and interpretation. 1. Title.
PQ6335.S35 1999   863'.3   C98-901149-6

Typeset in Adobe Garamond 11/13
by Caractéra inc., Quebec City

To my family,
with gratitude for their unflagging support

Contents

Figures

Preface

Don Quixote and Sancho Panza have undergone the curious transformation from characters in a novel to visual icons to an extent unparalleled in the history of Western literature. Pablo Picasso's famous black and white painting of the pair, in which Don Quixote is depicted as a stick figure and Sancho Panza as a rotund blob of ink, encapsulates the graphic abstraction of the pair: the fragile, skeletal silhouette of the ethereal dreamer and the abundant girth of the man of the world. Most of our contemporaries recognize this duo in their contrasting figures and personalities even if they have never read the novel. Don Quixote and Sancho Panza wander far from the pages of Cervantes' novel though paintings, sculptures, ballets, movies, musicals, cartoons, and comic books in settings and narratives that bear little if any relation to the author's work. The phenomenon by which the two protagonists were either stolen or freed from the constraints of the author's work had already begun in Cervantes' lifetime. By 1613, eight years after the publication of the first part, Don Quixote and Sancho Panza roamed in a carnival procession in Leipzig. By 1614 an apocryphal continuation of the pair's adventures, written by an anonymous writer using the pen-name Avellaneda, circulated in Spain. Theatrical and prose adaptations continually appeared, at first gradually and then in a virtual torrent, in seventeenth- and eighteenth-century England. The curious pair were even given voice by Telemann. Cervantes himself responded to the reproduction of his characters in the second book of *Don Quixote*, published in 1615, in his typically ambivalent way. The protagonist Don Quixote refuses to follow in the footsteps of his spurious manifestation in the Avellaneda adaptation, and thus eschews the road to Zaragoza. When he actually meets a character from the other work, he requires the man to sign a notarized statement that he, Cervantes' Don Quixote, is the real one. Thus, the character Don Quixote expresses his outrage at the imitator and usurper of his fame, or notoriety, if one will. But the author Cervantes realizes that this too is the stuff of literature, and further deepens his exploration of the blurred and porous boundary between the realms of the imagination and reality by interweaving readers of the first part of the "original" *Don Quixote,* as well as the apocryphal one, into the second part of his own literary creation.

At times the characters' escape from the novel disconcerts me as much as it does any student of the text, for its subtle irony rarely, if ever, finds its way into the work's re-visions, whatever the medium. Cervantes' socially acute portrait of an impoverished gentleman and his ambitious but naïve sidekick often does not translate into other forms, not to speak of his sly, humorous, depictions of the many and varied persons they encounter in shabby inns, luxurious palaces, arid mountains, and dusty crossroads. The richly detailed and pointedly satiric tapestry of sixteenth-century Spain across which Don Quixote and Sancho Panza meander in the novel does not serve as the backdrop for modern adaptations, but rather is replaced by a nostalgically bucolic countryside or an empty horizon. This idealized setting stages the romancing of *Don Quixote*, in which the novel's content and characters are represented in broadly sentimental strokes. In this sentimental theatre, Don Quixote's love for Dulcinea may actually be reciprocated, given the worthiness of his heart and the fantastic transformation of the rowdy peasant, Aldonza Lorenzo, into a bourgeois sweetheart. The characters surrounding the noble sentimentalist find themselves similarly uplifted and enjoined in a round of comedic purification of spirit and wedding of souls. Gustave Doré's immensely popular illustrations, first published in 1863, continue to reproduce the ennoblement of the misunderstood Don Quixote, the sweetly loyal Sancho Panza, and the fantastically enthralling details of a world populated by knights and dames rather than pig herders and inn prostitutes. In short, Don Quixote's mad vision, the result of too much ingenuous consumption of chivalric romances, overshadows Cervantes' satiric puncturing of the genre. *Don Quixote*, the parody of a romance genre, becomes a romance in the modern popular imagination.

The second setting for the modern Don Quixote and Sancho Panza is the broad sky and empty horizon of Picasso's painting. Against an empty landscape the pair stand out as abstractions desperately seeking significance: the ideal versus the real, mind versus body, will versus desire, bourgeoisie versus proletariat. These readings of the text as a philosophical or theoretical work are, obviously, far subtler and more compelling than the romancing of *Don Quixote*. None the less, the ambiguous narrative play, the dynamic interaction of the protagonists, the finely ironic shadings of social interaction across boundaries such as class and gender, and even the overwhelming enchantment of Don Quixote's madness reflected in all the characters' behaviour are found lacking in these erudite approaches to the novel. The dialogue that enlivens the novel's play is reduced to dialectic. Yet this general approach to *Don Quixote* appeared in the eighteenth century and was in fact responsible for the canonization of the novel. Neoclassical literary critics and Enlightenment thinkers found the novel to be a satire rather than a simple burlesque and thus asserted Cervantes' involvement in the critique of literature and society through the text. The protagonist Don Quixote became the author's weapon against perniciously fantastic literature, irrational thought, and excessive enthusiasm. The novel *Don Quixote*, bolstered by these intellectual readers, gained a place beside the other greats of Western literature. The erudite, elevating interpretations of the neo-classical critics, expressed in both visual images and text, informed the de luxe critical editions of the eighteenth century that graced the bookshelves of the cultured thinking man. The German Romantics, who furthered these readings into the dialectics mentioned above, only took the further step of assimilating satire to speculative thought.

Significantly for this study, both the sentimental and the satirical interpretations of *Don Quixote* shaped the graphic and literary components of these eighteenth-century de luxe editions and, therefore, were integrally involved in the canonization of the novel. By closely analysing both components of these books, this study proposes, first, to revise the history of the reception of Cervantes' work, which until now has been focused on the German Romantic era as a major turning-point. When one studies these editions as a whole, considering that both visual images and critical writings represent interpretations of the text, the coexistence, conflict, and development of these readings in the eighteenth century comes to light. We see how the very attempt to champion *Don Quixote* as a worthy piece of literature required that the text be read as a discourse on abstract matters. In the visual medium of book illustration this approach manifested itself in allegorical frontispieces and classicizing portraits of the author. By the same token, artists seeking to represent the material according to the norms of history painting resorted to standard depictions of heroes as either classical figures or Christ figures, and introduced elements of valour and sentimental purity into the ridiculous figure of Don Quixote. Thus we glimpse how the transfer of material from one medium to another can bring about change that, while seemingly formal, affects the substance itself.

Secondly, this study highlights the productive independence of the illustration from the literary text as an interpretation that can even recast the narrative content into different generic forms. The iconography used by the artist becomes, most graphically, a rewriting through imagery of the text. The aesthetic, social, and even political interests that gave form to these rewritings, whether visual or literary, emerge from a consideration of the different interpretations juxtaposed in the eighteenth-century editions when they are viewed in the light of the editorial conflicts and historical contexts giving rise to the book's production. An edition such as the one published in 1780 by the Real Academia Española, produced in order to establish the work as the masterpiece of Spanish literature, unfolds in its astounding variety and surrounding controversy a moment of conflicting interests and opinions from which Cervantes emerged as the nation's rival to Homer. The editors wrote of displaying Spain's glory in the monumental edition, although a few sly illustrators undercut their nationalistic intentions by slipping in a visual pun associating Don Quixote, Knight of the Lion, with the shield of Castilla-León. The biographer of Cervantes and analyst of the text Vicente de los Ríos characterized the author as both a man of Enlightenment and a sentimental hero of the heart, and noted in the novel a satirical attack on pernicious romances and the perspectivist irony of the narration. One artist, Antonio Carnicero, fell back upon established iconography, emphasizing that Don Quixote's delusions were folly, whereas another, José del Castillo, introduced innovation into his images through subtle explorations of the dynamic relationship between the would-be knight errant and his squire. A few illustrators managed to slip in grotesque images harking back to the original burlesque reading of the text, but Goya's illustration mocking common sense and reason through an uncompromising depiction of two towns' mutual folly was rejected. The edition that finally established *Don Quixote* as the foundation of the Spanish canon was, obviously, not hegemonic in its production or its interpretation of the text, but rather an arena of conflicting perspectives and interests. Finally, then, in this study I wish to recast the discussion of canonization by discarding as simplistic and ahistorical the supposition that the process involves an imposition of a dominant class's values and interpretations on to a work and its readers. Instead, the canonization of a novel emerges from a period and society in conflict, in which various interpreters find (or perhaps create) in a text meanings amenable to their interests, be they literary, aesthetic, social, political, or intellectual.

As I reflect on my engagement with these editions, I realize that the images and arguments contained within are still compelling. Indeed, by slipping in as often unbidden companions in the seemingly solitary act of reading, they have compelled me to reimagine my own understanding of the text. Like my teachers and colleagues, they have initiated me into traditions of interpreting *Don Quixote*. Like my students, they have served as interlocutors with whom to explore the complexities and even perversities of the novel. They proceed from a brief period in which the popular laughter at the novel still echoed along with scholarly rumination, in which the wisdom of the fool had still not been sentimentalized to the point of cheap consumption. I am aware of the nostalgia that tints my vision, and have striven to overcome this myopia by keeping in mind the various contexts in which these images and interpretations were produced. This nostalgia for a golden age in which both sides of a dispute resided in uneasy truce within the covers of a book may represent several elements of my own situation. Like Don Quixote himself, I experience the modern yearning for a seemingly lost moment in which disagreement did not necessarily lead to conflict, for difference existed without inequality in a just society. These editions themselves clearly contradict the supposition that the eighteenth century was such a time, for both Hogarth's and Goya's images were rejected, and surprisingly harsh controversy surrounded literary interpretation and production. None the less, like Jürgen Habermas, I glimpse a social space, the public sphere, in which venom was occasionally transformed into the spice of differing opinion. For me, the de luxe critical edition, albeit the expensive mark of education and class, did at times serve as a public forum for the disinterested, spirited consideration of ideas and perspectives.

Acknowledgments

This work has been supported by many institutions, research libraries, and funding agencies. I wish to acknowledge the Faculty of Arts and Sciences and the Spencer Research Library at the University of Kansas for funding and supporting research that led to an exhibition of illustrated editions of *Don Quixote* in 1984. A year's fellowship to Spain from the Institute of International Education/International Telephone and Telegraph program allowed me to continue my interaction with this material in 1985–86. In 1990 I received support from the Department of Romance Languages and Literatures at Princeton University and the Institute for Cooperation between United States' Universities and Spain to return to Madrid for another four months of investigation. The manuscript was completed with a starter grant from the University of Calgary.

I also wish to acknowledge the libraries whose Cervantes collections I have consulted, in particular Spencer Research Library at the University of Kansas, the Biblioteca Nacional in Madrid, Spain, the Rare Books Collection of Princeton University Library, and the University of Illinois Library, Urbana-Champaign. The Real Academia de la Lengua Española and the Academia de San Fernando de Bellas Arte in Madrid also graciously offered me access to their files and records. Since this work represents the culmination of over ten years of research on the illustrated editions of Don Quixote, it is impossible to acknowledge all the individuals who have contributed in one way or another to the project. Special thanks go to the individuals at the University of Kansas who encouraged my early encounters with this material, especially Elizabeth Schultz, Linda Stone-Ferrier, Andrew Debicki, and Elizabeth Mason. I am also grateful to those who directed and read my doctoral thesis at Princeton University, in particular Alban Forcione, Margaret Greer, and Ronald Surtz. Jonathan Brown of New York University has kindly read and commented on the introductory chapter of this manuscript. I would also like to thank Joan McGilvray and Susan Kent Davidson of McGill-Queen's University Press for their patience and diligent assistance at a time when my energies were otherwise engaged. Needless to say, all errors contained within are my own.

A Note on Citations

According to the custom among Hispanists, all quotations from *Don Quixote* are cited in the text of this study by book and chapter, as, for example, (1:8). In the notes I refer to quotations from both Spanish and English editions by book and page numbers, indicated thus (2:526).

All illustrations in the editions are cited by book and facing page of text, since the illustrations themselves were rarely numbered, and are indicated thus (1:fp26).

All quotations from the Spanish text of *Don Quixote* are from Martín de Riquer's edition (Barcelona: Editorial Juventud 1979). All English quotations are from Samuel Putnam's translation, *The Ingenious Gentleman Don Quixote de la Mancha* (New York: Viking 1949).

Critical Images

Book Illustration as Critical Interpretation of the Text

Retráteme el que quisiere, pero no me maltrate.
Don Quixote 2:59

In the course of the second book (2:59) of Cervantes' *Don Quixote* (1615), Don Quixote meets a reader of an apocryphal continuation of his own story, issued anonymously in 1614 under the pseudonym Avellaneda. The misappropriation of his person understandably disturbs the "original" Don Quixote, who goes so far as to change his itinerary in order to avoid Zaragoza, site of some of his illegitimate double's adventures. Even in Cervantes' continuation, however, Don Quixote already rides in the shadow of his literary incarnation in the legitimate Part 1, and, alongside Sancho Panza, suffers adventures created for him by the readers of the first book, especially the Duke and the Duchess. These two noble readers, with too much time on their hands and too much power at their disposition, invent and carry out a series of fictitious episodes designed to mock the would-be knight's calling to aid damsels and to right wrongs as well as the would-be squire's ambitions to govern a state (2:30–58, 69–70). In both the author's own time and in his work, Don Quixote begins to multiply into successive and different manifestations as his readers devise witty plots and artifices to fuel his mission and keep his weary figure on the road. During the discussion about the apocryphal text (2:59), in which Don Quixote argues for his primacy as the original, Sancho and Don Juan suggest that no one but Cide Hamete Benengeli should be allowed to "dare treat of the affairs of the great Don Quixote."[1] Perhaps with a sense of exasperation, futility, vulnerability, or powerlessness, Don Quixote exclaims, "Let him who will portray me ... but let him not mistreat me."[2] With an ironic flourish, Cervantes depicts his literary creation Don Quixote, resigning himself to his reincarnation in a series of representations. Accepting this pronouncement as a challenge, succeeding generations of authors and artists have continuously portrayed the deluded knight.

PRINTING AND AUTHORITY

This study concerns itself with representations of *Don Quixote* in print, which by their very nature as re-presentations of the text call into question the authority of the same. Of course, the characters and versions of the plot have also been represented in carnival, theatrical, musical, and dance performances, as well as on film and canvas. Yet print reproduction of the text and the accompanying visual illustrations offer a particularly complex and fertile field of study for the critic who chooses to question the reception and canonization of the novel. More than any other early modern text, *Don Quixote* arises from and problematizes print culture. Eisenstein describes a whole web of changes brought about by the advent of print, which range from the appearance of the atomistic, silent reader to the power of the reader to establish market demands, from the creation of the professional author as a cog in the print industry to the Romantic myth of the alienated author, from the democratizing free flow of information to the propagandistic control of "truth."[3] Cervantes' *Don Quixote,* as a fictitious friend of the author states in the prologue to the first book, is an invective against the literary genre of chivalric romances, which took some of its material from the oral ballads and epics of the Middle Ages but was popularized and rendered ornately fantastic in the medium of print in the sixteenth century. The genre met the demand of the sixteenth-century Spanish minor nobility (*hidalguía*) for literature that served to romanticize the already archaic ethical code and calling of their own class.[4] If one accepts the declaration in the prologue as a declaration of authorial intent, as eighteenth-century critics did, Cervantes proposed to destroy this print genre, responsible for the artificial preservation of an archaic culture, through the publication of another book.[5] His weapon is Don Quixote, a once sane but impoverished *hidalgo,* Alonso Quijano el Bueno, driven mad enough by his isolated reading to put to work the antiquated system of values conserved in the printed romances of chivalry. The result could only be comic chaos at the expense of the main character's overblown and deluded self-transformation into a hero of a literary genre.

Embedded in the parodic levels of narration employed by the author in his parody remains the initial conflict between the antiquated manuscript and modern print cultures. An anonymous narrator appears at the end of chapter 8 of Part 1 to announce that the story has ended, and then narrates his search for the continuation, culminating in the discovery of an Arabic manuscript written by Cide Hamete Benengeli. The narrative fictitiously originates within the medium of the manuscript, smelling of the past and giving off the "aura" of authenticity. Cide's manuscript is valuable because it must be actively sought and retrieved from oblivion by the reader within the novel, to whom it will then offer the grail of rare and special knowledge. None the less, the authority of the Arabic manuscript depends on the rather questionable character of the author, since Arabs were considered by Spaniards to be notorious liars. Don Quixote, upon learning that the narrator of his adventures is a Moor, "was a bit put out that the author was a Moor, if the appellation 'Cid' was to be taken as an indication, and from the Moors you could never hope for any work of truth, seeing that they are all of them cheats, forgers, and schemers."[6] In addition, the authority of the translation depends on the questionable competence and reliability of a *morisco*, a descendent of the Iberian Moors, who completes his work in merely six weeks in return for a payment of raisins and wheat. The anonymous owner of this manuscript and its translation, purporting to have given an unquestioned, unmediated account of his search, then passes it into print. The whole series of fictive persons separating the reader from the "original" text serves to throw into doubt the very authority of the same.[7]

The printed *Don Quixote* is then available to all, to a community of readers that ranges within the novel from the Duchess to a poor student, including the innkeeper if he would care to set aside his chivalric romance. Samson Carrasco boasts to Don Quixote, "Little children leaf through it, young people read it, adults appreciate it, and the aged sing its praises. In short, it is so thumbed and read and so well known to persons of every walk in life that no sooner do folks see some skinny nag than they at once cry, 'There goes Rocinante!'"[8] As a collective, the readers acquire the power to demand they be provided with what they want. The Duke and the Duchess have the power to create more adventures for Don Quixote because they have the knowledge acquired through reading the novel to take advantage of his condition, and the economic and social authority to create their own charades. Others have to wait for an author and publisher to meet their demands. Avellaneda, the anonymous author of a spurious continuation, does just that by printing his imagined charades, thus stealing authority from the original author, Cervantes. In fact, the result of the whole web of encounters, between manuscript and print, Arab and Spaniard, protagonist and reader, Cervantes and Avellaneda, is to cast doubt on the authority of the author. Ginés de Pasamonte, the *pícaro*, may actually be the most astute manipulator of this new print culture, since he seeks to control his own fortunes by taking authority into his own hands – he writes his autobiography.

The history of the reception of *Don Quixote* and its canonization in the eighteenth century centres on the problem of authority. Those who sought to represent the novel as a classic had to buttress the authority of Cervantes in order to establish as his the parodic, didactic goals upon which their interpretation of the work according to a neoclassical aesthetic depended. Their conception of authority rested on the identification of the whole nexus of the creative production and interpretive control of the text with the will and work of an individual: in this case, Miguel de Cervantes Saavedra, whoever he may have been and whatever he may have wished for his "dry child."[9] This focus on the author certainly appears to be another result of print culture, for the venerated object of the manuscript did not require a known author to enjoy authority. As Walter Benjamin writes of the unique object,

The authenticity of a thing is the essence of all that is transmissible from its beginning, ranging from its substantive duration to its testimony to the history which it has experienced. Since the historical testimony rests on the authenticity, the former, too, is jeopardized by reproduction when substantive duration ceases to matter. And what is really jeopardized when the historical testimony is affected is the authority of the object.[10]

The book, reproduced by printing and seen as without its own history or *provenance*, appears to be inauthentic, lacking authority in itself. Although Benjamin's denunciation of modern technologies of reproduction errs towards a romanticized veneration of the "original" object as almost iconic in its spell, he voices a general objection that could easily have been directed towards the printed book. An object that is no longer dear thanks to its uniqueness must then have a unique creator.

Yet the very authority of the author is called into question by the narrative play in Cervantes' novel and by the tendencies of print as a reproductive technology to affect the production and consumption of the text. Alvin Kernan has attributed three tendencies, at times co-existing and at times contending, to what he calls print logic: multiplicity, systematization, and fixity:

The way in which these print qualities manifest themselves in the world can be illustrated most immediately and obviously with print's most characteristic product, the book: multiplicity – the printing press makes many different books and many copies of the same book; systematization – a book is systematically produced and internally ordered, and in existence forces the systematic structuring of knowledge; fixity – the book is objectively, durably, there, always the same or moving toward a "true" form.[11]

These terms are useful to this study, for they describe the tensions inherent in the production of *Don Quixote* as a printed text. Multiplicity casts the author's work into the hands of many different readers from many different cultures, yet unlike the manuscript, which still appears through its "aura" to belong to different times and places, the book takes on the form of whichever culture reproduces it. For example, the eighteenth-century *Don Quixote*s published in England contain not only translations into idiomatic English but also illustrations of Don Quixote and Sancho Panza as English gentleman and peasant. The very multiplicity of the book thus feigns a superficial universality. The author Cervantes is not necessarily a representative sixteenth-century Spaniard but rather a man of reason and heart whose work could be understood according to the "universals" of the Enlightenment.

Systematization further invites that the novel be read as a treatise, in which the reader discovers an ordered message transcending the narrative. Thus, eighteenth-century critics such as Gregorio Mayans y Siscar and Vicente de los Ríos ignore the complications of the plot in order to discern moral lessons and social observations basic to the systematic societal critique of their enlightened, *ilustrado* ideology. Implicit in this approach to the text is the assumption that the reader can step into the place of the author to view the text from his vantage point as a vehicle of communication. The systematization of the book, then, downplays the story in favour of the "meaning." Fixity, in an ironic twist, offers the reader the temptation to step into the process of reproduction and fix the text for posterity. The Real Academia de la Lengua Española, for example, undertakes in the 1770s to restore the text to its "original" state and fix it for posterity through an authoritative critical edition. Authority now belongs to the editor and critic, who amend the text in the stead of the author. The author Cervantes exists, then, as the mirror image of the authoritative reader.

In order to systematize and fix their interpretation of the text, these authoritative readers of the eighteenth century undertake a re-presentation of *Don Quixote* as a classic through their own activities in print. Indeed, the three tendencies of print signalled by Kernan shape the historical reception of the text largely through the tension between multiplicity and fixity. Multiplicity allows access to the text to different readers and interpreters, whereas fixity fuels the movement to classify and classicize the text. One can easily characterize seventeenth-century reception of the text, in which the characters Don Quixote and Sancho Panza often leave the text to walk on stages and ride in carnivals, and in which printing makes the text itself available to the growing literate sector, as an example of the power of multiplicity. One can just as easily characterize the canonizing tendency of much eighteenth-century reception, marked by the appearance of the de luxe critical editions published for the educated aristocracy and bourgeoisie, in which the application of neoclassical standards fixes the meaning of *Don Quixote* to the exclusion of the popular burlesque reading, as an example of the power of fixity.

PRINTS AS REPRODUCTIONS AND REPRESENTATIONS

This study also considers the effect upon the text's reception of another aspect of print culture, the visual image printed alongside the text as a book illustration. William Ivins's description of printmaking as the "exact repetition of pictorial statements" clearly states the characteristic of print images basic to the technology by which they are produced and which defines them as a medium.[12] The individual print is, like the text, fixed through the exact reproduction of copy after copy. Prints thus function in the dissemination of visual information, through maps, scientific charts and diagrams, or prints reproducing paintings, sculptures, and architecture. In the early modern period the printed image, like the printed book, made available to a much larger audience familiarity with the monuments of high art, the discoveries of scientific inquiry, or the landscape and cultural artifacts of distant lands. Reproductive prints, those representing works of art, were widely used in the instruction of artists and contributed to the establishment of iconographic and stylistic traditions. Rubens, Raphael, and Michelangelo, among others, became the models for artists who could never see their original work; thus the language of history painting, to cite a genre important for this study, was fixed after their examples. The book illustrations, like the reproductive prints, shared in the same tendencies towards multiplicity and fixity. Certain sets, such as those of Bouttats and Coypel to be discussed later in this book, were printed in numerous editions throughout Europe, circulated freely as independent images, and copied by "pirates" to the point that they became images well known to readers and influential to artists. Through their multiplicity, they fixed certain traditions for the representation of the novel.

These visual images communicate through their own systematic use of elements of visual meaning: for example, the play of black line on white page, composition, use of frames, comparison and contrast of individual figures, and mimesis or the lack thereof. Dark line against light page defines the contours of the images, just as it defines the contours of the letter of the text. But all the linear techniques of mimetic representation, such as scientific perspective, foreshortening, and contour shading are used by the engraver through the web of lines peculiar to the medium to create an image that is abstracted into black and white in order to achieve the illusion of mimesis. The visual image differs from the printed text in that it offers a representation of the narrative that is not merely a reproduction of an authoritative original. The act of representation implies that the illustrator and/or the other persons involved in the supervision of the undertaking make a series of interpretive decisions regarding the narrative.

Edward Hodnett maintains that the most important decision for the artist is the *"moment of choice."*[13] "Before an illustration can be drawn, therefore, two related decisions have to be made – the passage, in a limited sense, and the precise moment at which, as in a still from a cinema film, the action is stopped."[14] Taking the infamous example of Don Quixote's battle with the windmills, he lists four different possible moments: the argument of Don Quixote and Sancho Panza over the identity of the strange objects; the ride towards the windmills; the clash with them; and the aftermath, each of which can be subdivided into smaller moments.[15] In the case of this episode, the choice of moments is intimately linked to different interpretative approaches to the text. In the case of a burlesque interpretation, the representation of the moment of violent impact would heighten the absurd humour of the protagonist's delusion. In the case of an enlightened satirical interpretion, either the argument beforehand, in which Sancho Panza acts as the voice of reason, or the pain thereafter, in which Don Quixote suffers the consequences of his act (more decorous than the actual moment of impact) would serve to underline the protagonist's folly. In the case of a sentimental interpretation, the moment of heroic approach, before the protagonist suffers his defeat, would present him at his most noble. In addition, the illustrator must elaborate on the physical description of landscapes, figures, gestures, facial expressions, clothing, and architecture, elements Hodnett classifies as supplementary to the text.[16]

Fig. 1 John Vanderbank. *Don Quixote and Sancho Panza Captured.* London 1738 (Lord Carteret edition). Department of Special Collections, Kenneth Spencer Research Library, University of Kansas.

Nevertheless, these seemingly innocuous "additions" and choices of the illustrator carry important interpretive impact – witness the distinction between John Vanderbank's presentation of a Don Quixote with a sentimental cast to the eye (see Figure 1) in contrast to José del Castillo's presentation of an Alonso Quijano with a maddened fury to the eye (see Figure 2). The distinction Hodnett draws between what he considers the three functions of illustration – representation, interpretation, and decoration – obscures the interpretive activity of the illustrator in every image, even that of a simple vignette. Representation involves, as Hodnett himself realizes, a whole series of choices, none of which can safely be considered naïve. The mere transferral of narrative content (if one can even conceive of this process as self-apparently simple) from a literary medium to a visual one implicates the artist in a process of transformation. The arbitrary black figures on white page of written text become in seventeenth- and eighteenth-century illustrations the representations of figures related to each other in a manner perceived as mimetic, although created

Fig. 2   José del Castillo. *Alonso Quijano Reading*.
Madrid 1780. Biblioteca Nacional, Madrid.

through a rationalizing series of lines. Representation itself cannot be seen from
the point of view of the artist as mindlessly mimetic. In short, as Stephen C.
Behrendt claims, quoting William Blake, "Imitation *is* Criticism."[17] By the same
token, neither is ornamentation the mere act of making pretty.

   Like the ornamentation of the body by jewellery, hairstyle, and dress, and that
of architectural spaces by painting, sculpture, and furnishings, the adornment of
a book functions within a semiotics of social status and power. The illustrated
book "states" to the viewer that this is a work worthy of the extra expense and
trouble of ornamentation. A series of burlesque woodcuts signifies that the book
is especially funny, whereas a series of neoclassical engravings signifies that the
book is especially instructive or noble. The ornamentation itself confers value
on the text, value for which the publisher believes the reader is willing to pay.
As Behrendt notes, by 1700 the word "illustrate" in English meant "to make
famous or noble" and "to unfold or explain."[18] The productive acts of representation and ornamentation both imply the most basic interpretation of the text
as worthy of consumption. The grounds for this valorization of the text are to
be found in the illustrations themselves when seen as interpretations.

ILLUSTRATIONS AND ICONOGRAPHY:
READING AND WRITING VISUAL IMAGES

The representation, or imitation, of the text in illustrations also takes form within a stream of multiple visual images, either the series of illustrations bound within the same volume or the current of visual images known by the reader and/or artist. In this way the illustration defies Lessing's generic description of visual representation as spatial rather than temporal. Among these multiple images grows a net of similar and contrasted figures, imitated compositions and innovative ruptures, even moods and atmospheres. In the case of the series of illustrations contained within a book, the person flipping the pages of the text (his/her eye generally drawn first to the image as shown by psychological studies)[19] learns to decipher these images for meaning. The eighteenth-century reader in particular was accustomed to searching for allegorical meaning in visual images, as evidenced by the commentaries written by their owners on series of Goya's prints. Thus, this study considers the relation of the viewer of a print to be analogous to that of the reader vis-à-vis the text – indeed, in the case of book illustrations, the viewer of the print and the reader of the text are presumably the same. The reader of the illustrations, while reading the text or thumbing through the pages, experiences the images within a sequence that forms a narrative, chronological order. The flow of images therein creates for the reader a second narrative embedded within the textual narrative.

The effect of this juxtaposition of visual and textual narratives upon a reader can be studied indirectly through the analysis of the historical artifacts of reception – the illustrations and commentaries on the text themselves. Certainly, a circularity of argumentation underlies this method, for it treats the illustrations and commentaries as both producers and reflections of interpretation. This circularity is nevertheless not only symptomatic but also constituent of the situation of the book illustration. Like the technology of printing itself, the book illustration circulates. That is its very strength, as the more-or-less same image passes from reader to reader, volume to volume, edition to edition. The technology makes possible the reproduction of the same – multiplies the same – to the extent that a set of images, or a single image, or a single element of an image becomes iconographic, forming a visual sign within a system of pictorial "writing." As W.J.T. Mitchell observes in defence of pictorial expression, "What expression amounts to is the artful planting of certain clues in a picture that allow us to form an act of ventriloquism, an act which endows the picture with eloquence, and particularly with a nonvisual and verbal eloquence."[20] The establishment of an iconography of *Don Quixote*, or any literary text, depends upon the multiplication, or reproduction, of a visual signifier that circulates to such an extent that its signified becomes fixed. For example, even persons who know nothing of Cervantes' text can recognize Don Quixote's attenuated stick figure and Sancho Panza's round blob in Picasso's famous black and white painting. Therefore, the figures of the novel's characters take on a pictorial existence as signs in an iconographic tradition that, by the twentieth century, has gained its independence from the text.

The history of illustration, though, like that of printing, is intimately linked in the West to production for a capitalist market. Publishers print what sells. The recirculation of certain sets of illustrations, both independently and in successive editions, from Gaspar Bouttats' burlesque to Gustave Doré's romantically sentimental ones, reflects market demand. For a variety of reasons, readers at certain times and places find certain images to be interesting, provocative, pleasurable, and sympathetic. Their taste, partially formed by the illustrations, also partially forms the illustrations by demanding through the publishing market images that respond to their own interests in the novel. The circulation of illustrations both creates and reinforces already existing interpretations. Not surprisingly, those images that proved to be most innovative in the history of the reception of *Don Quixote* were originally excluded by generally conservative and cautious publishers. In many cases innovative images reformed interpretation through other forms of circulation, as did William Hogarth's independently published prints or Francisco de Goya's private stash of drawings later reproduced as prints.

Book illustrations should not be understood, then, as depictions that are simply loyal or abusive to the text, for they in fact represent readings of the same. With a few notable exceptions of collaboration, such as that of Charles Dickens and George Cruikshank, illustrators have not worked with authors or for authors. Contrary to Hodnett's assertion, the majority of illustrators have neither the inclination nor the capability to "understand the author's intention and to imagine what legitimately can be visualized beyond the words he has used."[21] This is particularly true in the case of *Don Quixote,* whose illustrators have all been separated by time and/or culture from Cervantes. Illustrators are aligned not with the authors but with the readers, for their representation of the text arises from a reading of the text, not the author's mind. The images are not "swallowed" or "raped" by the text, to use Suzanne Langer's terminology for the assimilation of the product of one artistic medium by another,[22] precisely because the illustrator is *not* the author and does not insert the pliable images into the master text (note how Langer's sexualized language becomes inverted when the metaphor is forced to an extreme). The illustrator does not couple with the author but reads and creates a critical representation in response to the text. Circularity is unavoidable, for it characterizes the dialogue – at times even the conflict – of reading that gives form to the illustrations. As a representation and reading interpolated into the text, it also serves as mediator between reader and text. Illustrations reflect both the text and the reading, and affect both. The illustrations respond to the text, thus giving evidence of its reception, but they also represent the text and give new forms to its content, which in themselves shape the reception of the text. The illustrations consequently share in the tension of print logic between fixity and multiplicity.

The assertion that the illustration represents a reading of the text invites the question: how does a visual image embody what is presumably a thoughtful response to the literary text? Ernst Gombrich and Rudolf Arnheim, despite their fundamental disagreement concerning the determination of visual meaning according to cultural (Gombrich) or psychological (Arnheim) criteria, agree that visual meaning does exist. Arnheim argues more persistently, largely on the grounds of psychological experimentation on perception, for the recognition that visual perception and artistic creation constitute thought.

My contention is that the cognitive operations called thinking are not the privilege of mental processes above and beyond perception but the essential ingredients of perception itself. I am referring to such operations as active exploration, selection, grasping of essentials, simplification, abstraction, analysis and synthesis, completion, correction, comparison, problem solving, as well as combining, separating, putting in context. These operations are not the prerogative of any one mental function; they are the manner in which the minds of both man and animal treat cognitive material at any level. There is no basic difference in this respect between what happens when a person looks at the world directly and when he sits with his eyes closed and "thinks."[23]

This study, indeed any study in the history of art, is based on the belief that the visual elements of an image, composition, use of dark and light, figuration, and so on, constitute in the very act of representation an interpretation of the content.

For both Arnheim and Gombrich the strength of visual representation as opposed to linguistic is the capacity of the visual image to show a web of relationships between elements through their simultaneous juxtaposition, comparison, or contrast in two-dimensional pictorial space. In the very essay in which he denies the capacity of the visual image to express the creator's feeling or to make a statement, Gombrich none the less extols the capacity of the family tree to encapsulate knowledge spatially: "A relationship that would take so long to explain in words that we might lose the thread ... could be seen on a family tree at a glance."[24] For Arnheim, the visual image's capacity to organize information spatially is not only more efficient but also maximizes the qualities of what he terms "productive thought." The ordering of the visual image, based on lines or forces of relationship between objects, allows non-linear syntheses of objects in context to others, as well as linear analysis of the parts of an object. As Arnheim writes, "In fact, productive thinking is characterized, in the arts and in the sciences, by the interplay between the free interaction of forces within the field and the more or less solidified entities that persist as invariants in changing contexts."[25]

In the illustrations studied in this volume, the productive thinking about *Don Quixote* is found in the images in which interpretations of the text differ from those seen in written commentaries. This difference of interpretation often reveals itself in new juxtapositions within the single image, such as the paralleling of the supposedly rational characters with the irrational in William Hogarth's illustration (see Figure 3), which points towards a universalizing satirical reading of the novel. In other cases the interplay takes place between images within a set of illustrations, such as the contrasting of the gradually declining but emotionally softening figure of Don Quixote in John Vanderbank's illustrations (see Figures 1, 16, 20, 21). Indeed, this capacity to understand the changing character of the protagonist places Vanderbank's interpretation in opposition to that of eighteenth-century literary critics who insisted on the never-changing psychology of the decorous character. For Arnheim, the ability to understand change within an object that maintains its identity springs from visual perception, which "requires a mind that, in perceiving a thing, is not limited to the view it receives at a given moment but is able to see the momentary as an integral part of a larger whole, which unfolds in a sequence."[26] Even more innovative is José del Castillo's juxtaposition of the figures of Don Quixote and Sancho Panza within an ellipse, a form that abstracts the give-and-take of their relationship through its use of two foci (see Figure 4). In their active recombination of figures and objects in new spatial relationships, then, these illustrations suggest new meanings, critique the literary text proper. Through this active participation with the stuff of the text, the illustrators can thus transform its reading.

TRADITIONS AND ICONOGRAPHY

A dialogue that generates productive, interpretive thinking takes place not only between the text and the illustration but also between the illustration and the other elements of its various contexts, in particular that of the book and the various visual genres. In this study I view the illustrations to *Don Quixote* within interpretative traditions, structured patterns of reading and representation, according to the concept of the term "tradition" within art history. A visual tradition makes possible the creation and reading of visual images structured by and legible on account of a visual idiom recognized as such by a community. The different cultural constructions of visual meaning have been widely commented upon, but no one has integrated this concept into a theory of the visual arts as completely as Ernst Gombrich. Whereas Arnheim analyses best the role of the artist as an independently thoughtful creator of images, Gombrich describes the role of the artist and the viewer as readers of the images central to their cultural traditions of representing visual meaning. In *Art and Illusion* he accounts for the dependence on traditions of both the artist and the viewer. For the artist even mimesis, viewed in the West as naturalistic, is not a simple

Fig. 3 William Hogarth. *The Curate and Barber disguising themselves to convey Don Quixote Home*. Biblioteca Nacional, Madrid.

Fig. 4   José del Castillo. *Don Quixote and Sancho Panza.* Madrid 1780.
Biblioteca Nacional, Madrid.

reproduction of life but an artifice constructed through highly sophisticated techniques of looking and depicting:

The injunction to "copy appearances" is really meaningless unless the artist is first given something which is to be made like something else. Without making there can be no matching ... In fact, the achievement of the innocent eye ... turned out to be not only psychologically difficult but logically impossible. The stimulus, as we know, is of infinite ambiguity, and ambiguity as such ... cannot be seen – it can only be inferred by trying different readings that fit the same configuration. I believe, indeed, that the artist's gift is of this order. He is the man who has learned to look critically, to probe his perceptions by trying alternative interpretations both in play and in earnest.[27]

Gombrich's use of the term "reading" is significant for this study because it links the creation of a visual image to the act of interpretation. The artist must interpretatively analyse his subject, even a landscape – that is, take it apart and look for a way to put it back together according to established conventions or schema of visual expression, making the parts form a meaningful whole. The illustrator of a text undertakes a parallel task, except that his subject is another artifact infinitely ambiguous, the literary work. This image based on the text reproduces the narrative only in the broadest terms, as a landscape painter reproduces a seashore, by organizing his reading of the subject into its critical expression in a different medium. The artist's reading depends in turn on the traditions by which he/she has been trained to see and create. Note that these traditions are plural, for the languages of art, at least in a secularized culture – like the languages of literature – are many. The illustrator must choose, then, not only the episode of the text to be depicted but also the visual tradition, or language if you will, within which it will be depicted. This understanding of tradition as a system of representation implies the possibility of various systems and is thus pluralistic. Traditions as such can exist independently of "Tradition," understood as a hegemonic aesthetic canon reflecting the social interests of the dominant sector of society. These traditions or languages can, of course, be appropriated in the name of "Tradition," but, as will become clear in this study, different interpreters use different traditions to express and establish their interests in *Don Quixote* and its representation. The visual languages of the traditions are open to appropriation, adaptation, and transformation according to the intellectual and/or social interests of the artists and publishers.

The reader of the illustration (for the purposes of this study, also the reader of the text) must likewise use his/her knowledge of the tradition(s) within which the image is created to interpret it. Writing of psychological experiments on the spectator of the visual work of art, Gombrich notes, "What we called 'mental set' may be precisely that state of readiness to start projecting, to thrust out the tentacles of phantom colors and phantom images which always flicker around our perceptions. And what we call 'reading' an image may perhaps be better described as testing it for its potentialities, trying out what fits."[28] According to this description of the spectator or viewer, he/she also engages in critical activity, matching what is depicted to what is known of the traditions of art. In the case of the book illustration, the reader projects knowledge of both the text and the visual traditions used by the artist on to the image. For example, a reader of the 1780 Real Academia edition, upon encountering José del Castillo's depiction of Alonso Quijano/Don Quixote reading, would project on to the image what he/she had read in the text of the episode, as well as whatever knowledge he/she might possess of previous illustrations to *Don Quixote* or other books, and the many eighteenth-century portraits depicting the act of reading. The reader would also note the gestures, facial expression, figure, and clothing of the maddened country gentleman, comparing them to the various visual styles of representation known to him or her. Even knowledge of other literary texts could enter into the reader's act of interpretation, since images of readers abound in eighteenth-century novels, whose figures could be projected on to the illustration. In addition, the reader could naturally flip pages to compare this image to others of the same edition. Within the image, he/she would trace the lines of the composition, compare and contrast the antiquated armour on the wall with the bare wall itself, focus on the agitated lines around the eye and their relation to the character's state of mind.

Obviously, the contexts and meaningful traditions that inform an image can, from the reader's point of view, multiply to an astounding number. Thus, the act of looking for the reader as well as the artist is characterized by its very activity, as the spectator approaches the image as a wilfully constructed representation of the text that expresses an interpretation of the same through its use of elements common to visual traditions. In this respect the illustration participates in iconography, the writing of pictures, and, like the writing of text, seeks a reader conversant with its systems of representation and expression.

CANONIZATION OF *DON QUIXOTE* IN THE EIGHTEENTH CENTURY

Literary historians have traced a rather sketchy and broken history of *Don Quixote*'s reception, centred around two poles: Cervantes' contemporaries, who laughed heartily at what became the seventeenth-century equivalent of a best seller but failed to acknowledge any elevated literary qualities, and the German Romantics, who loudly proclaimed the madman to be a hero, a champion of the ideal, an individual alienated from a shallow world. According to Oscar Mandel's article "The Function of the Norm in *Don Quixote*," Cervantine scholars have divided themselves into the "hard" school of thought, largely Anglo-American, which insists that *Don Quixote* is basically a funny book, and the "soft" school, which follows the German Romantics in their search for a deep, hidden meaning behind the pratfalls of the hero.[29] The "hard" school accuses the other of anachronism, whereas the "soft" school accuses the first of simplistic reduction of the text. From these polarized positions, neither "school" has questioned sufficiently the process of canonization that has caused the novel to be deemed worthy of such a debate. The status of *Don Quixote* as a classic has been taken as a given by those of the "soft school," whereas the "hard school" has merely assumed that the transformation of *Don Quixote* from a funny book into a serious one, as achieved by neoclassical critics, was somehow an organic outgrowth of Cervantes' supposedly satirical intention. Nor has either group questioned the process of reception that has eventually led to the strange impasse they now experience. Instead, they have remained locked in mutual silence by their own failure to ask diachronic questions of the text and their own situation as readers and critics.

A study of the reception of *Don Quixote* in the manner suggested by Hans Robert Jauss in his article "Literary History as a Challenge to Literary Theory" could help to resolve this sterile debate by disclosing the tensions and tendencies informing the novel's history as an aesthetic object. As Jauss writes:

The perspective of the aesthetics of reception mediates between passive reception and active understanding, experience formative of norms, and new production. If the history of literature is viewed in this way within the horizon of a dialogue between work and audience that forms a continuity, the opposition between its aesthetic and its historical aspects is also continually mediated. Thus the thread from the past appearance to the present experience of literature, which historicism had cut, is tied back together.[30]

The concept of a dialogue between the text and its audience offers the theoretical aperture for a consideration of the illustrations as an example of the reception and the representation of the literary work. The illustration both represents a reading of the text by one or several readers and takes its place within the skyline of the hermeneutic horizon that makes possible certain interpretations of the text at given times and places. The reading, once erected in the form of illustrations or critical commentary, stands as a guidepost or sign for coming readers, who can always choose to follow or reject it, or to follow it only a certain way until their eyes are caught by other signs, or to opt for a middle course between two signs. Although this metaphor may appear to resemble T.S. Eliot's description of the monuments of tradition, the order is neither "ideal" nor "timeless."[31] The concept of traditions used here rejects the sempiternal universality attributed by Eliot to the canon of "great" works. Eliot fails to consider *how* the order is changed by the "introduction of the new (the really new) work of art among them."[32] By reintroducing the temporal dimension to the horizon of reception, Jauss calls attention to the construction of the monument to a "new" classic by given readers at a given time.

The term "classic" has too often been circulated without a critical inquiry into its meaning, as happens in the renewed call from certain sectors within and without academia for a return to the study of the "classics."[33] Obviously, the word itself, which lacks a study of its history similar to Walter Cahn's study of "masterpiece," harks back to the cultures perceived as the lost golden age of the West, ancient Greece and Rome. As such, the word "classic" entails an aesthetics based on the values early modern Europe discerned in the remains of the ancient world unearthed in ruins as fragments and truncated torsos from the very ground beneath their feet – clarity, unity, order, symmetry, and idealized beauty. As Cahn points out, the seventeenth- and eighteenth-century aestheticians and arbiters of taste were very aware of the historical mutability of standards of artistic value, and thus believed that the test of time, along with the universality of appeal beyond one specific nation or culture, must be passed in order for the work to merit status as a masterpiece.[34] Ancient Greece and Rome provided the models for the classic precisely because their literary, artistic, and architectural monuments could still inspire awe in viewers separated by the barriers of time and culture. From a materialist point of view the ancient classical world also offered a model of interest to an upper class, be it the aristocracy or the bourgeoisie, because its aesthetic order required that both the producer and the consumer of art and literature invest substantial amounts of education, time, and money, if not travel, to acquire the training and taste necessary for the appreciation and re-creation of the antique monuments of art, architecture, and literature. Nevertheless, the early modern neoclassicists struggled with the physical opposition of these decaying and distorted remains to the ideal schemata and reconstructions of ancient perfection in their own literary and visual images of the lost world.

The dialectic of restoration versus decadence that fuels much of the eighteenth-century reconstruction of the text of *Don Quixote* and Cervantes' authority underlies the very notion of the classic. The appearance of the first classicizing edition of the novel in 1738 in England (the Lord Carteret edition) signalled that the work had survived the hundred-year span recommended by Horace and repeated by Pope,[35] and the transferral from one nation and culture to another. Thus, the text deserved its restoration from its decadent popular reading as a burlesque depiction of a fool to a work fitting the standards of neoclassical aesthetics. The process by which Cervantes' very unclassical text was re-evaluated according to another standard exemplifies the convergence of the two modes of "maintaining a classic" outlined by Kermode.[36] The first, which attempts to reconstruct philologically the meaning of the work to its author and his contemporaries, functions within the neoclassical reassertion of Cervantes' supposed claim to parody the literature of knight errantry. But the second mode, "accommodation," "any method by which the old document may be induced to signify what it cannot be said to have expressly stated,"[37] functions within the universalizing claim that the work is also satirical, criticizing the follies common to all but subject to correction by Enlightenment. In this sense the canonization of *Don Quixote* serves as a prime example of the use of allegory to render a text "relevant" to another time and place.[38] Central to both the philological repair and cultural accommodation of the text is the suppression of *Don Quixote*'s earlier reception as a funny work according to the popular values of carnivalesque laughter, the grotesque body, and "art for entertainment's sake."

Canonization, the establishment of an order or list of classics, literary and artistic works worthy of serious, scholarly study and useful for instilling values and cultural truths in those members of society to be educated, has become the focus of much debate on university campuses and among literary scholars and cultural critics in the last decade. As the American scholar Cornel West insightfully observes, canon formation grows out of moments of crisis in a given society. The attempt to reform, discard, or replace the canon by himself and others is based first on "a historical reading of the present-day crisis of American civilization," just as the literary works "are themselves cultural responses to specific crises in particular historical moments."[39] The mere criterion of form for the creation of a canon is neither possible nor desirable. In order to understand the larger economic, social, and political interests at stake at any moment of canonization, West counsels that "the key here is not mere interdisciplinary work that traverses existing boundaries of disciplines but rather the more demanding efforts of pursuing dedisciplinizing modes of knowing that call into question the very boundaries of the disciplines themselves."[40] The dedisciplinizing effort of this study is to understand the canonizing editions of *Don Quixote* as physical constructions, composed of visual as well as verbal commentary on the text, and as cultural artifacts, produced by and for members of the elite and bourgeois classes of eighteenth-century Spain and England in response to a variety of cultural changes and conflicts, such as the elite attempt to introduce Enlightenment ideology into Spain and the middle-class demand for a more accessible ethics of spiritual nobility and capitalist industry in England.

The reconstruction of this context demands attention to the stuff of literary, art, and socio-political history because, as John Guillory remarks, "the canon participates centrally in the establishment of consensus as the embodiment of a collective valuation. Hence it is in the interest of canonical reformations to erase the conflictual prehistory of canon-formation or to represent such history as the narrative of error."[41] The current critical debate about the canon suffers, because of these erasures, from a lack of understanding of the process of canonization. In his latest work Guillory rightly observes that both camps share three questionable assumptions concerning the canon: "Canonical texts are the repositories of cultural values"; "The selection of texts is the selection of values"; and "Value must be either intrinsic or extrinsic to the work."[42] In the case of *Don Quixote*, as this study will show, the same text proves to be a repository for differing and conflicting sets of cultural values, be they carnivalesque, aristocratic, or bourgeois, which the interpreters of the text highlight for their own purposes and/or according to their own social positions and interests. The selection of *Don Quixote* as a neoclassical text does not mean that the text will necessarily communicate those values, and thus an apparatus composed of different interpretative devices, such as critical commentary, biographical information about the author, and allegorical frontispieces is set up to instruct the reader towards a neoclassical reading.

The assumption of a text's intrinsic value leads towards the liberal belief that a consensus of readers can be achieved in order to change the canon, and the materialist assumption of a text's fundamentally extrinsic value leads to the belief in a conspiracy of elites against oppressed sectors to enshrine their values in a work.[43] Both beliefs erase once again the traces of conflict, even among groups of elites, in the process of canonization. In the case of *Don Quixote* the canonization of the text takes place in Spain due to the struggle of one elite, those intellectuals and politicians wishing to introduce the Enlightenment model of bourgeois social and economic reform, against another elite, those protecting the old interests of the Catholic church and the landed aristocracy. These conflicts have been erased first by literary critics interested in the unquestioned establishment of a national literature, and later by the critical insistence on formal issues such as the "Romanticism" of the text or its essential identity as a literary parody. Nevertheless, they can be reconstructed, largely in the visual imagery of the very editions that first canonized the text.

CANONIZATION OF *DON QUIXOTE* WITHIN THE DE LUXE EDITIONS

The eighteenth-century de luxe editions contain within themselves traces of the conflicts and interests of various groups of readers, critics, and publishers who combined in often uneasy partnerships to canonize *Don Quixote*. In eighteenth-century editions in particular (typically so, for it is perhaps in that century that printing reached its most potent position) the printed book became a forum for differing responses to the literary text contained within, which might include a translator's preface, a publisher's dedication, a biography of the author, a critical commentary on the text, and even a critical response to the illustrations, in addition to illustrations of episodes, portraits of the author, and allegorical frontispieces. The illustrations must be understood within their space in an edition – *in situ*, so to speak – in order to analyse their largely dynamic relationship to their neighbouring interpretive elements. In this form the de luxe edition of a novel participates in the public debate signalled by Jürgen Habermas as central to eighteenth-century bourgeois culture.[44] Through rational discussion the publishers of a de luxe edition sought to educate those for whom it was produced, the emerging middle class who, alongside the aristocracy, now had access to it as a cultural commodity.[45] Very often, however, the edition in all its facets was not a space of reconciliation of

competing interests but an arena of disagreement and conflict, which undermines Habermas's utopic vision of enlightened public debate. This debate,
which raised *Don Quixote* from the popular sphere of the carnival and the inn
to the coffeehouse and the bourgeois home, did not extinguish the burlesque
popular reading, nor did it successfully incorporate the bourgeois sentimental
and satirical ones into a hegemonically overriding neoclassical interpretation.
The editions remained a site of conflict, a cultural arena of difference. These
editions did attain the elevation of the text to the public sphere, where it was
then worthy of dispute. The fixing of the novel's significance as an exemplary
lesson on moral courage, a demonstration of the eloquence of the Spanish
language, and a monument to the literary prowess of the Spanish nation would
be left to the philologists and educators of the nineteenth century.

None the less, these eighteenth-century disputes are crucial to this study, for
in them one can trace the differing structures of response to and interpretation
of the text that led to the canonization of the novel. The choice of *Don Quixote*
as an exemplary neoclassical text does not appear now (nor indeed did it appear
to many then) to have been self-evident, natural, or reasonable. First, the
author, Miguel de Cervantes Saavedra, was far from representative of the
Spanish elite. His life was a story of frustration and marginalization. As a young
soldier he was maimed in the battle of Lepanto and left to rot for five years
in Turkish captivity. Upon his return to Spain he was denied permission to go
to the Americas, and was later thrown in jail for coming up short on his
accounts as a tax collector. As a struggling author he was maligned by more
successful, younger authors, shamed by a suspicious murder that took place on
his doorstep, and buried in penury. The example of Cervantes belies, then, the
theory that the canon is informed by exclusion on the basis of sex, race, and
class, a theory criticized by Guillory for its incapacity really to consider the
problem of class.[46] It appears that Cervantes' only success was the popular
notoriety of *Don Quixote*. The story of a penniless *hidalgo* (minor gentleman)
driven crazy by the reading of chivalric romances, who wanders the dusty and
violent roads of sixteenth-century La Mancha with a peasant squire in search
of heroic adventure and in service of a peasant girl, was, quite simply, laughable.
The two main characters were comic in the Aristotelian sense – that is to say,
not of the upper class – and erred on the side of indecorum both in the content
of their violent "adventures" and in their sudden moments of wisdom and
lucidity. On the road they met coarse pig herders and lascivious maids, hedo-
nistic aristocrats and ridiculous scholars. The narrative wandered as much as
they, and the author erred at many turns.[47] In short, the novel was a popular
parody of a popular genre, the chivalric romance, itself offensive for its fantastic
content. This rambling and raucous narrative had to be recast into a neoclassical mold – and indeed was, mostly through the decisive and powerful efforts
of the publishers of two editions (1738 Lord Carteret and 1780 Real Academia)
to shape a new literary reputation for *Don Quixote*.[48]

These two editions gave the text the monumental form of a classic, replete
with learned critical commentary emphasizing the text as serious and didactic,
the physical accoutrements and ornaments of linen paper, high-quality type,
and expertly executed engravings, and the biography of Cervantes as an enlightened, learned author. John Guillory has rightly reminded us of the origin of
the canon "as an aristocracy of texts,"[49] for these editions were fit to be seen
in the library of an aristocrat. The creation of a niche in the eighteenth-century
canon for *Don Quixote* depended on the representation of Cervantes as an
author of authority, possessing the intellectual resources to speak from within
the lettered community to both a worldly elite and a growing middle class.
Thus the editions, as conceived by their publishers, presented the sixteenth-
century Spanish soldier, penniless writer, and jailed tax collector as a forebear
of the Enlightenment thinker. Indeed, Cervantes took on their image in his
neoclassical guise, for, as Hauser notes, "nothing is more typical of the transitional character of this semi-court, semi-bourgeois culture, than the thin intellectual stratum of writers and amateurs who try to distinguish themselves from
ordinary mortals by their classical education, their fastidious taste and their
playful and complacent wit."[50] Cervantes would join them in this literary
Parnassus; his words would then ring forth with authority from a lofty niche
to educate his readers. The physical embodiment of his place of honour among
the canonized authors is the de luxe edition, which works, in Kernan's term,
to fix Cervantes' authority. But these editions were also a commodity, thus
accessible to any literate public with sufficient disposable income, such as the
rising middle class in England or the isolated intellectual elite in Spain.[51]
Cervantes' authority was fixed, then, but not only for the lettered community
or titled aristocracy; it would enjoy the multiplication of its impact made
possible by the technology of printing.

TRADITIONS OF READING AND ILLUSTRATING
DON QUIXOTE

The conflict of interests, expressed as literary but often arising from social
interests, between the various interpretations of the novel reveals itself within
the editions in elements, usually visual, that subvert the neoclassical reading
and/or introduce within the monument alternative readings. In the case of *Don
Quixote* these readings can be roughly characterized as either distant and
laughing, thus taking burlesque and satirical forms, or sympathetic to the
protagonist or the author, thus taking sentimental and classicizing forms. The
traditions themselves ebb and flow, responding to historical demands and being
appropriated for historical needs. As demonstrated best by the burlesque, a
tradition does not necessarily always represent the interests of the social context
in which it originates but is often available for appropriation and adaptation
in other settings. The burlesque tradition, which originates in the seventeenth

century and highlights the humorous, often violent and carnivalesque conflict between the world and Don Quixote, remains a constant undercurrent linked to readings popular in so far as they refuse to view the text as didactic, serious, or authoritative. The burlesque approach to the text surfaces in unexpected contexts, such as in the vignettes in the classicizing 1780 Real Academia edition or the rococo images designed by the French court painter Charles Antoine Coypel. In these elite contexts it represents a parodic attitude towards the very attempt to render the popular text "aristocratic," or canonical. To the extent that it subverts and inverts any serious reading of the text as "high" literature, the burlesque follows in the stead of the earlier carnivalesque tradition, one of the formative currents of seventeenth-century reception of *Don Quixote*.

In the eighteenth century various interpreters sought just such an elevated meaning for the text by applying to it the available aesthetic models, such as neoclassical strictures or sentimental romance. Those who cast *Don Quixote* into the neoclassical mould represent, as stated above, the interests of a conservative elite attempting to preserve the values of an earlier court culture centred on aristocratic patronage. Few illustrations bear the marks of this neoclassical reading. Most instead use visual idioms representing alternative readings: either the popular burlesque or the bourgeois sentimental or caricatural readings. Those that do embody the neoclassical interpretation are usually confined by content to aggrandizing portraits of the author and allegorical frontispieces that use classical figures to establish the satirical, didactic purpose of the author. Those who reformed the novel according to the bourgeois models of the noble man of sentiment, as in Vanderbank's representation of Don Quixote in the classicizing 1738 Lord Carteret edition, or the self-made entrepreneur and family man, as in Hayman's representation of Sancho Panza in the 1755 Smollett edition, produced images congenial to the interests of the middle-class reader. These illustrators drew attention away from the author towards the characters, and thus encouraged the reader's play of identification with the literary text typical of eighteenth-century sentimentalism. In particular, Don Quixote was no longer his author's weapon against decadent literature but a poor gentleman transformed by his own will into a hero of the heart, in the image of eighteenth-century bourgeois nobility. Biographers of Cervantes influenced by sentimentalism, Tobias Smollett (1755 edition) and Vicente de los Ríos (1780 Real Academia edition), then reversed the mirror to cast the author in the image of the sentimental literary hero. As both the cases of the sentimental and the neoclassical readings of *Don Quixote* reveal, the process of canonization of the text required that an aesthetic system reflecting the values of the literate class(es) be applied to shape the text according to its own norms. Through this transformation of the literary text, which included its representation in visual form, the canonizers established its status as a serious, exemplary work.

But the satirical reading, which differs from the burlesque in its basis in the originally Horatian, neoclassical imperative to educate while entertaining, and its use of elevated rather than popular visual and literary idioms, served again to undermine the serious readings by taking them to their extremes. William Hogarth's illustrations, produced for and evidently rejected from the 1738 Lord Carteret edition, extended the satirical criticism of Don Quixote's folly, the foundational principle of the neoclassical reading, to all the characters. They undercut the authority of those who spoke for reason within the novel. Francisco de Goya's illustrations, some of them produced for and evidently rejected from the 1780 Real Academia edition, undermined the boundary between the rational and the irrational, the foundational principle of the Enlightenment, and thus questioned the very authority of reason. These illustrations, studied in comparison to the critical elements of the editions in which they did not appear, signal the conflicts and tensions that defy the canonization of *Don Quixote* on the grounds of any totalizing reading. Within them one catches sight of the cultural arena in which the canonization took place, not uncontested. Goya, as the artist most conscious of the interpretative traditions he was manipulating and increasingly aware of the social contradictions of his time, attained a critical viewpoint on both the text *Don Quixote* and the ideological grounds on which it was being canonized. In his image of the two towns engaged in the braying controversy, the one rejected from the 1780 Real Academia edition, he undermined *sensus communis* as the basis for rationality (see Figure 48). In his later private image of Don Quixote reading, he blurred the rationalized separation of reality and fantasy in earlier illustrations by allowing the nightmarish figures of imagination to enter the space of the feverish *hidalgo* (see Figure 49).

From the worn traditions of the *Don Quixote* iconography, Goya created images that called into question the very foundation of the Enlightenment. Does common sense establish what is reasonable? At what point do the irrational monsters of the imagination crowd in upon the rational reader? It is no accident that the image of Don Quixote reading so closely resembles Goya's well-known print *The Sleep of Reason* in both composition and ambiguity. His depiction of *Don Quixote* is not only critical but also ironic in the terms of the early Friedrich Schlegel. His images arise from an ironic hovering, distancing and freeing him to critique his society and also to investigate the more emotional, imaginative recesses of the frontier between reason and irrationality. Thus Goya's images depict most vividly how the eighteenth-century interpretations of *Don Quixote*, with their dual emphasis on Enlightenment and emotion, folded into nineteenth-century Romantic readings. Hogarth's eye for hypocrisy and pretension in all sectors, plus Goya's fearless plumbing of the depths of rationality and irrationality, manifest the link between a satirical Enlightenment reading of *Don Quixote* and its Romantic counterpart. Both read the text as a serious work on the potential capacities and limitations of imagination and reason.

The Book Errant:
Seventeenth-Century Readings and Depictions of
Don Quixote

Having returned home ignominiously in a cage at the end of the first book, Don Quixote takes heart to hear from the Bachelor Samson Carrasco that his adventures have already enjoyed the attention of young and old (2:3). The young man dutifully reports that, of course, people's tastes differ, for some prefer the fight with the windmills, others the liberation of the galley slaves, the description of the sheep herds as armies, the encounter with the fulling mills, the fight with the Basque, or the adventure of the dead body. What all these opinions shared, however, is a universal taste for the absurdly violent. The reception of the novel in the seventeenth and early eighteenth centuries differed from the subsequent canonizing interpretation in its understanding of the work's "universal" appeal as popular. The humour was universal because it was appreciated across class boundaries rather than temporal and national ones. The figures of the novel *Don Quixote*, freed from the pages of print, stepped on to the stage and into the carnival; in so doing, they spoke to the illiterate and marginally literate.[1] It was also universal because the laughter it elicited responded not so much to a weak mind depraved by the reading of fantastic literature but to an arrogant individual who took on airs as well as arms. The social hierarchy, with its elevation of certain codes of conduct and rituals above others, was as much the target of laughter as was the fantastic literature of knight errantry. The vestiges of carnivalesque culture, including burlesque theatre and mocking carnival figures, coloured early on the reception of the novel, adopted the characters into its own spectacles, and rendered it popular, encompassing the follies of all classes and provoking laughter at the same. Thus, the novel's violence served the cathartic and subversive laughter of popular seventeenth-century culture.

In order to appreciate the eighteenth-century cultural contest over the interpretation of *Don Quixote,* it should be placed in its own context between the earlier readings, which rejected any serious qualities of the novel to focus on the humour, and the Romantic reading, which took the serious Enlightenment

reading several steps further. Ironically, the sea change in interpretation attributed to the German Romantics that occurred at the end of the eighteenth
century resulted from a confluence of the earlier "serious" and "comical"
interpretations. These interpreters did not deny either the status of the text as
"classical" or its satirical humour, but rather, through irony, recast the satire
into opposition with idealization. In this bold interpretive move, the Romantics
joined the tradition of a laughing, burlesque or satirical reading with the process
of idealization begun early in the eighteenth century, canonizing *Don Quixote*
according to neoclassical criteria and and presenting Cervantes and his protagonist as sentimental heroes. In addition, like Goya, they found the very
questioning of the opposition between idea and reality, fantasy and reason, to
be central to the authority of *Don Quixote* as a classic. Finally, in the nineteenth
century the interpretation of *Don Quixote* was separated into that of the lettered
elite, who continued the neoclassical treatment of the text in philological
monographs, and that of the populace, who were introduced to the text
through the expanding educational system and preferred, by and large, a highly
sentimental reading.

THE BOOK ERRANT:
A SEVENTEENTH-CENTURY READING
OF *DON QUIXOTE*

For the seventeenth-century reader of *Don Quixote* the book was inseparably
linked to the genre it parodied, the literature of knight errantry. As a parody
of a minor genre, it shared the same status. Juan Mommarte, the publisher of
a 1662 edition of the work, wrote in an obligatory preface to a noble:

Great books have been printed, and are given to the world press everyday, about rare,
singular, and sublime subjects, divine as well as profane, which it is not necessary to
parade before one who has seen and read so much as Your Excellency. Among all these
[is] DON QUIXOTE OF LA MANCHA, which, though minor in substance, for being a
novel of knight errantry, is a complete parody of the old books and an enjoyable lesson
for the coming ones, invented only to pass leisure time ...[2]

Mommarte did not present the text solely as a satire or parody of chivalric
romances, belonging therefore to a separate genre, but as a member of the
genre itself. Knowles notes that the association of the parodic *Don Quixote* with
the works it purported to parody was also common in seventeenth-century
England.[3] For this seventeenth-century Spanish reader, a *burla* or a "joke" about
the genre shared in the status of chivalric romances as a popular genre intended
to entertain readers in their spare time. No mention of instruction through
parody is made. Nor did Mommarte reveal any unease concerning the unproductive passage of leisure time, whose transformation into productivity was

typical of eighteenth-century bourgeois society.[4] Indeed, the innovative position Mommarte claimed for *Don Quixote* as an example to future books of knight errantry implied that Cervantes parodied the genre in order to renovate it rather than to destroy it.

Nor was the renovation of the genre as such a small deed. Mommarte refrained from criticizing literature created only to pass the time of day, but rather argued that through this small success, *Don Quixote* had gained greater success throughout the world:

But through its very smallness it has acquired such greatness in the world, that the greatness of its artifice, praised by all and never sufficiently emphasized, is made public; its disposition in the dialogues is so similar to reality, that supposing such, DON QUIXOTE himself, reading them, would be so transported that he would lose his mind again, even more easily than with those of Don Belianis of Gaul, Don Roger of Greece, Don Splendian, etc.[5]

The greatness acquired by *Don Quixote,* its fame, is not immune from the hyperbolic language of parody itself, as Mommarte wrote with tongue firmly in cheek. According to him, the power of *Don Quixote* to entertain is such that it could deceive and madden its protagonist even more effectively than the chivalric romances did. As a work of fiction *Don Quixote* does not instructively warn against the power of literature to create a world of fantasy dangerous to the gullible reader, but participates in the same enchantment and deception. For the publisher, as Mommarte advised his reader, the transport of literature was quite profitable because it put food into the mouths of more booksellers. The publisher presumably would not be interested in shooting himself in the foot by publishing a book that would weaken his product's spell. Thus, this seventeenth-century publisher jokingly disarmed in advance any argument for *Don Quixote* as an instructive work, warning of the power of fiction by claiming for it the same power to enchant and deceive.

None the less, Mommarte did attribute to *Don Quixote* the power to instruct the reader to shun vanities and pride:

And jointly with so much propriety of language, full of moral documents, many cautionary lessons have been imbibed along with the jokes, and between giggles let them learn to despise vanities and pride; for with common applause [*Don Quixote*] has not only gained credit among the Spanish nation, which prides itself not only on its sobriety but also on its good and mature taste; but also among the other foreign nations, by whom it has been received with esteem, read with applause, and celebrated with universal acclaim.[6]

Despite his earlier qualification of *Don Quixote* as a parodic work of a minor genre, Mommarte acknowledged that the work might be read according to the criteria of high, serious literature, as a work both morally instructive and exemplary of good taste. In order to suggest that the text was more than a joking burlesque, Mommarte, like the eighteenth-century Spaniards who would seek to canonize the work, appealed to its "universal" – that is, European – reception. Once that door had been opened, the norms of neoclassicism could enter into the interpretation, norms that are, in this instance, only briefly implied in the allusion to its serious, tasteful quality. For Mommarte, the cautionary example provided by the text was not, however, the negative example of Don Quixote's deluded imagination but that of his mad pride and arrogance. Thus, the conservative tendency of popular culture to reinforce rather than undermine the class structure dovetailed with the suggestion of a neoclassical universality.[7]

After this flirtation with the neoclassical concept of the universal as crossing national boundaries, Mommarte turned towards a quite different definition of *Don Quixote*'s universal appeal. The comic deflation of the social airs of the protagonist, who did, after all, illegitimately add the honorific "don" to his name and squander what little money remained to him in his profligate consumption of chivalric romances, points towards a reading of the novel informed by popular laughter. The term "popular" is used here with the understanding that the "people" run the social gamut of the community. As Heers has observed, early modern references to the festival included the entire community, encompassing all social strata.[8] Mommarte in fact provided a catalogue of these readers that encompasses all classes and echoes Bachelor Samson Carrasco's report to Don Quixote:

By which [universal acclaim] it has been extended so much, as its repeated editions attest; for it seems to me (and it is the truth) that no book has been seen that has so many times sweated in the press, occupied officials, nor fed so many booksellers; sufficient proof that his author knew how to give it that final touch of seasoning for the wise and the ignorant, the small and the great, the young and the old, students and soldiers; preparing this dish to the taste of each palate, whereby it has aspired to more greatness ...[9]

A plate prepared for each and every taste represents a universality encompassing difference, rather than transcending it to present the one meaning of a neoclassical reading. Mommarte's catalogue of readers, which includes the poles of the seventeenth-century social spectrum, may in fact indicate the all-encompassing range of carnivalesque humour rather than any true inventory of readership. As Mikhail Bakhtin has described carnivalesque laughter, it is the "laughter of all people ... universal in scope."[10] This laughter, ambivalent in its joyous and derisive tone, as Bakhtin insisted, turns upon the very person who laughs.[11] Mommarte's attribution of *Don Quixote*'s success to its preparation for each taste functions according to the same reversal of comic thrust. Accordingly, Cervantes turned the laughter upon the reader, entering through his taste (a reference to the carnivalesque mouth?) in order to target his own point of presumptuousness.

The carnivalesque qualities of Don Quixote have been previously suggested by Bakhtin himself, who compares the literary character to the medieval clown, whose role it is to "transfer ... every high ceremonial gesture or ritual to the material sphere" in the "tradition of grotesque realism."[12] Speaking of the figure of the happy fool, Heers has advised that it is necessary to see beneath the trappings of the fool the bitterness *and* the sheer pleasure linking him to carnivalesque spectacle.[13] Don Quixote, of course, takes on the roles of the clown and the fool as his absurd figure parodies the aristocratic ritual and trappings of knight errantry. As understood within the popular tradition, his folly does not result from the reading of literature so much as the desire for social elevation. In fact, the very inversion of the knight errant embodied in Don Quixote parallels the inversion of the chivalric tournament common to many carnivalesque spectacles.[14] Nor is the character's foolishly deluded identity as a knight errant cured, for the laughter it causes is productive rather than destructive. As Mommarte noted, the madness enabled the novel *Don Quixote* to wander through Europe as a knight errant in search of adventures: "And finding itself among so many garments and weapons, fabricated and woven in the kingdoms of Spain of so much metal and paper, it has come to these states to look for new adventures, in order to be able to say that this book, like a knight errant and adventuring soldier, has also passed through the banks of Flanders."[15] Mommarte thus equated the book with its protagonist, applying the seventeenth-century characterization of Don Quixote as a *miles gloriosus*, bragging soldier, to the glory-seeking book itself.[16] His assertion that the work is autonomous and escapes from its author's control in order to take new forms and adventures seems incredibly modern when read outside the context of carnivalesque laughter. Yet in this context it explains the historical multiplication and reproduction of the characters of Don Quixote and Sancho Panza outside the text in the seventeenth century. The parodic humour was not destructive but generative, and the central joke of the deluded knight errant opened up to new representations. Unlike the printed text, the carnivalesque representation of the literary characters separated them from the controlling hand of the author and allowed them to wander abroad in spectacles and parades.

THEATRICAL BURLESQUE: BOUTTATS' ILLUSTRATIONS OF *DON QUIXOTE*

Just as Mommarte described *Don Quixote* as a work of *burlas*, jokes, so the seventeenth-century illustrators depicted it as burlesque. The use of the term "burlesque" to describe this tradition implies theatrical overtones to the interpretations offered by the illustrations. Like the seventeenth-century Spanish dramatists who actually transferred its characters to the stage, these artists generally viewed them as figures evoking laughter rather than carrying serious meaning.[17] The burlesque spectacle typical of carnival did contain didactic meaning at first, but with the passage of time its form became ever simpler.[18] The same primary emphasis on laughter shaped the early illustrations, seen in the interchangeability of characters, who are largely undifferentiated physically or psychologically, the preference for episodes of action, often violent, in which the slapstick humour is immediately accessible to a viewer possessing little literary knowledge, and the depiction of bawdy, sexually charged, or scatological moments. These illustrations are popular, then, in their accessibility to a barely literate or illiterate audience, for the content depicted requires little knowledge of the novel and its characters beyond what could be acquired viewing the antics of Don Quixote and Sancho Panza on the popular stage and in the carnival procession.[19] The lesson they convey is a simple one: foolishly deluded self-images will lead to deflationary and social, if not physical, beatings.

The illustrations that embody most fully the burlesque reading accompany Mommarte's edition, along with many others well into the eighteenth century.[20] On their first appearance in a Dutch translation published in Dordrecht in 1657, twenty-six illustrations were attributed to Jacobus Savery. In 1662 these same images appeared with sixteen new ones, all signed by Gaspar Bouttats, in Mommarte's Spanish edition published in Brussels, and all are thus referred to here as the Bouttats illustrations. Diego Obregón roughly engraved copies of many of Bouttats' illustrations, which were first published in Madrid in 1674 by Andrés García de la Iglesia and enjoyed subsequent reprintings themselves. Clearly, these illustrations struck a popular chord, warranting attention as examples of the popular reception of *Don Quixote* in the seventeenth and even eighteenth centuries. Bouttats chose most often to depict scenes of physical romps, wrestling, and brawls. The following illustrations from the first book of the novel compose a telling sample of Bouttats' narrative: the battle with the Basque; the blanket-tossing of Sancho; the fight between Cardenio and Don Quixote; the would-be knight errant slapping Sancho for his defamation of Dulcinea; Don Quixote's arrest by the officers of the Santa Hermandad; the wrestling match between Maritornes and Don Quixote; the attack upon the funeral procession; the battle of the galley slaves; Don Quixote's somersaulting penance in the Sierra Morena; his fight with the penitents; and his fight with the goatherd. Bouttats singled out the aspect of Cervantes' humour most troublesome to twentieth-century readers – the violence.[21]

THE CARNIVALESQUE BURLESQUE

It remains important to understand the function of violence within the burlesque tradition of reading and representing *Don Quixote* as the embodiment of comic deflation. The figure of Don Quixote in particular continuously suffers or inflicts beatings in all sorts of representations, theatrical, operatic, literary, or visual.[22] He often appears in visual depictions as if he were a doll or a puppet, undifferentiated facially or psychologically, thrown across a stage for laughs by a capricious puppet master.[23] Bakhtin makes the sweeping assertion that "the carnivalesque basic element in Cervantes' *Don Quixote* and in his novellas is quite obvious: his novel is directly organized as a grotesque play with all its attributes."[24] The many illustrations of the beatings and abuse pelted down upon Don Quixote grow out of the carnivalesque tradition of plays composed of "uncrowning, travesty, and thrashing" of the king.[25] Of course, the self-proclaimed knight errant is a fool masquerading as a king, voicing the aristocratic language and code of chivalry. Thus, his mock-crowning draws from the tradition of the "feast of fools" and his uncrowning from the tradition of the thrashing of the king. In the early modern period, fools, who repelled and attracted the sane because they were both feared and revered for an almost prophetic alienation from worldly wisdom, often served as sacrificial lambs for the community.[26] When viewed through such a lens, the illustrations, like the episodes, represent not sado-masochistic revellings in violence and suffering but rather parodic rituals that level social barriers and restrictions on free expression with laughter and exorcise the fears and anxieties of the community.

Bouttats' illustration of the adventure of the Wagon of Death, in which Don Quixote meets a travelling troupe of players dressed in their costumes as the King, Queen, Angel, Devil, Jester, and Death, illuminates the doubling of folly in the protagonist's character as uncrowning fool and uncrowned knight (see Figure 5; 2:fp89).[27] The foolish Don Quixote mistakes the players for the characters they represent, but is persuaded by the Devil that they are actually actors. Upon realizing his mistake, Don Quixote makes the ironically wise observation that one must touch appearances in order to unwork their deception (2:11). At this very moment his words of wisdom are deflated by a jester dressed in rags and armed with bells, the apparel of a fool,[28] who scares Rocinante, Don Quixote's horse, with his appearance. In the left background of Bouttats' depiction one views the effects of this mischief as Rocinante tumbles to his knees, throwing his rider forward. Sancho runs towards his master, leaving his ass unattended, only to be scared off by the demon. Although he looks slightly to the left, the triumphant jester rides straight towards the reader's space, thus defying the fictional wall of the picture plane between the image and the spectator. The action of the jester and the Devil, wilfully provocative and destructive, is similar to the *diablerie* of sixteenth-century festivals, in which actors disguised as devils ran through the streets wreaking havoc, themselves "exempt from the law."[29] Indeed, both Don Quixote and Sancho Panza appeared as characters attacking devils in a festival in honour of the beatification of St Teresa of Avila in Zaragoza in October 1614.[30] The encounter between Don Quixote, the jester, and the devil takes on a mirroring effect, as the jester reflects and plays upon the

Fig. 5   Gaspar Bouttats. *Encounter
with the Wagon of Death*. Brussels
1662. Biblioteca Nacional, Madrid.

protagonist's foolishness. Yet the figure of the jester reflects back upon the fool
he burlesques, who, because of his foolishness, was himself incorporated in the
seventeenth century into an actual *diablerie*.

The most salient feature of the *diablerie* for the study of this illustration is
that it "crossed the footlights to merge with the life of the marketplace and
enjoyed similar privileges of freedom."[31] The devil in Bouttats' image traverses
the frontier lit by footlights between theatre and life, the boundary between
fiction and fact so often overlooked by the foolish Don Quixote, to uncrown
the one moment in which the crazed protagonist wisely recognizes the difference between appearances and substance. The fools who reflect Don Quixote's
delusions then turn the reflection back upon him to reveal to the reader, if not
to the madman, the protagonist's folly. This inversion of folly, which enlightens
through play rather than reason, distinguishes burlesque mocking of the character from neoclassical satire. Foolishness does not reside in one figure alone,
who will then be cured by those around him who enjoy sanity. Instead, folly
is seen and reflected in all. Upon completion of his foolish mischief, the jester
in Bouttats' illustration approaches the boundary again as he rides towards the
reader's space. By foregrounding the presence of the frame through this figure,
the illustrator reveals through the use of elements from carnival and popular

theatre the root of Don Quixote's foolishness, his inability to differentiate fact and fiction, only to turn it upside down once again. The attempt to draw a lesson from the folly, if the reader does not recognize his own complicity, will only be attacked once more, like Don Quixote's serious words of Enlightenment, with laughter.

THE CARNIVALESQUE BODY

The carnivalesque elements of these illustrations extend from the theatrical presentation of the action to the representation of the bodies of the actors. They are not merely victims or perpetrators of uncrowning violence and play but represent the grotesque body of carnival. Stallybrass and White have listed these "discursive norms" of the Bakhtinian grotesque body thus: "impurity (both in the sense of dirt and mixed categories), heterogeneity, masking, protuberant distension, disproportion, exorbitancy, clamour, decentred or eccentric arrangements, a focus upon gaps, orifices and symbolic filth …, physical needs and pleasures of the 'lower bodily stratum,' materiality and parody."[32] In these illustrations the carnivalesque lower body reveals itself several times as the vehicle of bawdy humour undercutting the elevated code of chivalric honour. In particular, bare bottoms abound in these editions. Most notable are the illustrations of Sancho Panza defecating from fear at Don Quixote's side during the fulling mill adventure (1:20). Obregón illustrated this scene,[33] as did anonymous illustrators of the Frankfurt 1648 edition[34] and of the Frankfurt 1669 edition.[35] In the Madrid 1735 edition published by Antonio Sanz the anonymous illustrator copied Obregón's image but added a stream of excrement.[36] All the illustrators show Sancho Panza, his pants dropped to reveal a full view of his fat buttocks, standing at the side of the mounted Don Quixote. In the 1669 illustration his face is contorted in physical exertion or fear. As Bakhtin rightly insists about carnivalesque humour, the humour of Sancho's accident is ambivalent. "The image of defecation from fear is a traditional debasement not of the coward only but of fear itself."[37] Thus, the fear inspired by Don Quixote's elevated fantasy of a heroic confrontation with mysterious, menacing power is literally brought to earth by the stream of excrement. In this image Sancho appears, according to a Bakhtinian analysis, as the "bodily and popular corrective to individual idealistic and spiritual pretense."[38]

Don Quixote's own buttocks appear from time to time to debase his arrogant vision, particularly in his disembodied desire for Dulcinea, his idealized vision of the peasant girl Aldonza Lorenzo, whom Sancho Panza praises, in fine carnivalesque recognition of androgyny, for her strength equal to that of men (1:25). In Bouttats' illustration of the protagonist's penance in the Sierra Morena in imitation of Orlando, Sancho Panza, bearing a sheaf of grain perhaps representative of fertile, earthy abundance, discovers Don Quixote

Fig. 6   Gaspar Bouttats. *Don Quixote's*
Penance in the Sierra Morena. Antwerp
1673. Biblioteca Nacional, Madrid.

semi-nude, bent over acrobatically (see Figure 6; 1:fp255).[39] His bare buttocks
gleam in the foreground and inescapably catch the reader's eye as well as
Sancho's. His nakedness debases his lofty penance, and thus renders the
knight's disembodied code of chastity humorous. In another example of such
a response to the knight's sublimated sexuality, Guillén de Castro takes a similar
potshot at Don Quixote's chaste devotion to Dulcinea in his play *Don Quixote*
de la Mancha. In a scene parallel to the Sierra Morena penance in its
exaggeration of the character's amorous abasement, the playwright shows his
Don Quixote swimming across a meadow towards another woman as if he
were Leander and she Hero. This scene caused chagrin to a twentieth-century
critic,[40] but reveals the manner in which the seventeenth-century reader viewed
Don Quixote's fidelity to Dulcinea as a joke in itself. The self-proclaimed
knight's love for Dulcinea was funny to many seventeenth-century readers not
merely because Dulcinea was in fact a burly peasant but also because his very
chastity appeared ridiculous. Don Quixote's chastity received the same incredulous ridicule in England, as evidenced by Edmund Gayton, who "leers" at
Don Quixote's chastity in his *Pleasant Notes upon Don Quixote*, and Ned Ward,
who denied the character's celibacy in his play *The Life and Notable Adventures*
of that renowned Knight Don Quixote de la Mancha, Merrily translated into
Hudibrastic Verse.[41]

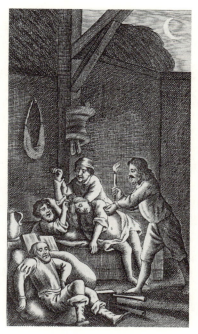

Fig. 7   Gaspar Bouttats.
Fight with Maritornes. Brussels 1662.
Biblioteca Nacional, Madrid.

The seventeenth-century illustrators also uncovered the flesh of the very unide-
alized women with whom Don Quixote crossed paths in his adventures, in order
to bring the protagonist's elevated sexual code back down to earth. In Bouttats'
depiction of his midnight encounter with Doña Rodríguez, the chaste knight
again suffers a carnivalesque paddling moments after proclaiming his unswerving
devotion to Dulcinea.[42] In the midnight darkness the Duchess's maids paddle and
pinch the middle-aged couple, a scene dominated by the duenna's white buttocks
glowing in the foreground. The midnight tussle with Maritornes gave Bouttats
occasion to lay bare the woman's breasts (see Figure 7; 1:fp133).[43] The reader cannot
ignore what Don Quixote does – the female flesh tempting him in the night. As
is clear from these images, the protagonist's chastity, the very quality for which
he would be so esteemed and elevated in sentimental readings of the eighteenth
century, invited excited laughter from early readers as yet another form of folly
manifesting the proud delusions of a love based on literary codes. This laughter
can be characterized as popular in so far as it expressed the reaction of the people,
including a spectrum of classes, towards elevated ethical and social codes of conduct perceived as ridiculously removed from common sense and material reality.
The folly was inspired by literature, but the literary representation of antiquated
aristocratic modes of behaviour also appeared ridiculous to an upper class far
removed socially from the lower-class viewer of Don Quixote in a carnival procession and far removed historically from the ethos of a once military aristocracy.[44]

THE COURTLY BURLESQUE:
COYPEL'S ILLUSTRATIONS

Another series of engraved illustrations, appearing first in 1724, was soon widely reproduced across Europe, replacing the roughly executed but energetic prints of Bouttats, Obregón, and their counterparts. Designed originally by the French court painter Charles Antoine Coypel as tapestry cartoons destined for the Château de Compiègne, these illustrations lent a new elegance and charm to the novel's characters and episodes.[45] The artist paid much attention to the episodes that took place among spectacle and luxury, such as Camacho's wedding and the adventures in the palace of the Duke and Duchess. In addition to his depiction of elegant courtiers and courtesans, he endowed peasant girls with round, sweet faces, simple elegant dresses with low-cut bodices revealing perfect shoulders, and tresses falling in gentle curls or neat coils. Flourishes of drapery, plumage, or clothing are often echoed in swirls of clouds or foliage. For example, even the innkeeper, a simple, almost sadistic brute in most illustrations, sports a ruffle about his very round face and a large plume in his hat.[46] In the illustration of his knighting of Don Quixote, he wields the sword with a flourish and looks benevolently upon the novice knight. Rococo elegance and refinement permeate almost all the images. Nothing could seem more different from Bouttats' illustrations, in which charm has no part in a rough and tumble world. As Hauser has stated, referring to Antoine Coypel's statement that painting changes with fashion, "art becomes more human, more accessible, more unassuming."[47]

Nevertheless, in spite of the new cast of characters, costumes, and settings, the interpretation of the text illustrated by Coypel had not changed so much.[48] Coypel, a would-be dramatist whose play *Don Quichotte* has been lost, was still basically engaged in a theatrical illustration of the text, although adapted for a "finer" taste.[49] Charles Antoine's father and teacher, the court painter Antoine Coypel, stated that "everything contributes in spectacles to the painter's instruction."[50] Of course, Antoine qualified the spectacle as Aristotelian tragedy when he described what the painter should learn from theatre: expression through action and gesture.[51] In a lecture Charles Antoine identified the painter's language with the actor's language of gesture and facial expression.[52] Despite his grounding in neoclassical aesthetics, Charles Antoine largely continued to represent the action of *Don Quixote* in the burlesque theatrical manner used by Bouttats and others. He also chose the same episodes of the novel for depiction as had his popular predecessors, with a few obvious omissions such as the fulling-mills episode and the tumble with Maritornes, both of which would have been deemed too grossly earthy for a rococo audience. But other episodes remained: Don Quixote's knighting; the battle for Mambrino's helmet; Don Quixote bound to a window by Maritornes and the innkeeper's daughter; Sancho Panza hiding in a tree during the boar hunt; Don Quixote and Doña

Rodríguez's paddling by the maids of the Duke and the Duchess, etc. What Stallybrass and White call the "low Other" – in this case, the burlesque representation of a popular text – is not excluded from the high culture of the court. Instead, the content of the burlesque reading enters into the genteel form of the rococo.

THE TRANSFORMATION OF CARNIVALESQUE LAUGHTER INTO SUPERIOR GIGGLES

The difference between Bouttats' and Coypel's illustrations resides not so much in the action depicted as in the nature of the laughter elicited by the action. In the case of Coypel's imagery this laughter does not arise from the overt, physical deflation of Don Quixote's folly undertaken by the carnivalesque figure of the jester, who afterwards turns his mocking visage with the same uncrowning intention towards the viewer. Rather, it is the stifled giggle of the courtier or courtesan who catches the viewer's eye with a complicitous glance hidden patronizingly from the figure of ridicule. The episodes from the ducal palace rather than the dusty road and dirty inn better suit this sense of humour, for in them the court sets up a whole series of tests and adventures for both Don Quixote and Sancho Panza to provide mocking entertainment. Coypel arranged these scenes as a director would a *tableau*, with the various spectators of the court displayed about the central action of the protagonists in a semi-circle, fully open to the view of the public beyond the picture frame. The *tableau* itself often represents the theatrical machinations of the Duke and the Duchess, arranged for the leisurely pleasure of court and reader alike. A prime example of the staging of this *mîse en abyme* is the illustration entitled *The Afflicted Matron complains to Don Quixote of her Enchanted Beard* (see Figure 8; 3:fp364).[53] In the centre the Countess Trifaldi, actually a lady-in-waiting, reveals her facial hair, a moustache, to the horrified Don Quixote and the amazed Sancho Panza. A line of similarly afflicted women to the left and a cluster of giggling maids silenced by the Duchess to the right frame the central trio. But a figure to the left captures the reader's attention by holding up his/her veil to reveal directly to the reader a long white beard and a broad smile as he/she lets the reader in on the joke. The reader shares the privileged point of view of those in the know in the court, and thus shares in the joke played on the gullible knight and squire, who make the mistake of believing their eyes and imagining themselves to be noble hero and wise governor.

This distanced perspective represents neither an Enlightenment one, focused from a superior point of view on the intellectual cause and cure of the folly, nor the carnivalesque, focused on the uncrowning of folly from below, but what I will call courtly, focused from a superior point of view on the laughable absurdity of the social drama created by the characters. Don Quixote, who desires the noble identity of a knight, and Sancho Panza, who desires the

Fig. 8 Charles Antoine Coypel. *The Afflicted Matron complains to Don Quixote of her Enchanted Beard.* London 1731. Biblioteca Nacional, Madrid.

political power of a squire, are manipulated as pawns, even court fools, for the leisurely enjoyment of those who really possess nobility and power. Heers has defined the function of the court fool as principally that of diverting the nobility and breaking the monotony of their daily existence, as "gratuitous spectacle *par excellence*."[54] The cure of the folly would be no fun, as evidenced in the novel by the Duchess's impetuous anger towards those who attempt to end the charade. A similar figure pierces the fourth wall between the *tableau* and the reader in the illustration entitled *Don Quixote attended by the Duchess's Women* (see Figure 9; 3:fp235).[55] Leaning on a table in the left foreground, her dark dress blending in with the drapery, the lady looks over her shoulder at the reader with a smile that functions as an aside, pointing out the ridiculous scene taking place in the centre. She shares with the reader the knowledge that this is a play, a spectacle performed for the amusement of the audience, except, of course, that the two leading men believe it to be real. This *burla*, or joke, is the source of the humour, expressed theatrically. Hauser has written convincingly of the rococo as a mediating style, in which the grand style of the court begins to cede, in its new sweetness and intimacy, to the intrusive claims to

Fig. 9   Charles Antoine Coypel. *Don Quixote Attended*
by the Duchess's Women. London 1731.
Biblioteca Nacional, Madrid.

cultural power of the growing middle class, expressed through sentimentalism.[56]
Yet the harsh vision of Don Quixote evident in these rococo illustrations
negates any tie to the sentimentalism emerging in Vanderbank's illustrations,
designed in the 1720s. Instead, they represent the assimilation of a popular
burlesque reading, based on theatrical action and an unflinching laughter at
the defeats of the protagonists, transferred into an elite visual idiom that strips
the burlesque of its regenerative carnivalesque undercurrents.

THE MOCK-HEROIC MODE:
THE BOUTTATS AND COYPEL FRONTISPIECES

Despite the difference in perspective between the courtly Coypel and the more
carnivalesque Bouttats, the two work with the same burlesque attitude towards
the protagonist's assumption of the heroic identity of a knight errant – they
mock him. The mock-heroic mode informs the burlesque tradition of illustration whenever the decision is made to use an elevated literary or visual language
to represent Don Quixote, and then to undercut the same by depicting his
deflation, either through laughter or violence inflicted upon the protagonist by
the other characters. Producing illustrations for a public still conversant with
the conventions of chivalric romance, the artists were often able to accentuate
Cervantes' jesting pokes at these straw knights visually.[57] Their parodic frontispieces to the novel reveal expectations of just such knowledge of heroic imagery
on the part of the readers. The Bouttats frontispiece, originally signed by Jacobus Savery, depicts Amadís de Gaula and Orlando clad in the gear of Roman

Fig. 10   Jacobus Savery (?) and Gaspar
Bouttats. Frontispiece. Brussels 1662.
Biblioteca Nacional, Madrid.

soldiers on two pedestals that bear their names and frame the image.[58] Amadís
brandishes his sword as he casts a challenging glance outside the frame towards
the reader, whereas Orlando gazes down upon Don Quixote and Sancho Panza.
The two chivalric heroes stand in niches set above the two would-be heroes,
thus occupying the space of the "classical body" as statues. As Stallybrass and
White note in general reference to the burlesque in carnivalesque culture, "The
presence of the statue is a problematic presence in that it immediately retroflects
us to the heroic past, it is a *memento classici* for which we are the eternal late-
comers, and for whom meditative imitation is the appropriate contrition."[59] Yet
the imitation of the two heroes is the work of the two fools, whose very presence
in the same image mocks Amadís and Roland. As if the juxtaposition of heroes
and fools were not parodic enough, the profile of Dulcinea as a coarse peasant
woman clad in classicizing drapery and coifed in a Roman manner graces a
roundel above the figures. Bouttats has deflated the trappings of heroic history

Fig. 11   Charles Antoine Coypel. *Don Quixote led by Folly, & Inflam'd by
an Extravagant Passion for Dulciana sets out upon Knight Errantry.* London 1731.
Biblioteca Nacional, Madrid.

painting (as well as literature) simply by placing Cervantes' characters within
their frame. In the frontispiece to the second volume, Dulcinea and Sancho
Panza take the places of the chivalric heroes and gaze down in approval on the
figure of Don Quixote, now glorified as Knight of the Lions. The inversion of
the heoric is complete; fools grace the elevated space of the valorous, and Don
Quixote stands memorialized with the lion that refused to meet him in battle.

Nor did Coypel take seriously the protagonists or any satirical intent on the
part of the author, despite his use of the elevated visual language of allegory.
Entitled *Don Quixote led by Folly, & Inflam'd by an Extravagant Passion for
Dulciana sets out upon Knight Errantry,* this image serves as a frontispiece in its
presentation of the premise underlying the story (see Figure 11; 1:fp8).[60] Folly
personified as a woman hovers over Don Quixote, whereas Love personified as
Cupid touches his heart with a torch as the would-be hero rides out in pursuit
of Dulcinea and adventure. Dulcinea, cutting an absurd figure as her round
body bursts out of her dress and the large, starched collar sets off her double
chin, smiles coyly at Don Quixote. Thus, the figures of his own overheated

imagination, including a windmill/giant, surround the character. About the
machine swirl dark clouds, among which the forms of a stern, bearded face
and hands holding a scimitar and cudgel take shape, personifying the windmill.
The transformation of the windmill is as much a humorous example of the
madman's delusion as is his adoration of the peasant Aldonza Lorenzo as
Dulcinea. His visions are ridiculed in their depiction, and no attempt is made
to represent any form of Enlightenment or the cause of his madness. The artist
clearly preferred the theatrical aim of entertaining the reader rather than
instructing him. Coypel has even parodied the high form of allegory in his
attempt to provoke laughter through a fully mock-presentation of the heroic
code of chivalry. It is this preference for entertainment rather than instruction,
the dedication to art that is not elevated and didactic but popular or charming,
that marks the burlesque against the satirical. Almost contemporaneously, John
Vanderbank was designing an allegorical frontispiece that would elevate the
same text to the status of satire.

THE CHARM OF FOLLY?

The danger of the burlesque for the neoclassical thinkers of the eighteenth
century who sought to canonize *Don Quixote* as an example of serious didactic
literature rested in its failure to insist upon Enlightenment as an outcome of
reading the novel. Dr John Oldfield, in a commentary upon book illustrations
published in the 1738 Lord Carteret edition of *Don Quixote*, objected to
precisely this burlesque tone in Coypel's images.[61] It was the superior ridicule
of Coypel's illustrations, denying any serious meaning to Don Quixote's
actions, that offended Dr Oldfield. If no transcendent explanation was given
to the protagonist's folly, he and his author suffered the ridicule. The protagonist seemed a mere fool, saved from his own absurd visage by no overriding
mission. His author seemed a mere panderer to popular laughter, who could
certainly lay no claim to the status of a learned, important author. Even worse,
the author's representation of folly without overtly criticizing it ran the danger
of inviting the reader to imitate folly.[62] Of particular concern to Oldfield was
the indiscriminate representation of the windmill as a giant. Central to the
neoclassical justification of book illustration was the fear that the reader's
imagination, left free to wander, or led astray by frivolous imagery, would
actually fall victim to the same power of literature that afflicted Don Quixote
– the power to enchant and delude.

This power of literature was indeed depicted uncritically by Coypel in the
very image that purports to depict the triumph of reason. The last illustration
of Coypel's series, entitled *Don Quixote's Deliverance out of Folly by Wisdom*,
represents the protagonist's final Enlightenment (see Figure 12; 4:fp253).[63] The
armoured Don Quixote slumps limply in a chair, as Wisdom hovering above
him offers to bestow upon him her gift. To the right her counterpart and enemy

Fig. 12   Charles Antoine Coypel. *Don Quixote's Deliverance out of Folly by Wisdom.*
London 1731. Biblioteca Nacional, Madrid.

Folly directs her gaze to Sancho Panza, who stares with awe and enchantment
at the proffered castle. Of the two protagonists, the chastened but wiser Don
Quixote and the dreaming but deluded Sancho Panza, the second looks by far
the happier. It is the similar enchantment, worked by the pair's folly upon the
reader, that fuels Coypel's illustrations. If Folly can be so charming, then
perhaps it is not so bad; and thus Cervantes' stated intention – to destroy the
literature of knight errantry by parodying it with a foolish protagonist – is
undercut. Even when Wisdom wrests the mad knight from Folly, the latter
retains her hold on Sancho Panza – and perhaps on the reader. Indeed, St
Evremond expressed the charm of folly in an anecdote relating his own moment
of identification with Don Quixote, in which he is tranformed into a fool.
Glimpsing two approaching figures, he took them for knights errant, "transported as I was, and more Don Quixote than Don Quixote himself."[64] St
Evremond, like Coypel's Sancho Panza, chose to delight in the enchanting
delusion at least for a moment, in spite of the triumph of reason.

The enchantment of the novel's humour was obviously popular, in the sense
of being widespread enough that it crossed class and national boundaries, since

these illustrations appeared in eighteenth-century editions throughout Europe. The burlesque tradition continued in its courtly form of Coypel's imagery and its popular (in the sense of belonging to the culture of the lower classes) form of Bouttats' imagery. The enchantment would soon dovetail with the new cult of sentimentalism, representing the taste and interests of the emerging middle class, just as the laughter would soon dovetail with the neoclassical satirical interpretation of the novel's canonizers. Central to the change was the transformation of the book from its popular status to a public one. As a popular book it had enjoyed universal appeal across social and political borders, and become well-known through the media of the carnival, popular theatre, and eventually, court spectacle. It existed without critical commentary or debate as a work of entertainment, and shared the lowly status of a book useful for passing pleasantly the time of day — much like the chivalric romances themselves. As a public work it would move into the newly formed cultural space of the public, defined by Jürgen Habermas as the mediating space between the bourgeois home and the state.[65] There it became the object of critical debate seeking to establish a didactic meaning for the work, upon which its canonization depended for an intellectual basis. Consequently it was found, according to both a neoclassical aesthetic and a sentimental ethics, to be a morally exemplary work as well as a cautionary tale, and was promulgated as a work fit for consumption by the new class to be educated. In short, as a public work rather than a popular one, it became a classic.

Cervantes as Hercules Musagetes: The First Neoclassical Edition

The publication in Spanish in London in 1738 of the first de luxe edition of *Don Quixote* by J.R. Tonson, at the behest of Lord Carteret, marks a turning-point in the reception and interpretation of the text unnoticed by literary historians more concerned by the "revolutionary" Romantic reading.[1] Whereas the German Romantics offered a new approach to the text already perceived as a literary masterpiece, the producers of this earlier edition actually conferred classical status on the popular work. Thus, the 1738 Lord Carteret edition signals a hermeneutic shift that elevates the work from the lowly genre of popular literature to the elevated stratum of texts representing the elite, learned values of neoclassicism. The production of a *classic* entails the "packaging" of the text within a physical vehicle worthy of it: the de luxe book, complete with such critical apparatus as a biography of Cervantes, commentary on the literary aspects of the work, and visual components such as frontispieces, a portrait of the author, and illustrations.[2] This edition obviously tailors the text, through both its physical and literary presentation, for consumption intended for instructional as well as entertainment purposes by the upper and emerging middle classes. Although anecdotal evidence exists for the enjoyment of *Don Quixote* by all classes in the seventeenth century, there is little indication that an affluent, learned reader would have approached the text as other than an example of popular humour. None the less, in the eighteenth century the editions themselves bespeak the elevation of the novel from a funny but insignificant book to a classic discreetly instructive for an educated public.

The semantic link between the terms "classic," as applied to a canonized work, and "neoclassicism," as applied to the early modern aesthetic, reveals the crucial connection between *Don Quixote*'s new status and the aesthetic that informs it. As Frank Kermode has so aptly shown, a classic is made, not born.[3] According to J.A. Mayans y Siscar, Lord Carteret proposed that a volume of the work, "the most pleasant and discreet fable written in the world," be added to the English Queen Caroline's library of the wise Merlin, composed of a select collection of "books of invention."[4] Apocryphal or not, this anecdote reveals the nobleman's effort to present the text on all levels as a classic according to the aristocratic standards of neoclassicism, an endeavour that brought about the inclusion of the novel within the library of good taste – that is, the canon. The making of *Don Quixote* into a classic, its canonization, fell – ironically – to adherents of an aesthetic parodied by Cervantes within the novel. Neoclassicism, grounded in the Aristotelian precepts of unity of action, subordination of character to plot, and decorum, suffers from the same poverty of imagination for which Cervantes teased his neo-Aristotelian contemporaries in the Canon of Toledo's discourse on theatre.[5] In fact it is hard to imagine a less neoclassical work than *Don Quixote*, characterized by its rambling plot, violent and bawdy humour, and indecorous comic deflation of the self-appointed knight and gradual ennoblement of the peasant Sancho Panza. The espousal of *Don Quixote* by eighteenth-century neoclassical men of letters was by no means "natural," and therefore calls for an analysis of the various contexts that made possible this strange coupling.

Seen from a socio-political point of view, *Don Quixote* offered Spanish neoclassicists a foundational text with which to establish the stature of their culture within European civilization. Suffering from their own vision of Spain as a land colonized for seven hundred years by an Islamic, Oriental culture, these scholars fought to protect their national honour from the propagators of the "black legend" and from their own chronic sense of cultural inferiority.[6] The adoption of a neoclassical aesthetic by various scholars placed them firmly within the Western tradition of classical Greece and contemporary France. Encouraged by Cervantes' supposed intention to parody the romances of knight errantry, Gregorio Mayans y Siscar represented the author in the first Cervantine biography as a champion of European neoclassical values against the decadent, fantastic "Oriental" fiction of the imagination. For Mayans, this Moorish contamination extended to Spanish social values such as valour and civil conduct, and thus transformed Cervantes' literary parody into an act of national reform and defence. The author became, to some Spanish eyes, a national hero, displacing the decadence that marked Spain's imperial fall with the clear values of reason and proportion.[7] The text subsequently became a classic, authoritative to the extent that its author had used it to fight for good (that is, neoclassical) taste and a reformed national character. The burlesque humour that had characterized earlier readings was subjected to this authority, and marginalized in favour of didactic satire.

In England *Don Quixote* offered the producers of the 1738 Lord Carteret edition a text pliable to the edification of the newly emerging reading public. As an extended work of prose it appealed to the private leisure reader of the new genre of the novel.[8] For the neoclassical thinker, such as Dr John Oldfield, the text taught a satirical lesson concerning the perils of naïve reading through the negative example of a leisured reader, Alonso Quijano, the country gentleman who became Don Quixote. For a reader influenced by sentimentalism, such as John Vanderbank, the knight, although deluded, represented a positive example of the suffering but noble man of heart, and Sancho Panza represented the accessibility of this spiritual nobility to a man of the lower classes. In general, the extratextual components of this edition joined together in the display of interpretive approaches to the text, intended to instruct and orient the reader by creating within the edition a forum for the discussion of the text. Viewed positively, the eighteenth-century de luxe edition participated in the critical debate that instructed, according to Habermas, the emerging and expanding reading public, and informed the public spaces of discussion, such as the newspaper and the coffeehouse.[9] Viewed negatively, this interpretive material, in particular Oldfield's instructions to the viewer of the illustrations, sought to limit the reader's imagination according to the strictures of rational representation.[10] From both perspectives the eighteenth-century critical edition encapsulated the strains and tensions of interpretation that effectively canonized *Don Quixote* and simultaneously opened the novel to new readings based on the critical assumption that the text, the product of a worthy author, was serious as well as humorous.

Conceived and executed according to a neoclassical vision of a unified interpretation and presentation of *Don Quixote*, this two-volume edition deserves to be considered the first monument to the novel's author, Cervantes. In addition to Mayan's biography, the "Vida de Miguel de Cervantes Saavedra por D. Gregorio Mayans y Siscar," it contains the first portrait of the author, designed by William Kent, and an allegorical frontispiece, designed by John Vanderbank, that represents Cervantes as Hercules Musagetes liberating Mount Parnassus from the monstrous invaders of fantastic literature. The publication of the first Cervantine biography and portrait, as well as the sheer size and physical sumptuousness of the book, paper, binding, print type, and illustrations, mark this edition as a physical and intellectual venture intended to launch Cervantes from the realm of popular literature on to the ethereal heights of Parnassus. In order to analyse this edition as a whole, it is necessary to take into account all its components, literary and graphic. In general the verbal elements of the book serve to lionize the author, transforming the beaten soldier Cervantes into a literary soldier, the hero of decorous, serious, and reasonable literature who expels the excesses of imagination and fantasy from his homeland. None the less, the illustrations themselves provide evidence of the inception of a sentimentalizing reading that glorifies the protagonist as well as the author as fallen soldiers triumphing spiritually through noble suffering. In the very first monument to Cervantes as a neoclassical writer of didactic satire are to be found the seeds of the Romantic reading, given that both oppose themselves to the burlesque reading in their insistence upon a serious, didactic content, which either aggressively attacks a decadent literature through satire or more peacefully expounds a model for living in a base world.

CERVANTES AS THE CHAMPION OF SPAIN: MAYANS' DEDICATORY LETTER

The author of *Don Quixote*, Miguel de Cervantes Saavedra, enjoyed relatively little fame or approbation through the seventeenth century, in spite of his creation's rollicking success. Alternately maligned and overlooked by his contemporaries, he never achieved the literary recognition nor the reasonable monetary recompense to which he aspired. Perhaps the greatest insult he suffered was the publication in 1614 of a spurious continuation of Part I of *Don Quixote* by an anonymous writer using the pseudonym of Avellaneda. Through the century Cervantes' novel enjoyed uninterrupted popularity and publication, whereas Avellaneda's unauthorized text fell into oblivion. None the less, as an author of a burlesque prose work parodying the maligned genre of the chivalric romance, Cervantes himself merited no critical or biographical recognition until the 1730s. The Valencian scholar Gregorio Mayans y Siscar began his biography of the author in an attempt to recuperate Cervantes' literary reputation in the face of renewed publication and praise of Avellaneda's work by the French writer Alain René Lesage and his Castilian counterparts.

In his dedicatory letter to the Countess of Montijo, Mayans proclaims Cervantes a literary giant who, "by the fertility of his wit produced (although burlesquely) the most serious, useful, and salutory effects that one could imagine."[11] The movement to cast Cervantes as a hero and to canonize his most widely read work thus received its initial push in this monumental edition. The phrase "although burlesquely" encapsulates the challenge to Mayans and reveals how the old reading of the novel must be incorporated and transcended in the new neoclassical interpretation. The parentheses indicate that the burlesque qualities of the text must first be marginalized from the didactic, "useful" and "serious" qualities. The concessive "although" further indicates that they must then be subjugated to the higher literary goal of education. The assertion that such a goal exists depends subsequently on the author's supposed intention to elevate the text beyond a merely romping and rowdy burlesque of the conventions of chivalric literature to a satirical parody of the same. Whereas the burlesque reading merely makes fun of the genre, as indicated by the Spanish verb *burlar*, "to make fun of," the neoclassical reading insists that a socially responsible, educational purpose to eradicate the genre grounds the parody. Cervantes did suggest such a parodic intention in the first prologue through the voice of a visiting friend. Although one can argue that this statement is ironic due to its embedding within an ironic statement on the necessity of the prologue for a work of literature and within the voice of one other than the author, Mayans y Siscar implicitly attributes these words to Cervantes himself.

In addition, Mayans assumes that the parodic attack on a decadent literary form includes a patriotic defence of what he perceives as Spanish culture against the continued effects of an invading, decadent culture.[12] In this dedicatory letter he specifically lauds the old soldier's successful expulsion of Moorish ideas from Spain, which remained to be done after the physical expulsions of the Moorish king of Granada in 1492 and the remaining Moriscos, beginning in 1609.

One can say of him, without having recourse to his inimitable art of irony, that a poor old soldier, maimed and imprisoned, was the greatest instrument of the expulsion of the Moors from Spain, without the shedding of blood, ruin of families, nor any inconvenience at all, which did occur in the two famous expulsions.[13]

Drawing upon the early modern ideal of the young courtly poet-soldier, epitomized in Spain by the sixteenth-century lyric poet Garcilaso de la Vega, Mayans y Siscar places Cervantes, although poor, maimed, and old, into the same noble tradition. He is metaphorically knighted, and then credited with the honour of dealing the final blow in the Spanish *reconquista*, the centuries-long struggle to win Iberia back from the Moors:

Only he was capable of exiling the fantastic and extravagant ideas that had infected the ideal of valor and civil conduct; and if one could truthfully say that he who enhances a nation's genius and makes it so outstanding, does more good for a kingdom than one who extends its borders ...[14]

Mayans y Siscar clearly equates the fantastic content of the literature of knight errantry with the invading Oriental forces of the Moors and juxtaposes them to the values of the noble Christian conquerors, valour and civil conduct. By logical extension, the fantastic and extravagant ideas of the Moors are also opposed to the rational and proportional ideas of the West, those propounded by the neoclassical literary aesthetic. The eighteenth-century critic thus recasts Cervantes as a noble champion of Christian Spain and, consequently, launches the radically new, but conservative, neoclassical reading of *Don Quixote*. This reading is innovative to the extent that it reforms the status of the text and recasts it in the mold of neoclassicism; yet it is deeply conservative to the extent that it reinforces the vision of Spain predominant since the days of Ferdinand and Isabel as an essentially Catholic land besieged by infidels. Cervantes' work of ideological purification, as proposed by Mayans, represents the apotheosis of arms by letters in the defence of the nation.

CERVANTES AS CHAMPION OF NEOCLASSICAL LITERARY VALUES: THE ALLEGORICAL FRONTISPIECE AND KENT'S PORTRAIT OF CERVANTES

The desire to ennoble the author extends to the publication of the edition as a whole, including the visual imagery such as the portraits. The frontispiece to

the first volume of the edition, designed by John Vanderbank, manifests the
ambitious aim of the publishers to read the novel as a neoclassical satire upon
the genre of chivalric romance. The artist seems to have adopted the well-
known image of the choice of Hercules, in which Virtue offers the classical
hero the high road as "hero and civilizer."[15] Cervantes, who would be unrec-
ognizable but for the explanation of the allegory in the "Advertisement concerning the Prints, by John Oldfield, MD,"[16] strides up the path of Mount
Parnassus as Hercules Musagetes, avenger of the Muses (see Figure 13).[17] Never
before and never again will Cervantes appear so heroic. Clothed by a mere
lion's skin about his waist, he enjoys the physique of a classical statue, with
tautly muscular torso, arms, and legs. Already bearing a lyre in one hand, he
accepts his weapons from a satyr – a club and the mask of Don Quixote.[18]
These attributes neatly incorporate in this surprising figure the offices of
Cervantes' character that will be used to exalt him in the coming decades:
soldier and scholar, satirist and restorer, gentleman and enlightener. Of most
interest is the mask, for it reveals the deceptive guise Cervantes must take on
in order to defeat the grotesque antagonists of chivalric literature. Oldfield
identifies this mask as "the proper implement for accomplishing his end, *viz.*
those of raillery and satire, expressed by the *Mask*, which he presents him
with."[19] This gift is none other than a mask representing the profile of Don
Quixote. In order to enlighten and reform, he must mask himself with the
deluded visage of his protagonist. The Muses stand languishing below, having
been expelled from their aerie and awaiting restoration to their seats by their
avenger. A giant, a three-headed man, and a multi-headed serpent occupy the
summit won unjustly through force, and threaten the hero, who, in his second
manifestation in the same image, appears as a simple *hidalgo*, or country
gentleman.

As Oldfield writes, Cervantes has won the victory:

The main scope and endeavour of the author, in this performance, was, to banish from
the writings of imagination and fancy the chimerical, unnatural, and absurd conceits,
that prevailed so much in his time, and which, in consequence, had infected the world
and common life with a tincture of them, and to restore the ancient, natural, and
genuine way of treating the subjects that fall within this province.

In order to represent this by delineation to the sight, *Mount Parnassus*, the seat of
the *Muses*, here expressed and shown in the possession of the monsters and chimeras
of the books of chivalry, will sufficiently serve to intimate the preposterous and
disorderly state of the poetical world at that time, and the reform it stood in need of.[20]

Oldfield reads the image as an illustration of Mayans' interpretation in the
most literal terms. Mount Parnassus is society overrun by the fantastic monsters
of chivalric romance. The victims of this invasion include not only good taste
and neoclassical literary standards but also bravery and civil conduct, the same

Fig. 13   John Vanderbank. Frontispiece. London 1738. Department of Special Collections, Kenneth Spencer Research, University of Kansas.

Fig. 14   William Kent. Portrait of Cervantes.
London 1738. Department of Special Collections,
Kenneth Spencer Research Library, University of Kansas.

noble warrior virtues signalled earlier by Mayans as attributes of Cervantes.
Not only these are to be restored but also their literary equivalent, decorum.
A concept adapted from Aristotle's *Poetics*, requiring that characters remain true
to their stations in life and psychologically consistent throughout the temporal
progression of the literary work, the problem of decorum dominates early
eighteenth-century interpretations of *Don Quixote*. As a concept decorum
implies the complete control of the author over his characters as he uses them
to express his own intended meaning. A less-than-decorous character undermines authorial intention by failing to conform to the social status and
personality inherent in its literary conception. Literary disorder and extravagance, as understood by Oldfield, then work to subvert not only authorial
intention but also the authority to reform society through literature.

Accordingly, the second portrait of Cervantes in this edition emphasizes both
the dignity of the author and his control over the novel's protagonists (see
Figure 14).[21] This image, the first extant portrait of Cervantes, establishes the
image of Cervantes as both soldier and author, an iconographic constant in

the eighteenth century.[22] The author sits in the right foreground, holding quill to paper and discreetly hiding his hand, injured in the battle of Lepanto, from the viewer. Framed by folds of drapery (typical of the portraiture of dignitaries undertaken by artists such as Van Dyck), he appears to be a self-contained and dignified man as he looks fixedly into the distance. On the walls about him are pieces of armour and against them are piles of books, the attributes of his two offices. But more curious is an ambiguous space that extends behind him in the upper left-hand corner. Logically speaking, this would be a picture, but the perspective of the vaulted Gothic room it represents is enough askew to raise a doubt. Through this hall, pierced by tall Gothic windows, ride Don Quixote and Sancho Panza, unmistakable despite their small size. Armour clads the knight's tall, skinny frame, while his crooked, knobby nose dominates his profile. Rocinante, his horse, appears duly skeletal and overburdened. Sancho Panza is embodied in a tubby figure with a square, featureless face atop Rucio, his donkey. Kent has drawn the characters' figures from the author's textual descriptions, unlike those seen in earlier illustrations.[23] Cervantes and his characters now sport the forms that will create the iconographic tradition in which they still exist, forms that purport to transfer to paper and line the words of the author. This edition draws from Cervantes' authority, understood to be the text read literally, in order to establish the visual tradition. In the light of what will follow, it is interesting to note that the author's satirical intent, as stated in the first prologue to *Don Quixote* and depicted in the allegorical frontispiece, will not retain its authority, given that these figures will ride off into even the most unauthoritative popular representations, such as *aleluyas*, comic books, and Broadway shows.

AN APOLOGY FOR A NEOCLASSICAL AUTHOR: MAYANS' BIOGRAPHY OF CERVANTES

Not even by rigid neoclassical standards, however, could critics reach an agreement on the value or meaning of Cervantes' *Don Quixote*. Upon the appearance of Lesage's translation of Avellaneda's spurious continuation of the novel, a debate arose concerning the relative merit of the anonymous author's imitation as opposed to Cervantes' original. Nor did Cervantes always come out on top. The general disregard in which Spanish intellectuals held Cervantes at this time is not particularly surprising when one takes into account the seventeenth-century reception of his most widely read novel. Françoise Etienvre refers to the law of silence around the popular *Don Quixote* that still prevailed, pointing out that Feijoo never mentioned Cervantes in his *Teatro crítico*.[24] The most blatant insult to Cervantes' literary fame was, of course, Lesage's transla-tion of Avellaneda's continuation in 1704 and its republication in Spain in 1732.[25] In Lesage's preface to the translation one notes the importance of decorum as a criterion for literary worth in his assessment of Avellaneda's protagonists. As far as Don Quixote is concerned, "he created a knight errant who is overall grave, and thus all his speeches are magnificent, pompous, and flowery."[26] But Avellaneda's rendering of Sancho Panza far exceeds Cervantes' depiction of the squire: "This one is a peasant who has all the good sense of the other, but he is even simpler."[27] Cervantes' Sancho, in contrast, violates decorum by showing traces of wit: "I forget that it is Sancho who speaks; and I sense, in spite of myself, that it is the Author under the name of Sancho."[28] Cervantes' error, then, is to have used Sancho as his mask, or his mouthpiece, since a peasant could not possibly speak for or as an author.

Influenced by the Lesage translation of 1704, Blas Antonio Nasarre, chief librarian of the king, and Agustín Montiano y Luyando, director of the Real Academia de la Historia and a member of the Real Academia de la Lengua, were the moving forces behind this lone Spanish eighteenth-century republication of Avellaneda's *Don Quixote*, a sure index of the work's plunge in popularity.[29] In his "Aprobación" to the edition Montiano judges Avellaneda's continuation to be superior to Cervantes' original. He considers the adventures of Avellaneda's protagonist, as well as the characters themselves, very natural, since they are portrayed according to the rigorous rule of verisimilitude.[30] He objects to the lack of decorum of Cervantes' Sancho, writing that "it does not seem easy to reconcile the extreme simplicity that he displays at times with the delicate picaresque ingenuity he uses in other occasions, and the particular discretion he often manifests; unless we say that Sancho speaks and works at times like the author, instead of working and speaking always as Sancho."[31]

Montiano specifically casts down the gauntlet for the supporters of Cervantes to defend their own evident lack of good taste:

Probably there is no lack today of supporters of his opinion, although for a different cause, because good taste is very debilitated, and ignorance enjoys the larger band of supporters. None the less, such opponents should cause little concern, least of all for being people who celebrate only what makes them laugh and do not know where too much humour sins.[32]

Paolo Cherchi attributes this surprising preference for Avellaneda, first expressed by Torres Villarroel, to "that particularly mechanical and dogmatic mode of understanding the concept of *mimesis*, satisfied by a gross realism that provides a shadowy sketch of characters, and inspired by a tendency towards a taste for the picaresque romance, the same taste Lesage had used to justify his own preference."[33] None the less, Montiano names this particular taste *buen gusto*, and thus attributes the preference for Avellaneda to those in the elite circle of taste. He blames this error in taste on the presumptuous critics of his century who fail to appreciate the harmony of proportion and medium that constitutes a work's success, as seen best in Augustan Latin literature. In his defence of Avellaneda, Montiano uses the same neoclassical terminology of taste and decorum that Mayans uses to argue for Cervantes. How and why, then, do the two contemporaries end up at odds with each other?

THE INTELLECTUAL CONTEXT OF THE PRODUCTION OF THE CARTERET EDITION

A discussion of Mayans' and Montiano's personal antipathy is necessary to elucidate the larger literary quarrel that contributes to Mayans' espousal of Cervantes and his participation in the production of the Lord Carteret edition. Due primarily to his methodological differences of opinion with Feijoo and to a subsequent series of intrigues among the circle of royal librarians, Mayans, affiliated with the Biblioteca Real in Madrid at the time, found himself in disfavour with Nasarre, Montiano, and others of their circle. As a young man he had established contact with Feijoo but soon became disillusioned with what he considered a lack of academic rigour on the part of the older scholar. He criticized Feijoo's work for its debt to foreign secondary sources rather than to original research on primary sources. Feijoo, in the eyes of the younger scholar, thereby passed on errors to the popular audience while at the same time abdicating his scholarly responsibility in order to investigate controversial topics.[34] In this criticism of the more traditional thinker, one glimpses Mayans' approach to *Don Quixote*, in which he insists on overlooking the earlier reception of the text in favour of his own, more analytical reading.

The relationship worsened upon a series of misunderstandings, exchanged criticisms, and political manoeuvrings that often placed Mayans at odds with other intellectuals. By the time he wrote his biography of Cervantes, he was engaged in disputes both with Feijoo and with the circle of intellectuals in the Madrid court. Whether he was mistreated, as Mestre assumes, is not a question of importance to this study. Indeed, Mayans was a self-appointed authority on the Castilian language and literature, and a fierce participant in the fiery debates that raged among the lettered elite in Madrid in the 1730s. More importantly, Mayans adopted the position of champion of Cervantes in opposition to the intellectual powers-that-were in Madrid. Despite his alienation from his Spanish peers (or perhaps because of it) he maintained extensive correspondence with European intellectuals and was acquainted with many foreigners in Madrid. Through his long-standing friendship with Benjamin Keene, an affiliate of the British Embassy in Madrid, he was contacted by Lord Carteret to include his biography of Cervantes in the edition of *Don Quixote* to be published by Tonson in London. Mestre assumes that part of Keene's and Carteret's concern was that Mayans' biography counteract the championing of Avellaneda at the expense of Cervantes.[35]

Mayans did champion Cervantes, and at the cost of Avellaneda. It is no accident that this edition contains one of the very few illustrations of Don Alvaro Tarfe's certification that Avellaneda's character Don Quixote was indeed

a fake (2:72). Mestre insists that the biography was a direct attack upon the
latter writer and his supporters.[36] As Mestre documents, Nasarre and Montiano
indeed considered it a personal attack. Thus, counterattacks against Mayans
increased, the most interesting of which accused the Valencian of being anti-
Spanish for his support of the author who had attacked the Spanish *hidalguía*,
or lower nobility.[37] Cervantes' professed satiric targets, chivalric romances, were
not necessarily held in low esteem by all. Even leaving aside the vitriolic
conservative voices defending this genre as an element of Spain's vanished
valour, more central voices lamented its passing. In a review of Lesage's translation published in the *Diario de los sabios* (31 March 1704) the anonymous
journalist (perhaps Nasarre) largely repeated, at times even translated, Lesage's
criticism of Cervantes' *Don Quixote*. This author insisted that both Cervantes'
and Avellaneda's goal was to amuse rather than to exile chivalric romances from
Spain. He even cited the approval granted some chivalric romances by the priest
and the barber in their scrutiny of Don Quixote's library as evidence that
Cervantes did not intend to proscribe the genre. At the end of the article,
however, he digressed to question Cervantes' and Avellaneda's parodic attack
on chivalric romances: "There is no lack of those who believe that youth have
lost a very useful source of instruction through the chivalric romances (which
are now very rare) in the heroism that encouraged the generosity and valour
represented by the well-imagined fables."[38] He continued to argue that the
books of knight errantry were required instructional reading for Spanish *caballeros*, who learned matters both of arms and of the heart by imitating their
example. Thus Cervantes, whom Mayans wished to set forth as a national hero,
was disparaged as a traitor to the values of his own country.[39]

   In order to argue for the worth and superiority of the original *Don Quixote*
Mayans appropriated the terms of the debate set forth by the anti-Cervantes
camp. In response to the criticism of Cervantes as a traitor to Spanish values,
he argued that the chivalric romances represented a barbaric vision of civilization. In response to the aesthetic criticism of Cervantes' *Don Quixote* as
indecorous, he adopted the three qualities of perfection in traditional rhetoric:
invention, disposition, and style.[40] In short, Mayans argued for Cervantes' work
in the same neoclassical terms used by Avellaneda's supporters and even those
indifferent to either, such as Ignacio de Luzán.[41] As a demonstration of Mayans'
ultimate success, when Nasarre finally did edit and print Cervantes' theatrical
works in 1749, he praised Cervantes in Mayans' terms, for his invention and
his attempt to rid Spain of non-classicizing literary genres:

And he tried through these eight comedies and *entremeses*, as if with so many other
Don Quixotes and Sanchos, who exiled the strange and unreasonable chivalric
romances, that destroyed the judgment of many men; he tried, I repeat, to mend the
errors of comedy with comedy, and to purge the theatre of bad taste and immorality,

returning to the reason and authority which had been discarded to please the base public, without respecting the remaining and healthier part of the people.[42]

Mayans won primacy for his interpretation of *Don Quixote* as a neoclassical work by rescuing it from the contempt of neoclassical intellectuals in Spain.

As the allegorical frontispiece to the 1738 Lord Carteret edition has already shown, Cervantes had to be clothed in the garb (or lack thereof) of a classical hero in order that his canonization as the author of a neoclassical work should take place. Mayans undertook this task in a similar manner. In the dedication to the 1738 Lord Carteret edition Mayans lamented the lack of information concerning Cervantes' life (in fact, the information was so scarce that he mistakenly assumed Madrid to be his birthplace), and stated that a discussion of the author's work would have to serve to clothe him.[43] His biography of Cervantes represents an effort to clothe the vulnerable author metaphorically in the respectable garb of neoclassicism, "in order to cover in some way with such rich and beautiful clothing the poverty and nudity of that person supremely worthy of a better century; because, although they say that the age in which he lived was golden, I know that for him and others worthy of better, it was an age of iron."[44] This sympathy for the man Cervantes, the desire to cover his nudity with this biography and this edition, indicates a more than didactic, academic appreciation of the novel. Perhaps it would not be too speculative to suggest that Mayans' sympathy derived in part from his own position as an outsider to the dominant literary and intellectual circles of Madrid.[45] Granting the author the final word, Mayans chose to end his biography with Cervantes' self-description from his prologue to the *Exemplary Novels.*

Within the context described above, Mayans' desire, identical to that of the others involved in the publication of this edition, was to produce an authoritative biography and edition to protect and honour the author whom they perceived as unjustly maligned and forgotten. The Spaniard clearly stated this aim in his dedicatory letter to Lord Carteret:

Your Excellency justly deserves his works, for you have shown yourself to be the most liberal supporter and propagator of his memory; and it is due to you that *Cervantes* and his *Ingenious* Gentleman attain today the greatest appreciation and esteem. Then, let the Great *Don Quixote de la Mancha,* if up until now a disgraced knight errant, henceforth happily fortunate on account of you, sally forth anew into the light of day. Long live the memory of the incomparable *Miguel de Cervantes Saavedra!*[46]

This exultant outburst championing the knight Don Quixote rings surprisingly enthusiastic, yet the character is secondary to the author, for whom it is the vehicle of fame. Authority is always presented in this edition as a function of the author's good character, writing skills, and controlled, instructive use of the imagination to create the novel and characters, for which he is to be praised and remembered.

CERVANTES AS A NEOCLASSICAL SATIRIST OF PERNICIOUS LITERATURE

Mayans y Siscar's biography was, therefore, largely concerned with saving Cervantes' reputation and buttressing his authority.[47] Part of this task was to recover what he believed to be Cervantes' voice within the novel. First, he must establish the importance of the author's presumed goal of satirizing and emas-culating the popular literature of knight errantry. This may not seem so different from the burlesque seventeenth-century reception of the novel as a parody, but one should remember that as a parody *Don Quixote* quickly entered the realm of popular literature instead of changing it from above. Part of the intellectual disdain in which the novel was held stemmed undoubtedly from its apparent popularity among the lower, uneducated classes. Thus, Mayans first had to establish the importance and necessity of the satirical aim to destroy the genre of chivalric romance through parody. He therefore wrote a history of pernicious literature, beginning with its effect in the classical world by referring to the role of the Milesian tales in the fall of Rome. Of most concern, however, was the role of the literature of knight errantry in the Christian era. Mayans mistakenly believed the legends of King Arthur to be contemporaneous with a historical king of that identity, ca 640. He saw the chivalric romance as vitally linked to the new society of the Dark Ages after the fall of Rome, one based on brute strength, which replaced the lost classical civilization.

According to Mayans the chivalric romances were the literary offspring of barbarism, the enemy of classical civilization.[48] To attack this monstrous issue as Cervantes did was to avenge the entire system of values that eighteenth-century thinkers believed to be classical:

He who had the most power, was worthiest. Barbarism had more power, and emerged winning and triumphant; the study of letters was viciously attacked, and good taste annihilated. When those things are lacking, they are necessarily missed; false doctrine and depraved taste took their place. They wrote histories that were fabulous, because the memory of past events had been lost, or it was not known how to look for them. Some men who suddenly desired to be the teachers of life could hardly teach their readers what they had never learned. Such was Theletinus Helius, an English writer, who around the year 640, during the reign of Arthur in Britain, fabulously transcribed the deeds of this king.[49]

Mayans established a whole web of concepts associated either with civilization or barbarism. Brute power belonged to barbarism, exiled the reason of civilization, and left an ideological vacuum into which authors ignorant of better poured their fabulous stories of power. Cervantes' counterattack, pitting reasonable literature against the marvellous, constituted not only a literary reform but also a just act of war against the barbaric vestiges of imagination and raw power left in society.

Mayans chose to emphasize as the most pernicious effect of this barbaric literature the confusion of fiction with history, or "mentira" with "verdad," that it created in the reader's mind.[50] Within the culture that produced chivalric romances, fictional tales gained authority through time. Therefore, these same texts were considered to be historically true, and were thus included in works of history such as the *Crónica general de España*, compiled at royal request by Florián Ocampo and Ambrosio Morales in the sixteenth century. Mayans considered this example particularly pernicious, since it led Fray Antonio de Guevara to say, "Outside of divine letters there is nothing to affirm, nor to deny in any work."[51] History thus found itself outside the authority of reason, subject to the demands of political power and besmirched by fiction's lack of veracity. As a historian who charged himself with the task of introducing new standards of historical research and documentation into Spain, Mayans found this mixture of lore and history particularly galling. The Aristotelian concept of fiction as a source of general truth, superior to the particular truths of history, had been discarded in favour of a more positivist preference for fact. Very much concerned with reviving the status of sixteenth-century Spanish intellectuals whom he considered his intellectual forefathers, Mayans continued by citing Juan de Valdés's critique in the *Diálogo de la lengua* of the author of *Amadís de Gaula* for calling truths what are obviously lies or offences against verisimilitude. Like Luis Vives, whose disapproval of chivalric romance he also cited, Mayans feared that the naïve reader would be unable to discern truth from fiction.

The goal of Cervantes, then, as presented by Mayans, was to educate the reader rather than actually to eradicate the literature of knight errantry. According to Mayans, Cervantes believed the best method was to fight fire with fire – or rather, fiction with fiction:

Cervantes believed that one nail pulls out another; and that given the inclination of the greater part of the leisured people towards similar books, using the force of reason, which usually only moves thoughtful minds, was not the best way to avert them from such reading; but rather a book of similar inventiveness and honest entertainment, which, by exceeding all others in the delightfulness of its reading, would attract all kinds of people, both intelligent and foolish.[52]

This statement of Cervantes' goal and methods is replete with implications. First, Mayans neatly classifies the author's work according to the Horatian precept of instruction and entertainment. Of more interest is his assumption that reason, the great weapon of so many Enlightenment thinkers, would not reach the common people. The concept of the vulgar public is still clearly at work, yet Cervantes' popularity among the uneducated can be explained as evidence of his didactic success. Instead of surpassing the capacity of the stupid and becoming the intellectual property only of the intelligent, good literature will educate the former about the excesses of chivalric literature and form in them good taste. Ironically, in his conception of the need to educate the common people, Mayans does not differ so greatly from his antagonist Feijoo. But it is clear that Mayans must justify Cervantes' popularity with the uneducated lower classes by cloaking him in the robe of the educator in order to argue that he is not one of them. Unlike his contemporary Spanish neoclassical scholars, Mayans has not dethroned the popular author Cervantes in favour of the forgotten Avellaneda but rather robed him in a neoclassical aesthetic more acceptable to the educated elite.

DON QUIXOTE AS THE MOUTHPIECE OF CERVANTES

Mayans believed that Cervantes, in his role as a literary educator, often spoke through his characters, in particular the Canon of Toledo and Don Quixote. Whether the literary precepts put forward by the Canon are to be read as Cervantes' beliefs or as yet another target of his satirical quill is still a matter of critical debate.[53] That the Canon was generally accepted as Cervantes' mouthpiece among later eighteenth-century critics should be of no surprise, since the cleric offered a critique of the *comedia*, Spanish theatre, based on its lacks of verisimilitude and decorum and its use for entertainment to the exclusion of instruction.[54] More surprising is that Mayans at times considers Don Quixote the mouthpiece of the author:

Aside from his manias, Don Quixote speaks as a sane man, and his discourses conform well to reason. Very worthy of reading are those he gave on the Golden Age, the first age of the world, poetically described; ... on the lifestyle of the student and soldiers; ... on the distinctions among gentlemen and lineages; ... on the use of poetry; ... and the two lessons, one political, ... and the other economic, ... which he gave to Sancho Panza, when he was going to be the governor of the island Barataria, are such, that they can be given to true governors, who certainly should put them into practice.[55]

The observation that Don Quixote enjoyed his sane moments is certainly not new, but it represents a distinct change from the earlier reading of the character as a fool. Lesage and Montiano objected to these moments as breaches in decorum. But for Mayans, Don Quixote is at times reasonable and dignified despite his singular delusion; and the lessons offered through him by Cervantes are as relevant to the governing elite on matters of economics and law as they are to the people on matters of literary taste.

This elevation of the character makes it proper for Cervantes to speak through Don Quixote and still maintain his dignity and authority as a serious writer. Because he avoids the fantastic excesses of imagination and creates a decorously eloquent character in his protagonist, Cervantes, unlike the authors of chivalric romances, can express truth through fiction. If Don Quixote is merely a buffoon, then his author is discredited. For this reason, Mayans objects to the base characters created by Avellaneda. Not only are they stolen from the author; they also rob the author of his dignity. The biographer quotes the passage in which Don Quixote meets Don Alvaro Tarfe, who has met the false characters, and then exclaims:

Admirable criticism! One of the precepts of the fable is to depict things as they are reputed to be, or to invent things such that they fit together. Cervantes had depicted Don Quixote as a knight errant, valiant, discreet, and enamoured; and this fame he had when the so-called Fernández de Avellaneda sat down to continue his story; and in it he paints him as a coward and fool, no longer in love ... Cervantes conceived Sancho Panza as simple, humorous, and neither gluttonous nor drunken; Fernández de Avellaneda conceived him, yes, as simple, but not at all humorous, as gluttonous and drunken. And thus he neither depicted things as they were reputed to be, nor invented with uniformity.[56]

In this passage Mayans privileges the original Don Quixote, unlike the anonymous author of the previously mentioned article in the *Diario de los sabios*, who privileged imitation over original creation. According to the principle of imitation, the anonymous writer using the pen-name Avellaneda has neither followed nor surpassed his model. Thus Cervantes' work stands superior, not only in being the model but also in its unity of character and action, which causes the novel to conform to itself. Through this shift in standards of evaluation Mayans successfully undercuts the preference for Avellaneda's Don Quixote and Sancho Panza on the grounds of decorum.

As a concept, decorum depends on continuity and uniformity, for the characters remain "true" to themselves and their station in life. Mayans charges Avellaneda with discontinuity by accusing him of not following the original. In fact, he rather pedantically insists that Avellaneda's characters are the polar opposites of Cervantes' originals. His reversal of the judgment concerning the comparative *gracia*, witty humour, of the two Sanchos directly rebuts Lesage's and Montiano's earlier charge that Cervantes' creation was indecorous and unhumorous. This sharp difference of opinion may throw a different light on the assertion made by recent critics that Cervantes' *Don Quixote* is correctly read primarily as a funny book.[57] Evidently, for Lesage and Montiano, Cervantes' novel was simply not as funny as Avellaneda's. Mayans links the *gracia* of Cervantes' Sancho to his relative moderation in eating and drinking, whereas the unbridled gluttony and thirst of Avellaneda's character would seem to diminish rather than increase any humour. There may be two phenomena at play here: a change in taste from burlesque to more cultivated, sensitive humour, and/or an ambiguity in the term *gracia*, which applies to festive and joking humour but also to the pleasantly attractive. Even more salient is Mayans' very positive description of Don Quixote as valiant and sensitive. In order to achieve his project of defending Cervantes as an author worthy of critical attention, the critic defends his literary protagonists as characters who, although funny, transcend humour in their nobler qualities. The elevation of the character Don Quixote is necessary for the ennoblement of the author Cervantes within this context of neoclassical interpretation. That the author is the hero of this edition is left in no doubt – the portrait of Cervantes, the allegorical frontispiece, and the biography proclaim this. Yet a first step has been taken towards the elevation of the character Don Quixote to hero, a characteristic of the Romantic reading. The Enlightenment and Romantic readings resemble each other to the extent that they both elevate the text, its characters, and its author, either from the burlesque semi-oblivion of its popular reception in the seventeenth century or from its stilted interpretation according to neoclassical standards by intellectuals in the later eighteenth century.

GESTURE AS AN ELEVATING DEVICE IN VANDERBANK'S ILLUSTRATIONS

Perhaps John Vanderbank's illustrations best demonstrate the effect of applying a neoclassical idiom, in this case pictorial, to the novel's episodes and characters. There is no doubt that the illustrations for this edition were conceived to participate in and supplement this exalted vision of *Don Quixote* and its author. According to a letter written by Mayans to Carteret upon receipt of a published copy of his *Vida de Cervantes* and copies of the illustrations, "the prints are admirable, first one attends to the selection of episodes, then the execution of the engraving. One only notices what you, with such good judgment, have already pointed out to me, that perhaps decorum is sometimes lacking with reference to national clothing … But these are things that should pass unnoticed in view of so much perfection in all the rest."[58] These illustrations, designed by John Vanderbank, engraved by John Vandergucht, and supervised by John Oldfield, are indeed remarkable for the technical expertise exhibited by both artists.[59] With the exception of the Coypel illustrations, these stand in relief against the generally poorly drawn, executed, and printed illustrations of earlier editions. The mere inclusion of these prints marks the edition as one of physical grandeur intended for an affluent and presumably discerning reader.

An index of the stylistic elevation of the subject-matter is the treatment of the hands. Artists have generally considered the hands and the face the most expressive elements of the body. For this reason, in workshops such as Rubens' the master would paint the hands and faces. The viewer's eye is automatically drawn to the face and hand, a fact acknowledged even by a twentieth-century avant-garde artist such as Picasso in his fracturing of the face and hand during his Cubist period. In the Carteret edition the repetition of a single hand gesture in the representation of a variety of characters is most striking. The same hand, in a terribly unnatural but refined gesture, with the two middle fingers held together and the outside ones spread apart, appears on the character central to the composition in seven illustrations in the fourth volume alone: the Duchess looking on Sancho Panza (fp2); Don Quixote receiving the fainting Altisidora (fp108); Teresa Panza receiving Sancho's envoy (fp152); Doña Rodríguez looking on Tosilos as he offers to fight for her daughter (fp213); the king holding the sceptre at Altisidora's funeral (fp326); and the notary taking down Don Quixote's last will and testament and the priest looking on the deathbed (fp363). This elevating gesture is none other than that of Venus in Botticelli's *Birth of Venus* and so belongs to the pictorial tradition of the Venus Coelestis, representative of the higher qualities and capacities of humanity within neoclassical iconography.[60] The indecorous representation of a peasant woman, Teresa Panza, employing such an elevating gesture must be explained.

All the characters depicted in this manner share the role of an interested spectator, often one dispensing largesse towards another character who expresses humility, service, or contrition. Most notable is the wide social disparity of the characters imparting *noblesse oblige* with this same hand gesture. Spanning the social classes, the artist attributes this gesture to the Duchess, Doña Rodríguez, and Teresa Panza. In this context the gesture tends to equalize the characters, not by lowering the Duchess but by elevating Doña Rodríguez and Teresa Panza. The dignity of Teresa's figure, despite her mop, rags, and rather sharp profile, is expressed not only by the gesture but by her statuesque girth. It would be easy to have used her corporality in parody or as as expression of carnivalesque humour towards the grotesque body. Nevertheless, in addition to not parodying the mother, the artist also graces the teen-aged daughter with a Cupid-like air as her drapery falls from one small breast. This classicizing, Rubenesque depiction of the two characters is surprising, both when compared to other, earlier burlesque illustrations and also when seen alongside the text, which pokes fun at the peasant woman's attempt to speak as a lady. Yet these classicizing elements continue to appear. All the characters, including Don Quixote and Sancho, sport statuesque proportions and weight, often distributed in *contrapposto* stances, rather than a more grotesquely exaggerated roundness or flatness. Even Don Quixote has shapely, muscular legs when glimpsed beneath his nightshirt in the comic bedroom encounter with Doña Rodríguez (4:fp129). Non-parodic elevation of comic characters is rare, but it is necessary to transform *Don Quixote* from a burlesque novel deflating the illusions of lowly people to a classic instructive for the educated classes.

OLDFIELD ON THE ILLUSTRATION AS A VEHICLE OF
INSTRUCTION AND INTERPRETATION

Vanderbank's illustrations are accompanied by the "Advertisements concerning the Prints, by John Oldfield, MD," a discussion of the same that also offers a discourse upon the correct design and interpretation of book illustrations in general. As will become clear in an analysis of Oldfield's writings, his concern with the illustrations stems from his desire to control and guide the reader's interpretation according to his own view of the text as a satirically didactic work. These concerns about the correct interpretation of visual images had already been stated by Jonathan Richardson in the *Theory of Painting* in 1715.[61] Richardson conceived of painting as a form of language capable of expression and of the painter as a student of this language.[62] As Lawrence Lipking writes, "Like modern psychologists, Richardson is arguing that we perceive according to the formulae made by our expectations, and that by storing our minds with certain kinds of images we can quite literally revise our visions. 'Knowing' or 'conceiving' are not separable from 'seeing,' nor the mind from the eye, and therefore every painter may be trained to see according to intellectually respectable visual traditions."[63] Certainly, the application of the above-mentioned hand gesture is evidence of the artist's use of the respectable tradition of history painting to depict a subject previously seen as common. The influence of the use of these elevating pictorial idioms on the canonization of the text cannot be overlooked. Oldfield's concern in the "Advertisement" is to educate the viewer rather than the artist according to the ideals of neoclassicism, based on the Italian Renaissance.[64] But Vanderbank's representation of the text according to these very same ideals leads to a quite different interpretation, particularly in its emphasis on Sancho's development and its tendency to present Don Quixote as a sentimental hero in spite of the neoclassical, allegorical frame.

For Oldfield, as indicated also by his explication of the allegorical frontispiece, the hero of the novel is the author Cervantes, not the protagonist. Oldfield, like Mayans, sees Don Quixote as the instrument of the parody, a view he states once again in the "Advertisement." Cervantes has completed his work of literary reform "in his inimitable performance, by erecting a scheme of the like fabrick and texture with those of the writers of romance, where he has foiled and vanquished all the brood of monsters of knight-errantry, with their patrons, and the whole band of necromancers, to assist them, at their own weapons."[65] The Spanish translator adds to this assertion the comment that Cervantes' literary "scheme" depends on the creation of a protagonist as marvellous, although decorous, as the heroes of chivalric romances.[66] If the hero is equally fantastic, although decorous, then it is easy to imagine how the careless reader might miss the parodic intent of the author. The addition to the Spanish version is remarkable, for it reveals the so-called Romantic reading to be implicit in the neoclassical reading, although lurking as a dangerous shadow on the other side of the tapestry. Or, to use the metaphor of the allegorical frontispiece, the Don Quixote mask might hide too completely the hero Hercules behind it. The use of heroic language, be it verbal or pictorial, runs the risk of conflating the satire with the object satirized and, subsequently, confusing the didactic message.

The illustrations, because they represent the activities of Don Quixote and not those of the author Cervantes, could potentially lead the reader astray if they are limited to depicting burlesquely funny scenes, for they do not make clear Cervantes' parodic intent. Oldfield particularly criticizes Coypel for having indulged his fancy in the depiction of the misadventures and visions of the literary character. Due to the ridiculous nature of these images and their lack of verisimilitude, their illustration results in a "kind of ocular demonstration of the falsity of them, and has the same effect upon the knight's own performances, as *they* were intended by the author to have upon *those* of the former champions in romance, by heightening and aggravating the extravagance and improbability of them."[67] The object of ridicule, then, becomes Cervantes' work rather than the chivalric romances he parodies. What particular measures does Mr Oldfield urge the illustrator to take to overcome this danger? He proposes an alternative to the depiction of action – the depiction of setting and characters – and recommends the illustration of gestures, costumes, facial expressions, and character as a means to use the language of visual imagery to create a more interesting and, one supposes, verisimilar image. This recommendation, although it seems rather obvious today, was in fact a departure from the seventeenth-century practice of illustration, notable for its lack of subtle detail, character differentiation, and unique settings. Illustrators of the text previous to Coypel emphasized the action and not the interaction – certainly not the dialogue – of the characters. That Oldfield suggested this change demonstrates his conception of illustration as an elevated art, akin to history painting, capable of more completely imitating the action and interaction of the novel's characters through the visual elements of gesture and facial expression. As Lipking points out, painting enjoys a special status among the arts since it "most clearly illustrates the doctrine that the arts are imitative, and because psychological analysis of the imagination took its pattern, after Hobbes, from the sense of sight."[68] Illustration, as a branch of painting, can constitute a worthy part of a critical edition of a classical author if it follows the conventions of history painting rather than the earlier popular burlesque woodcuts.

Oldfield offers his reader a discussion of the various moments of an episode suitable for depiction in order to illustrate his new conception of the visual genre. In the episode of the midnight encounter of Doña Rodríguez and Don Quixote he pinpoints four moments, slices of time suitable to be frozen in the two-dimensional space of the illustration: the moment when Don Quixote first sees the woman in her glasses and believes her to be a witch; the second moment when he then believes she is threatening his honour; the third when he takes her hand to promise his services; and the fourth when they converse. Notably absent is the paddling of the pair by the Duchess's maids. Oldfield recommends the illustration of the third moment, which is indeed the moment depicted in this edition. Don Quixote ceremoniously takes the woman's right hand to kiss it, as she offers it in turn with the same sense of delicacy. As Oldfield writes,

This solemnity, of that of his conducting her towards the bed, to which this is the introduction, or part of the same action, would perhaps afford a more entertaining picture than any other particular in the whole story, and accordingly it seems, in a manner, to be pointed out by the author for that purpose, by what he says in the next paragraph in the following humorous words. "Here Cid Hamete, making a parenthesis, swears by Mahomet, that he would have given the best of two coats he had, only to have seen the knight and the matron walk thus, hand in hand, from the chamber door to the bedside."[69]

Oldfield recognizes the joke, but perhaps not the irony in the aside. First of all, he unquestioningly aligns Cide Hamete's voice with Cervantes', thus ignoring the fictional space between the two. His comment, ironically providing a glimpse of another narrative mask, is taken as Cervantes' directive to the reader and the illustrator. It becomes a word of authority, which is indeed ironic, given the extreme questioning of authority and authorship in the novel.[70]

THE MARGINALIZATION OF THE FANTASTIC: THE CAVE OF MONTESINOS EPISODE

Authority is of great concern to Oldfield. He also specifically discusses the illustration of the Cave of Montesinos, dangerous because it opens up towards the marvellous. Don Quixote, after descending by rope into a cavern, returns with a tale of having met the great knight Durandarte, who affirms his own mission as a knight errant, consulted with the wizard Montesinos, and seen with his own eyes the enchanted Dulcinea. Oldfield's interpretation of the episode is simple and authoritative:

The recital of this transformation is made to a certain curious scholar, a collector of wonders, and a great dealer in the marvellous and improbable, and to his own squire, the original inventor of it, who had framed the story, to serve his own purpose, upon the plan of his master's romantic ideas; who, in conformity to them, readily believed, and, by natural consequence, when he was properly illuminated by the vapours and exhalations of the cavern, as distinctly saw all the particulars of it.[71]

Oldfield is careful to point out the physical and psychological factors: affected by the scholar's chatterings, Sancho's fictitious story of Dulcinea's enchantment, and the fumes of the cave, Don Quixote hallucinates. His desire creates a fantastic cave which he imagines himself exploring. In order that the reader not miss the crucial point that all was imagined, the narrator, Cide Hamete Benengeli, mentions it in parentheses. His meaning, taken to be that of the author, is not to be missed. Oldfield then charges the illustrator to take similar care to present the imagination in parentheses:

[The episode] will be sufficiently distinguished by the drawing of it, as we have ordered the matter in the print, in the hollow of the cave there represented, to be seen through the mouth of it. Examples of this kind are frequent enough with painters and engravers, of which one may be seen in a print of *Rembrandt's*, where he has told the story, which a conjurer or fortune-teller is supposed to be relating to his correspondent, by a faint sketch of it on the wall of his cell: and the same method is made use of by *Raphael* in a picture on the subject of *Pharaoh's* dream.[72]

Significantly, Oldfield draws upon a mode of representation of the marvellous already authorized by Rembrandt and Raphael.[73] One observes that depiction might be dangerous, since it could grant the marvellous an unsuitable power. The frame used by the two masters indicates clearly to the viewer that a marvellous tale is placed within another, more reasonably and verisimilarly represented setting.

In this edition the Cave of Montesinos episode is illustrated twice in order to inscribe the marvellous within a pictorially rational frame. In the first (3:fp204) appears a dark shadow in the lower left-hand corner, in which darker, more deeply engraved shadows hint at some mystery in the cave. Don Quixote, rope in hand, ignores Sancho's attempts to persuade him to give up the descent. In the second illustration (see Figure 15; 2:fp218), the mouth of the cave appears in the lower right-hand corner, this time more lightly sketched and luminous. Weightless, barely delineated figures look on from the background as Montesinos kneels with a cross before the supine figure of Durandarte, who supports himself on one elbow. Don Quixote stands armourless immediately behind Montesinos, with his hand on his chest in the elegant, elevating gesture seen in so many of Vanderbank's illustrations of noble personages. This is the key moment of Don Quixote's narration, when Durandarte stirs from the slumber of death to relay a message to Montesinos and the knight. This oracle proclaims that Don Quixote's deeds have been prophesied by none other than Merlin, and that he has revived the forgotten art of knight errantry to disenchant those lost in the semi-oblivion of the cave's underworld, including his beloved Dulcinea.[74] Perhaps Oldfield perceives this moment as particularly dangerous to the satirical reading, since this is the moment when Don Quixote seizes authorship – actually narrates his own adventure – and justifies his calling to the knighthood. Care must be taken to guide the reader away from precisely that justification. As will be discussed further, in this image Sancho Panza, who

Fig. 15   John Vanderbank. *Cave of Montesinos.*
London 1738. Biblioteca Nacional, Madrid.

sceptically listens to his master's fantastic account, provides the enlightened point of view for the reader to adopt. And yet the marvellous still appears, albeit literally marginalized and faint. Even this apparition of the marvellous would be eschewed by later eighteenth-century illustrators until Daniel Chodowiecki would present it in his boldly burlesque fashion at the end of the century.

THE BANISHMENT OF THE BURLESQUE: THE ADVENTURE OF THE WINDMILLS

Whereas Oldfield calls for the marginalization of the fantastic, he banishes the burlesque. Interestingly enough, he roundly criticizes Charles Antoine Coypel, the most famous illustrator to this date, for having indulged himself and the readers with the depiction of the more burlesque elements of *Don Quixote*. He finds particularly offensive Coypel's illustrations of the battles with the windmills (see Figure 11) and the herd of sheep, "which, though they are very

entertaining in the author's description of them, as they serve to show the
bewitching influence of romances on the imagination, yet, by being set immediately before the eye, become too shocking for belief."[75] Notably, these episodes are not illustrated in this edition, although their representation is standard
in earlier editions. Cervantes, it would appear, has more control over his writing
and succeeds in using the burlesque as a transparent medium of parody through
which his satirical message is always visible. By contrast, the illustrator has less
control over his medium, perhaps because of its two-dimensionality. The
temporal dimension of literature allows the author first to show the sheep as
giants and then to draw away the fantastic screen of Don Quixote's vision to
show the sheep as sheep. The illustrator is limited to one spatial frame. Thus,
Oldfield seems to be manipulating the same spatial/temporal distinction
between the visual arts and literature that Lessing would expound slightly later
in the century, one that in this case works in the favour of literature.[76] Unlike
many of his contemporaries, such as Pope, Oldfield does not necessarily cede
the laurels to painting as the superior of the muses.

   According to Oldfield, the visual representation of Don Quixote's adventures
renders them absurd, "particularly in dramatick representations, where several
of the subjects of the highest and perfectest kinds of narration will not bear to
be shewn to the naked sight, where the eye is the immediate judge."[77] Oldfield
again insists that what may be proper in literary narration is improper in visual
representation. In order to speak of this distinct decorum he equates the
illustration to dramatic representations. Many things that can be written cannot
be manifested to the eyes. This deep distrust of the eyes seems to hinge on the
immediacy of vision, "the immediate judge" that removes the filtering dimension of time. A literary judgment made in time places a burlesque episode
within a series that reveals its serious purpose, the satirical one. A depiction of
Don Quixote attacking the windmills isolates the entertaining fall of the hero
from the episodes that illuminate the satirical reason for the fall and fixes this
image in the undiscerning reader's mind. Without the benefit of the satirical
explanation, the reader, assumed to be naïve by Oldfield, is led to a hasty,
incomplete judgment of the work as a burlesque romp. Oldfield's objection to
the illustration of these episodes is indeed another element of the classicizing
project of this entire edition. Just as Mayans' biography refutes the intellectual
preference for Avellaneda, Oldfield's "Advertisement" to the illustrations refutes
the popular preference for slapstick humour and burlesque.

   The importance of the illustration is, then, to encourage this critical reading
expounded by Oldfield. As he asserts, book illustrations are traditionally seen
as mere ornaments "and to serve only for the amusement of those, who are
satisfied with such kind of beauties of an author."[78] And yet they are "capable
of answering a higher purpose, by representing and illustrating many things,
which cannot be so perfectly expressed by words."[79] In this sense Oldfield

conceives of the illustration as "ilustración," or Enlightenment, a casting of light that drives back the shadows of the reader's mind:

And as there are a great many instances, especially in writers of this kind, where the reader's fancy leads him to imagine how the passions and affections discover themselves upon particular occasions to the eye, and to figure to himself the appearances of them in the features and gestures of the persons concerned; in these circumstances the assistance of an artist, who knows how the countenance and outward deportment are influenced by the inward movements of the mind, and is able to represent the various effects of this kind by the lively expression of the pencil, will supply the imperfection of the reader's imagination, and the deficiency of the description in the author, which must, in many cases, be tedious and ineffectual.[80]

The illustration's function, then, is to fill in the gaps left by the narration, to round it out visually. These verbal gaps are dangerous, for the imagination and passions of the reader can surge through to affect the reading. The illustrations should not encourage the imagination, as they do when Coypel represents windmills as giants, but rather bridle the imagination. The reader should see windmills, if they are even to be depicted – and that is not advised. Instead, decorous moments of conversation between characters, for example, are to be illustrated. Depicting a series of tasteful encounters instead of bawdy, burlesque adventures changes markedly the reader's perception of the text.

ILLUSTRATION AS THEATRE

This change is not only one of interpretation but also of genre. As Oldfield claims, "by the introduction, as it were, of the actors in the treatise, in their proper attitudes and gestures, a written narrative may, in some measure, receive the advantages of a dramatick representation."[81] When writing of the necessity of affixing the meaning of such fabulous scenes as the Cave of Montesinos episode through the use of gesture, posture, and facial expression, Oldfield actually speaks of the meaning as being "determined by the scene of action."[82] What would be the advantages of a dramatic representation? First, one can safely assume that Oldfield refers to neoclassical theater, in which verisimilitude is preferred to the fantastic and the burlesque, quite different from actual theatrical presentations of *Don Quixote* of the previous century. Secondly, the figures would take on bodies, filling out the visual gaps left for the imagination to fill in the text. Thirdly, a sort of *Gesamtkunst,* very different from the Romantic conception of the phenomenon, would be achieved, in which word and image, voice and figure would coexist in a verisimilar manner. The reader would become a spectator and listener. This complete absorption of the *senses* would draw his/her energies away from the imagination. In addition, the manner of representation would control the emotional responses.

Finally, the metaphor of the theatre emphasizes the reader's experience of the novel not as an individual reader but as a member of an audience. Through the image of the theatre public, reading is transformed from a solitary act into a communal one, reminiscent of earlier reading practices. The practice of communal reading would seem to diminish the reader's critical capacity to participate in the group's reaction, but in fact appeared to many eighteenth-century thinkers an exemplary method of instruction. Roger Chartier has commented on the growing nostalgia for communal reading in this period as a response to the perception of private reading as a primarily sensual and escapist pastime. "In the idealized and mythical representation of peasant life widespread among the learned elite, communal reading signified a world in which nothing was hidden, in which knowledge was shared fraternally, and in which the book was revered. There is something here like an inverted portrait of the private, individual, and nonchalant reading habits of the city dwellers."[83] In the case of communal reading, the instruction intended by the author is bolstered by the similar reactions of the people at the listener's side, which in turn discourage intensely individual emotional and imaginative responses. Eventually, this instruction would lead to a change in the community's mores. As Mayans states in the dedication, through his work Cervantes was "capable of exiling the fantastic and extravagant ideas that had infected that of valour and civil conduct."[84] The renewed insistence of Oldfield and the publishers of this edition on Cervantes' supposed intention to reform Spanish society indicates a tendency on their part to see the text as still capable of community reform. It is a short step from Oldfield's discourse on the proper illustration of the work to Herder's assertion that the novel is a critique and satire of *Schwärmerei*, excessive enthusiasms of all kinds. The illustrations and the text, together in an almost dramatic presentation, should shape and critique the community of readers in addition to entertaining them. Again, Mayans makes explicit this instructional intention in the dedication: "But if books of humour have to be accompanied in order to please the eyes, the commentaries will be able to give some indication as to how to better them [that is, the eyes] in the future."[85]

THE ILLUSTRATION AS AN ALTERNATIVE INTERPRETATION: VANDERBANK'S SANCHO

The illustrations to this edition, as to many, confirm Oldfield's deep distrust of the visual image, based on its capacity to supplement the text with meanings perhaps not intended by the author or the editors. Although Vanderbank at times reinforces the neoclassical interpretation of the novel in his illustrations, his images in themselves present a very different interpretation when studied as they appear in the book – as a series. Perhaps most revealing is his characterization of Sancho Panza through the course of the illustrations, particularly since it stands in contrast to Mayans' characterization of the squire. The critic reduces the squire to a symbol, a hieroglyph for the simplicity of the peasant who continues in the error of his beliefs even though he may recognize them to be wrong.[86] Oldfield refers to an example of this blind simplicity when he wonders why Sancho continues to hope for his island even after witnessing Don Quixote's delusions and failures. Nevertheless, he also points to Sancho as the focus of the enlightened point of view in the Cave of Montesinos episode. There are times, then, when Sancho's perspective is to be shared rather than ridiculed. His character takes on a new, weightier side as the clownish peasant is recognized at times to be a source of instruction. Vanderbank's illustrations, more than any other component of this edition, serve to bestow upon the rotund Sancho this three-dimensionality.

In accordance with the more common interpretations of the peasant, Vanderbank at times reveals and deflates his folly. For example, an illustration depicts his terrified flight up a tree on seeing the Squire of the Wood's deformed nose, and represents the cowardice of the character, a quality so funny to many readers and yet objectionable to many critics in the seventeenth and eighteenth centuries (3:fp123). Sancho is also mocked in more peripheral interchanges with secondary characters when Don Quixote occupies centre stage. Sancho's thirst, appetite, and concern for physical comfort most often provide targets for satirical deflation. In the illustration of Don Quixote's discourse on the Golden Age with the goatherds, the inattentive, stout Sancho stands in sharp contrast to the muscular, even classical figure of a young goatherd (see Figure 16; 1:fp78). The materialistic peasant, as he is so often referred to by critics in the eighteenth century, turns his back to his speaking master as he chugs from a jug of wine. The goatherd, in contrast to Sancho, appears as a noble savage; with his strong physique clad in skins, his mind attempts to penetrate the lofty oration. Mayans, anxious to demonstrate Cervantes' erudition and good taste, points to this discourse when he writes of the intelligence and refinement of Don Quixote's opinions in spite of the deluded man's blind spot concerning knight errantry. In this episode Sancho's simple viewpoint is to be shunned, not followed, whereas his reverse image, the young goatherd, represents the person eager to be enlightened.

Vanderbank more often represents Sancho's foolishness as a function of his relationship to Don Quixote. The first illustration in which Sancho appears represents the scene in which the knight invites him to join in the search for adventures as a seduction of the innocent peasant (1:fp49). The squire holds his head in a gesture of appraisal and coyness as Don Quixote steps towards him, his left hand outstretched to the sky, the other extended towards his intended squire. The promise of the island certainly rests on his lips. Scenes that depict this relationship and the promise on which it is based are common in this set of illustrations. The very next illustration, that of the episode of the

Fig. 16   John Vanderbank. *Discourse on the Golden Age*. London 1738. Department of Special Collections, Kenneth Spencer Research Library, University of Kansas.

battle with the Basque, represents the moment after battle when Sancho falls to his knees at his victorious master's feet and pleads for his island (1:fp70). Don Quixote replies that this adventure is one in which only crossroads, not islands, are won. The defeated Basque and the astonished ladies remain in the background as this exchange takes place. Normally an illustrator would depict the battle, with the drama of the clash between the two combatants, as is suggested by the text itself in the description of the frontispiece to the second manuscript. Yet this illustration represents a scene showing both the folly of the master and the credulity of the squire. Action is to be sacrificed to enlightenment (and perhaps decorum). The critical vision centres on the relationship of Don Quixote and Sancho Panza, for within it their respectively fantastical and simple visions throw contrasting lights upon one another. Other episodes that depict Sancho Panza's greed and gullibility include the reception of Princess Micomicona (2:fp28) and Bachelor Samson Carrasco's request to become Don Quixote's squire (3:fp23).

Sancho Panza acts as both fool and foil to his master's delusions in Vanderbank's illustrations. Not surprisingly, several deflate the squire as cowardly and easily deceived. As R.M. Flores writes, "the Age of Enlightenment continued the critical trend set by the previous century and split Sancho's personality in two alien halves: one half, a laughable buffoon, the other, a wise judge."[87] As we have already seen, Vanderbank uses Sancho in the same compositional manner of framing and opposition with other characters, as both buffoon and wise judge. Particularly noteworthy for its potentially dangerous fantastic content is Vanderbank's depiction of the cave of Montesinos episode. In this illustration Sancho Panza takes a central position in the composition, mediating between the foolish student and the foolish knight. In the upper left-hand half of the frame the student stands seriously and attentively, while an incredulous Sancho Panza looks on as Don Quixote recounts his experience. Through the gestures of Don Quixote, his right hand pointing straight up to the sky and his left down towards the cave, the illustrator has taken pains to emphasize that the apparition of shadowy figures in the cave below belongs to the protagonist's tale, not to Cervantes' or the illustrator's account. The discerning reader must take into account the author and, consequently, the authority of the marvellous story of the adventures with Montesinos, Belerma, and Durandarte. The smirking reaction of Sancho Panza, in part due to his own authorship of the enchantment of Dulcinea so central to Don Quixote's adventures in the cave, serves to undermine his master's authority. Oldfield approves of this use of Sancho's perspective as a visual balance to the illusions of the deluded Don Quixote, in particular when compared to the student's gullibility:

Of his two auditors, to whom he makes a most faithful and serious relation of all that his chimerical imagination suggested to him upon this occasion, the one believes every tittle of it; but the other, who knew that he himself had been the lady's only enchanter, could not help entertaining some scruple very prejudicial to his master's veracity, of which however it imported him to conceal the reasons.[88]

Sancho Panza and the student, then, serve as sample receptors of the tale, the one more exemplary than the other. In fact, Oldfield recommends the visual expression of their reactions to the story as a means by which to fix the episode's meaning for the reader through the depiction of the scholar's stupidity, expressing his gullible belief in the fantastic story, and Sancho's stifled leer, expressing and uncovering his disbelief. Two models of reading are offered, the ingenuous and the critical, the one censured as naïve and foolish and the other encouraged as knowing and critical. Sancho Panza takes this same critical position in three other illustrations: the capture of Mambrino's helmet (1:fp190), the questioning of the galley slaves (1:fp213), and the adventure of the penitents (2:fp322). The use of the squire to present an enlightened, *desengañado* point of view constitutes quite a coming-up in the world for the buffoonish creature of material vices presented in earlier readings and illustrations. Sancho begins to represent that common sense available to every man according to the philosophers of sensibility, a new characteristic that would be developed further by the illustrator Francis Hayman twenty years later.

VANDERBANK'S DIGNIFIED, DEFIANT SANCHO

The figure of Sancho Panza takes on a more active role in Book 2 of *Don Quixote*, one suitable to his greater participation in the novel. The illustrators, because they manifest the episodes, seem to be much more aware of this growing strength of character than literary critics or authors of the same period. Flores notes that seventeenth-century writers demonstrate a certain "class consciousness" by presenting Sancho as wise and dignified while pronouncing his judgments, yet "crass, deformed, pigheaded and avaricious" on all other occasions.[89] Vanderbank's illustration of Sancho as judge would seem to follow this pattern, as he occupies an elevated position in the centre of the composition and sports a regal girth enveloped in fine robes. Within the series of illustrations this emerging dignity of Sancho is not, however, a momentary attribute. Thus Sancho Panza, like his wife Teresa, enjoys a promotion in rank to the middle class, a characterization that marks English eighteenth-century reception of the text. Although Vanderbank's Sancho must continue to suffer the abuses of the Duke and the Duchess, he does not accept such treatment. The first indication of his defiant attitude appears in the illustration in which Don Quixote and Sancho are captured by the Duke's men on the road and forcibly taken back to the palace (see Figure 2; 4:fp323). The beaten figure of the knight occupies the centre of the picture, but the inclusion of the squire is just as fascinating. He follows on foot, surrounded by two men, one of whom holds his finger to his mouth to silence Sancho, the irate ex-governor. Sancho's figure is lightly engraved to indicate recession into the background, but his facial expression is anything but receding. He holds himself with a sense of insulted dignity left over from his experience as governor. In this pose he is visually akin to a proud businessman or local official in an English eighteenth-century print.

The series of three illustrations depicting the mock rituals of Altisidora's funeral focus on Sancho's defiant attitude towards his tormentors. Normally, an illustrator would illustrate only one moment or episode from this encounter. Yet in Vanderbank's illustrations there is a crescendo of images towards the end of the novel. Obviously, this was made possible by the bankroll of Lord Carteret, who could afford to overlook the more commercial problems of finances. But even given the increased number of plates, the choice of episodes to be depicted is still remarkable. In the illustration following the kidnapping of Don Quixote and Sancho Panza, Vanderbank represents the first scene of Altisidora's funeral, whose mock-death was allegedly provoked by the chaste knight's rejection of her (see Figure 17; 4:fp326). Therefore, the relationship between the knight and the lady-in-waiting is often the focus of illustrations, but here Sancho's plight is the focus, since he is the central figure of the Duchess's sadistic spectacle. In the first of the three illustrations Altisidora's supine, semi-nude body dominates the foreground. The depiction of her stony

Fig. 17   John Vanderbank. *Altisidora's
Funeral*. London 1738. Department of Special
Collections, Kenneth Spencer Research
Library, University of Kansas.

features and sculpturally moulded breasts is testimony to the classicizing style
the illustrator chooses to adopt at times. Sancho, however, is not allowed such
noble treatment, since this is the scene of his humiliation. Clad in a *sambenito*,
the robe worn by those tried and convicted by the Inquisition, and a cloven
mitre, he stands at Altisidora's feet, lifts up a corner of her robe, and surveys
her with an expression mixed with pity and disbelief. In the following illustration his enemies, the *duennas* (waiting maids), rendered hideous by their dark
spectacles, assail him and prick his ample bottom (see Figure 18; 4:fp329). This
he will not stand for, as he grabs a torch from a page at his left to defend
himself, thus defying the machinations of the Duke and Duchess. In reaction
to Sancho's words and actions of defiance, Altisidora resurrects herself in
disgust, as depicted in the next illustration (see Figure 19; 4:fp330). Sancho
Panza barely contains his fury as he fumes at the young woman.

Like the narrator of the text, Vanderbank has clearly marked Sancho's
defiance as the climax of this episode. Sancho has broken the enchantment by
refusing to play the game any longer. The illustrator hints at this defiance in
the first illustration in order to develop it in the second and third. The
trajectory of images reveals a skeletal plot unfolding: the first introduces the
enigma of the capture and Sancho's new sense of dignity; the second reveals
the enigma to be Altisidora's death as she is unveiled; the third shows Sancho's
revolt against the control of the stage directors; and the fourth depicts the

Fig. 18   John Vanderbank. *Altisidora's Funeral.* London 1738. Department of Special Collections, Kenneth Spencer Research Library, University of Kansas.

denouement. The illustrations literally re-present the narrative, and in so doing focus on Sancho's insistence on his own independence.

"NI QUITO REY, NI PONGO REY": SANCHO'S DECLARATION OF INDEPENDENCE

Just as Vanderbank's depiction of Sancho's defiance represents a more multifaceted interpretation of the character, his illustrations also show dynamic changes in the character's relationship with Don Quixote, particularly as Sancho's newfound dignity challenges the balance of power. This new sense of self-confidence leads Sancho to assert and move himself up towards the level of his master. The first illustration of the squire's independent spirit shows a moment in the fulling-mill episode when Sancho ties the legs of Rocinante to the bridle of his ass (1:fp174). At this point in the narration of both the text and the illustrations, this small act might seem insignificant, an amusing example of Sancho's ingenuity when driven by fear. Yet in Book 2 of the novel both Vanderbank and Cervantes more frequently present such independent actions, one of which is the enchantment of Dulcinea by Sancho Panza (3:fp84). Book illustrators have normally depicted moments focused on Don Quixote, such as his humble supplication at the peasant girl's feet, or her violent rejection of him. Yet Vanderbank depicts Sancho Panza in his crucial role as creator of this deception.

Fig. 19   John Vanderbank. *Altisidora's Funeral.* London 1738.
Department of Special Collections, Kenneth Spencer
Research Library, University of Kansas.

Feigning a look of reverence and hazarding the girl's stick, Sancho, fallen to one knee, clings to the rein of "Dulcinea's" mount. Don Quixote at the right also falls accordingly to one knee, but his face reveals his astonishment and disbelief, and manifests the squire's persuasive power over his master.

Sancho's power as an enchanter did not go unnoticed by either Mayans or John Oldfield in their contributions to this edition. But Vanderbank takes this interpretation a step further, for as the enchantment of Dulcinea grows to ensnare its creator Sancho in its plot, the struggle between master and squire intensifies. The disenchantment of Dulcinea, as prescribed by the Duke and the Duchess, can only be achieved by Sancho Panza's self-castigation. A power struggle ensues, as Don Quixote coerces Sancho to whip himself and perform the disenchantment, and the squire resists. A physical fight actually takes places in an episode rarely depicted even after the eighteenth century (see Figure 20; 4:fp247). Sancho, of course, overcomes his master, who has been greatly weakened in spirit and body by the events of this last sally. As the episode is narrated in the novel:

Fig. 20   John Vanderbank. *Don Quixote and Sancho Panza Fight*. London 1738. Department of Special Collections, Kenneth Spencer Research Library, University of Kansas.

He [Don Quixote] kept on struggling to undo his squire's trousers; seeing which, Sancho leaped to his feet and charged at him. Grappling with him man to man, he tripped him up and brought him down flat on his back, and then placing his right knee on the knight's chest, he grasped his master's hands and held them in such a way that the poor fellow could neither stir nor breathe.

   "How now, traitor?" cried Don Quixote. "So you would rebel against your lord and master, would you, and dare to raise your hand against the one who feeds you?"

   "I neither unmake nor make a king," replied Sancho, "but am simply standing up for myself, for I am my own lord."[90]

As is clear in both the text and the illustration, Sancho Panza physically attacks the hierarchy implicit in the relationship by attacking Don Quixote. He demands not only that he not be forced to undergo the whipping but also that he be granted mastery over his own person. A war of independence, certainly furthered by Sancho's experience of governorship, is taking place within the master-servant relationship. Vanderbank, as always surprisingly faithful to the

Fig. 21 John Vanderbank. *Don Quixote Stops Sancho Panza's Whipping.* London 1738. Department of Special Collections, Kenneth Spencer Research Library, University of Kansas.

text, depicts Sancho astride the prone Don Quixote, firmly holding his wrists in the air to render his master even more helpless. The relationship has clearly undergone a reversal, quite literally represented in this image.

The companion illustration depicts the moment when Don Quixote momentarily frees Sancho Panza from his obligation to whip himself and also from his obligation to serve his master before his family (see Figure 21; 4:fp344). Sancho stands nude to the waist, swinging the arched whip over his bare back. Don Quixote rushes forward from the left to catch the end of the whip. As the text reads:

At the sound of this agonized wail and the thud of the cruel lash, Don Quixote came running up and snatched from Sancho's hand the twisted halter that served as a whip. "Fate, my dear Sancho," he said, "will not have you lose your life to please me, for you need it to support your wife and children."[91]

Of course, at this point Sancho Panza has not actually been striking himself, but the trees; yet Don Quixote's gesture is crucial. The illustrator's depiction is simple but powerful, using only a moon in the sky and deep engraving strokes to indicate the darkness of night. The emphasis clearly falls on the conflict between these two characters. Sancho's face is full of anger, underlining the humiliation that he has endured within this period of the relationship. The unrelenting, dignified anger of Sancho Panza throughout all these episodes contrasts with the increasing weariness and spiritual lethargy of his master. Don Quixote's face is full of frustration, clearly expressing the toll that growing disillusionment is taking on his spirit. These elegantly executed but rather simple illustrations alone would not constitute a critical denunciation of the master-servant relationship, yet the psychological depth of these representations of the knight and his squire is surprising.

Such an outright critique of the old feudal order would be much more typical of William Hogarth, Vanderbank's colleague in the St Martin Academy. Hogarth, so fascinated by *Don Quixote* that his wife claimed his depiction of Sancho Panza was in fact a self-portrait, submitted engravings to this edition which were rejected and later circulated as independent prints. Clearly Hogarth's interpretation was too satirically cutting for Lord Carteret, who chose Vanderbank's more psychologically interpretive engravings. Yet this interest in character, along with Vanderbank's remarkable fidelity to the text (the exact sentences he chooses to represent can easily be pinpointed), represents an interpretation much closer to our own psychological readings of the twentieth century. Sancho Panza and Don Quixote have become novelistic characters, representing an interior integrity of personality rather than decorum. As Habermas has elucidated, this sense of psychological integrity and interiority depends on the introduction of the public sphere, in which the individual man asserts his economic and political independence, leaving the intimate sphere of the bourgeois self and home private.[92] Habermas writes of the changed reading public's demands of literature: "The relations between author, work, and public changed. They became intimate mutual relationships between privatized individuals who were psychologically interested in what was 'human,' in self-knowledge, and in empathy."[93]

THE VISUAL FRAME OF
THE NEOCLASSICAL *DON QUIXOTE*:
ALONSO QUIJANO READING AND DYING

The 1738 Lord Carteret edition is revealing precisely because it embodies the transitional moment between an aristocratic neoclassical aesthetic presented by Mayans y Siscar and Oldfield, and the new sentimental aesthetic created by and for the new middle-class reading public glimpsed in Vanderbank's illustrations. According to the neoclassical interpretation, the elevation of Don Quixote

Fig. 22   John Vanderbank. *Alonso Quijano Reading.*
London 1738. Biblioteca Nacional, Madrid.

is most delicately achieved in order to preserve the comic quality of his folly
and the distance between the character and the author, who, according to this
interpretation, uses him as a tool for satirical purposes. Intending better to
guide the reader of this edition, Mayans, Oldfield, and presumably Lord
Carteret all find the overriding meaning of the novel to lie in the statement of
intention placed by Cervantes in his fictional friend's mouth, in the first
prologue, as an invective against the books of knight errantry. Don Quixote,
in the guise of a maddened reader, is Cervantes' weapon, the club and the mask
handed to Hercules by a satyr as he approaches Mount Parnassus. The first
and last illustrations of the narrative, of central importance to the interpretation
of an illustrated novel,[94] serve graphically to establish Don Quixote's identity
as a fool used as an instrument of satire. These illustrations act as visual frames
for the character as well as for the novel. The first represents Alonso Quijano
reading the pernicious books of chivalric romance in his library before the
impoverished gentleman transforms himself into Don Quixote (see Figure 22;
1:fp1). Although this scene is now standard in Don Quixote iconography and
has been taken to its fantastic extreme by Gustave Doré, this is the earliest

graphic illustration of the scene. Earlier illustrators, less interested in the didactic purpose of the satire, sped to the burlesque action and focused first on the windmill episode, thus earning Dr Oldfield's censure for taking burlesque delight in pratfalls and bruisings. Instead, a depiction of Alonso Quijano reading ideally underscores the neoclassical belief that reading bad literature caused the country gentleman to transform himself into Don Quixote. Mayans states:

The reading of bad books is one of the things that most corrupt customs and in all aspects destroy the republics. And, if the books, which only relate bad examples, cause so much harm, what will those who deceive on purpose not do to introduce into incautious spirits venom sugar-coated with the sweetness of style?[95]

In the illustration, the seated Alonso Quijano sits lost in his reading, propped up against another pile of books, and pointing with his long, elegant finger to a sentence in the open book before him. His mind is obviously engaged in the fantasy world created by the text, as his wide eyes sunken beneath his brow stare into the distance towards the old family armour hung on the walls. The room is remarkably bare except for the armour and the books, the same attributes of the soldier and the poet that appear in Cervantes' portrait by Kent. Yet in this image the imbalance and the predominance of the books over the the armour suggest that the concept of the soldier-poet has fallen into decay. The posture of Alonso Quijano leads the reader's eye in an elegant curve from the hand on the book to the eyes of the *hidalgo* and then, following the character's gaze, towards the armour, a movement that hints at his coming transformation into Don Quixote. None the less, Alonso Quijano appears so much the poet that Givanel Mas and Gaziel write, "If in that right hand, fine and slender, that rests over the open book, we put nothing more than a bird's plume, like those used in those times, we will have a perfect image of some very famous writer."[96] Hartau furthers the comparison by pointing to the "surprisingly certain resemblance with the statue of Shakespeare designed by Kent in Westminster Abbey."[97] Thus, the maddened reader as portrayed by Vanderbank vibrates with intimations of poetic creativity and undercuts the rationalistic interpretation offered by Oldfield. The boundary between author, character, and reader is further blurred as Alonso Quijano, the leisurely reader, elicits sympathy rather than derision.

The last illustration of the edition, the representation of Don Quixote's death, acts as the other side of the frame to the text (4:fp363). Again, the death scene became standard in Don Quixote iconography, and had already been represented by Diego Obregón (Madrid 1674) and Charles Antoine Coypel (London 1731). Obregón showed Alonso Quijano dictating his last will, thus reconciling himself with society. Coypel showed him reconciling himself to Reason, who appears to him as an allegorical figure seated on a puff of smoke or cloud. Vanderbank places emphasis on Alonso Quijano's reconciliation with the authority of the church as well as that of reason. As the text recounts, Alonso Quijano renounces his adventures as Don Quixote as a sham brought on by madness, and leaves a notarized statement to that effect. The notary is duly presented, looking on in wonder, as is the priest, who scornfully condescends to the dying man as he offers him the crucifix. To the right stands Sancho Panza, who alone rubs away tears with his clenched fist. The room is full of other witnesses lined up along Don Quixote's deathbed, the only notable one being the niece. As she leans forward from the corner, her figure and profile enjoy the stature and dignity of a classicizing figure, adding a touch of solemnity to the picture. As his life drains from him, Alonso Quijano, his face exaggeratedly gaunt and eyes half-closed, reaches towards the crucifix held in the centre of the frame by the priest. Don Quixote, the weapon used by the author to combat the literature of knight errantry, must be sacrificed to win the war. Except for the restrained tears of his squire and niece, the witnesses meet the death of Don Quixote and the final return of Alonso Quijano with little emotion as a necessary death. Authority and reason are restored, as even the niece's sorrow is contained within her stolid, classicizing posture.

DON QUIXOTE AS A MAN OF SENTIMENT

Vanderbank shares more with his contemporary Samuel Richardson than with Henry Fielding, thus presenting a sentimental reading of *Don Quixote* to offset the harsh satirical readings of Hogarth and Fielding or the neoclassical one of Mayans.[98] The figure of Don Quixote, of course, bears discussion within this sentimental framework. In comparison to earlier depictions of the text, these illustrations more closely follow the text's descriptions of the character as a tall, thin man of fifty years with a gaunt face and prominent nose. Yet his figure has a certain heroic bearing. As Hartau writes, "Vanderbank's interpretation of the figure of Don Quixote stresses his heroic side and solemnity. In one sketch …, which is described by Horace Walpole as the 'ideal study for the portrait of Don Quixote,' the hero of La Mancha is indistinguishable from a Roman soldier."[99] Just as Sancho Panza's person manifests the gradual growth and strengthening of his character, Don Quixote's manifests the diminishment and beating of his. The most notable depiction of the degradation suffered by the would-be knight errant is his capture by the Duke and Duchess's men. In this image (see Figure 1; 4:fp323) Don Quixote, his long locks of hair spilling unkempt over his shoulders, rides slumped and beaten on Rocinante. In the Western tradition this image resembles none other so much as that of Christ being led through the streets of Jerusalem with the cross, as the hero looks calmly at his discreetly mocking captors. This observation does not seem so far-fetched in light of Eric Ziolkowski's exploration of Fielding's use of the figure of Don Quixote as the model for Parson Adams, the good Christian man who suffers alienation from his world.[100] But the enunciation by Romantic literary critics of the implications of this resemblance is still distant.

Two contexts in which to understand this surprisingly early transformation of Don Quixote into a victim, sacrificial or otherwise, offer themselves. The first derives from the ideology of sentimentalism, which proved attractive to the English eighteenth-century middle-class public as a consequence of the spiritual nobility it offered non-aristocrats. Describing a madman, fooled by his own senses, Shaftesbury cautioned against derision and laughter:

For if we will suppose a Man, who being sound and intire both in his Reason and Affection, has nevertheless so deprav'd a Constitution or Frame of Body, that the natural Objects are, thro his organs of Sense, as thro Ill Glasses, falsely convey'd and mis-represented; 'twill be soon observ'd, in such a Person's Case, that since his Failure is not in his principal or leading Part; he cannot in himself be esteemed *iniquitous*, or unjust.[101]

Of course, Don Quixote's madness finds its roots in his reading and misapplication of his imagination, yet he displays soundness of reason in his sane discourses, and rightness of affection in his protection of women and his final sympathy for his squire. By sentimental standards Don Quixote practises a nobility of heart towards those less than he, and is a hero of sorts. His madness manifests itself through his misinterpretation of the world around him – his senses deceive him, albeit distorted by the lens of his imagination. The reader, like Don Quixote, should treat those lesser than he, none other than the deluded knight errant, with the same nobility of sentiment. Thus began the century-long ennoblement of the fool and madman that would mark many of the illustrations, and later the literary criticism itself. The eighteenth-century public, consumers of these de luxe editions, would gradually transform the protagonist into a hero.

A darker context also shapes this metamorphosis, as Don Quixote becomes not only hero but sacrificial victim. For the neoclassical, enlightened thinker, a man who did not always converge in his reading of *Don Quixote* with his more sentimental contemporaries, the protagonist is the instrument of Enlightenment. Don Quixote, who represents and expresses irrationality, is merely the tool of authority to be used for the instruction of others. In this manner the eighteenth-century classicizing interpretation of *Don Quixote* participates in the dialectic of Enlightenment analysed by Horkheimer and Adorno. The world of unreason, enchantment, which Don Quixote inhabits, must be illuminated and thus destroyed. The madman must renounce his delusion and his very identity in order to return to the side of his deathbed. The dialectic of Alonso Quijano/Don Quixote manifests the dialectic of reason and irrationality in all its forms: "The nimble-witted survives only at the price of his own dream, which he wins only by demystifying himself as well as the powers without."[102] This renunciation involves, of course, the sacrificial death of Don Quixote. Thus, the would-be knight errant appears already in the guise of the sacrificial victim, Christ on the road to Golgotha.

Don Quixote Every Man: Eighteenth-Century English Illustrators

Peter Motteux, in the preface to his 1700 translation of *Don Quixote*, voices a universalizing interpretation of Cervantes' satirical objective that dominated the novel's reception outside Spain in the eighteenth century. As he exclaims,

Every Man has something of *Don Quixote* in his Humour, some darling *Dulcinea* of his Thoughts, that sets him very often upon mad Adventures. What *Quixotes* does not every Age produce in Politicks and Religion, who fancying themselves to be in the right of something, which all the world tells 'em is wrong, make very good sport to the Publick, and shew them that they themselves need the chiefest Amendment![1]

This telling quote sets the stage for the crucial readings of the novel in Enlightenment England.[2] As the producers of the Carteret edition strove so mightily to elevate *Don Quixote* from the realm of every man, the popular sphere of the lower classes, certain English contemporaries sought to elevate it *to* the realm of Every Man, the public sphere of the newly emerging middle class. This new social construct, a product of a depersonalized state and a capitalist economy in which private persons gained power and autonomy through the acquisiton of property and education, is described by Jürgen Habermas as "the sphere of private people come together as a public."[3] This sphere, elevated above that of the lower classes as the *bourgeoisie*, none the less depended on the fiction of universal access, for it represented Every Man as opposed to the aristocrat. Thus, Every Man emerged as the bourgeois participant in the commerce of economic and cultural exchange, whose participation in the public market and coffeehouse depended upon the possession of personal property and education.[4] The reception of *Don Quixote* in England was intimately tied to the instruction of this new public of middle-class readers.

As Motteux indicates, this Every Man had to learn to dispel from his "humour" the desires, "Dulcineas," that impelled him towards irrational behaviour. The chief realms of these desires, politics and religion, represented the very institutions whose authority was to be mediated and diminished for the general good of the bourgeois public to allow the free commerce of goods and the rational commerce of ideas by private persons. "*Public debate was supposed to transform* voluntas *into a* ratio *that in the public competition of private arguments came into being as the consensus about what was practically necessary in the interest of all.*"[5] *Don Quixote* was to circulate within that realm of debate as a cautionary example of the disruptive nature of all idiosyncratic, irrational beliefs not tested and approved by "all the world." Motteux's "all the world" was that of the bourgeois public, which arrived at public opinion through the use of reason. His mention of the sport enjoyed by the community at the expense of the individual who followed a different course, departing from the path of "self-evident" and "natural" *ratio,* undermines Habermas's idealized view of the enlightened public as it points towards the dialectic of the same studied by Horkheimer and Adorno. Writing of the authoritative power of reason when perceived as self-evident and natural, they observe, "The spirit of Enlightenment replaced the fire and the rack by the stigma it attached to all irrationality, because it led to corruption."[6]

The "Every Man" at the beginning of Motteux's quote stands in contrast to the deluded individual separated from the community of "all the world" at the end. The opposition between communal reason and individual belief remains unresolved in Motteux's thought and, indeed, in that of the subsequent eighteenth-century English commentators and illustrators of *Don Quixote.* The producers of the 1738 Lord Carteret edition (with the exception of the illustrator, John Vanderbank) espoused an unabashedly aristocratic, neoclassical vision of Don Quixote as a foolish country gentleman led astray by the excesses of popular, extravagant, and indecorous fiction. In many respects the Lord Carteret edition, although subscribing to the novel's new claim to that of the status of a classic, was essentially conservative in its use of a neoclassical aesthetic to achieve this aim. At the same time in England *Don Quixote* became an instrument for reform-minded artists and authors of the emerging English middle class. These readers and producers of the new cultural public struggled to reconcile their sympathy for Don Quixote as an Every Man with the novel's instructive use for bourgeois Enlightenment at the expense of its protagonist's dignity. Like the neoclassical thinkers Mayans and Oldfield, all would proclaim the satirical intention of the novel, as stated in the prologue to Book 1 of *Don Quixote.* Yet the satire would begin to crack under its own cultural weight. As it was extended "universally" to portray follies in all the characters and throughout all strains of society, as in the case of William Hogarth and Henry Fielding's interpretations, the authoritative effect of the figures representing Enlightenment was undercut. Don Quixote became just one of many fools. By the same token, the tendency to view the characters as negative examples gave way to the force of identification with characters required of readers. Tobias Smollett and Francis Hayman, respectively the translator and the illustrator of the 1755

London edition, both perceived sympathetic, even exemplary traits in Don Quixote and Sancho Panza, and began to note similarities between Cervantes and Don Quixote as well as between the deluded gentleman and his readers.

Two major genre shifts accompanied the establishment of a middle-class public that produced and consumed culture as a commodity, available to all with the prerequisite price of a book or a theatre ticket, and demanded cultural products based on their own subjective experiences as private individuals.[7] In literature, the emergence of the sentimental novel heralded the establishment of the middle-class man of virtue, a man who rose to equality with the aristocrats through his own meritorious spirit and heart.[8] In the visual arts, the emergence of a new form of history painting, the satirical narrative exemplified by Hogarth's prints, heralded the same, although by emphasizing the man of virtue's darker sibling, the Every Man of folly. Both these new genres, consciously representative of a new "middle" layer of culture, contributed to the reception of *Don Quixote* by casting the novel's characters into new literary and artistic contexts. The voices of reason, such as the barber and the priest, began to resonate with hypocrisy. Don Quixote and Sancho Panza, as already glimpsed in Vanderbank's illustrations to the 1738 Lord Carteret edition, took on new figures, respectively those of the man ennobled by his sentiments and the self-made man of the bourgeois marketplace.

Ronald Paulson argues that the appropriation of *Don Quixote* was essential to these developments in both literature and art because it demonstrated a new understanding of the comic within a framework that allowed these artists to explore their contemporary society, unfettered by the restraints of neoclassical theory.[9]

What *Don Quixote* embodied was the essence of comic structure, the incongruous. It was constructed on a combined intellectual and formal incongruity, which was to organize much of eighteenth-century comic writing and art, setting both Hogarth and Fielding on their respective ways. This was an incongruity between the aspiration or illusion of a Don Quixote and the reality of his surroundings, between the image of a knight-errant with his heroic steed and the tall, bony, decrepit old shapes of both Quixote and Rosinante; and in formal terms between these lanky shapes and the short, earthy, well-fed shape of Sancho, amid inns, herds of sheep, and windmills.[10]

Paulson delineates well the manner in which *Don Quixote* was not merely passively received but also actively incorporated into a new aesthetic, mediating between the high and low forms of neoclassicism by the artists and writers of eighteenth-century England. It was a highly visual appropriation of the images of Don Quixote and Sancho Panza in relationship and contrast to each other, an appropriation rich in both its satirical and its sentimental potential. Just as the young Vanderbank began to explore the psychology of the two characters in his strangely incongruous illustrations to the 1738 Lord Carteret edition, so would his countrymen follow in one way or the other in his footsteps.

THE EXCLUSION OF HOGARTH FROM THE 1738
LORD CARTERET EDITION

Chief among Vanderbank's peers was William Hogarth, a figure central to this history despite the fact that his illustrations for the 1738 Lord Carteret edition were not published there. At this point one can only speculate whether they were rejected by John Oldfield, author of the commentaries on the Vanderbank illustrations, or whether Hogarth himself withdrew from the project.[11] Nor can one know whether Vanderbank and Hogarth consulted with each other, although the similarities in several illustrations are surprising.[12] As Mayans' letter indicates, publishers such as Tonson exercised great control over the content of the illustrations.[13] Thus, the similarity may be the result of the publisher's influence, possibly mediated through Oldfield. Regardless of the circumstances, something occurred to cause Hogarth to withdraw from the project and to make the publisher reject his engravings for the edition. Although Hogarth had been a student at Louis Cheron's and Vanderbank's Academy in St Martin's Lane from its inception in 1720, he quickly became disillusioned with Cheron's classicizing tendencies and later denied ever having studied there. Nevertheless, Hogarth was "influenced" by Vanderbank in his drawing from live models, a practice he later taught when he opened an academy in the same site in the 1730s.[14] In addition, Hogarth's relations were friendly enough with the other artist that Vanderbank testified on his behalf in a court case.[15] Yet Hogarth established in the St Martin Academy a long-lasting enmity with his fellow student William Kent, the artist who designed Cervantes' portrait for the Carteret edition and who, along with Carteret, belonged to Lord Burlington's circle of neoclassical artists and aestheticians. The conflict between the two artists was cemented by Hogarth's engraving "Burlesque on Kent's Altarpiece at St Clement Danes" (1725), which led Kent to retaliate in a much more effective manner by preventing Hogarth from realizing his ambitions to become a court painter.[16] If Kent enjoyed such influence at court, it is not hard to imagine that he also had a hand in preventing Hogarth's inclusion in the 1738 Lord Carteret edition.

As in the case of Mayans' conflict with Feijoo and his supporters, one must emphasize that the conflict between Kent and Hogarth rested mainly on intellectual differences, this time concerning the proper tenets of painting. Cheron and Kent took their Italicizing posture to such an extreme that they drew mainly from Renaissance masters such as Raphael and eschewed drawing from live models. This practice was anathema to Hogarth, who boasted a superb visual memory on which he based his fascination with the details, often irregular and bordering on the grotesque, of "life." Kent's frustration of Hogarth's aspiration to paint for the court had the broad effect of heightening other tendencies of Hogarth's artistic vision as he grew suspicious of study in Italy and more patriotic in his promotion of English art.[17] His failure to subsist financially on the patronage of the aristocratic class also contributed to Hogarth's espousal of the print, a medium financially accessible to the middle class. His suspicion of Italian art led him to develop further his eye for what he considered the imitation of life, an imitation much more suited to a satirical vision than to a neoclassical one. Thus, Hogarth occupied a unique position outside the circles of fine art created for the upper classes. This allowed him to develop his singular vision of his class and to profit from the newly gained wealth of this English middle class through the sale of prints, now conceived of not merely as reproductive but also as productive.

That Hogarth considered his sharply satirical vision to be an accurate imitation of life should not be passed over without more careful consideration, for it places Hogarth's work in relationship to both the neoclassical impulse of Vanderbank's art (see chapter 3) and the burlesque tendencies of more naïve, earlier English printmakers and the courtly Coypel (see chapter 2). As a student at Cheron's and Vanderbank's academy Hogarth would have been acquainted with the two major treatises on neoclassical painting predominant in England at the time, Dryden's translation of Du Fresnoy's *De Arte Graphica* (1695) and Jonathan Richardson's *The Theory of Painting* (1715). Richardson, like Du Fresnoy, insisted that "common nature is no more fit for a picture than plain narration is for a poem" and that "a painter must raise his ideas beyond what he sees, and form a model of perfection in his own mind which is not to be found in reality; but yet such a one as is probable and rational."[18] This perfect, rational model is precisely what Hogarth rejected when he insisted on imitation of nature as he saw it. None the less, the young artist sought not merely to copy objects but to discover through observation a language, or grammar, underlying them.[19] The mental image of perfection, the true object of mimesis for the neoclassical artist, would be replaced by a functional visual idiom based on the imitation of nature through which the artist would communicate with his viewers. The neoplatonic basis of neoclassical art theory, which valorized the ideal, disappeared in Hogarth's practice before his deductive creation of a visual idiom through the forms he copied almost obsessively from his surroundings.

It must be remarked that his surroundings were those of the urban marketplace, shop, and street, the realm of the newly emerging middle class. Thus, the shift from a neoclassical literary idiom to a less ideal, more mimetic one signified a shift downward in the socially determined hierarchy of the arts. As Dryden stated so clearly in his preface to *De Arte Graphica*, the lower forms of art, both literary and visual, proceeded from the imitation of nature, seen more often than not to be the realm of the grotesque as opposed to the ideal. Citing Horace's famous image of the grotesque figure with the head of a man, neck of a horse, wings of a bird, and tail of a fish, the poet argued that farce and grotesque painting were unnatural (unnatural, one assumes, because irrational) deformations of nature intended merely to provoke laughter. This was the art of the mob, "a very Monster in a Bartholomew-Fair, for the Mob to gape at for their Twopence."[20] The usually implicit social division of art into high and low forms thus reveals itself explicitly in this quote. The high, neoclassical form was, of course, the art of the court, the aristocrats, and the intellectual elite. The low, grotesquely comic form was the art of the market-place and the vulgar mob (as viewed from above) who traded and socialized there. Any possibly carnivalesque understanding of the marketplace as a dem-ocratic meeting-place for all the classes had disappeared.[21] Instead, the market-place had become a capitalist market, occupied and managed by the new middle class. This new public, composed of traders, women, and students, "endangered the established order in polite letters" and demanded new genres.[22] Most of the artists and authors of eighteenth-century England, like Samuel Johnson, belonged to the emergent middle class, and struggled to define a new, respectable place for themselves.

"IN IMITATION OF THE MANNER OF CERVANTES": FIELDING'S DEFINITION OF THE COMIC

Henry Fielding, himself an aristocrat with progressive leanings, attempted to define his own – and Hogarth's – humorous art in contrast to this very concept of a grotesque, deforming, and comic art in his preface to *Joseph Andrews* (1742). The author's acknowledged debt to Cervantes has proved difficult to gauge, yet Fielding claimed that this novel was written in "the manner of Cervantes" and had already used the characters of Don Quixote and Sancho Panza as his satirical mouthpieces in the play *Don Quixote in England* (1733).[23] Like Mot-teux, the novelist asserted, in the closing lines to his play, that Quixotism was a universal malady – "All mankind are mad, 'tis plain" – and concluded with an encyclopedic list of maniacs, including lovers, spendthrifts, misers, believers, deceivers, traitors of the state, preservers of the state, lawyers, rogues, poets, and women.[24] This catalogue, of course, included the spectators of the play, since to laugh at a character without recognizing one's own implication in the laughter was widely considered mean-spirited and unbecoming to the new gentleman of virtue. As Coburn explains, for Fielding, Don Quixote and his own characters were "mixed comic types – neither wholly damnable nor wholly laudable – much, in fact, like people in the real world. The source of our respect is the recognition that good-natured motives go far to atone for ineptitude."[25] The ideals of sentimentalism, unlike those of neoclassicism, thus tempered the raucous humour of Dryden's mob by intermingling pity with laughter. Fielding's public laughed as a middle-class audience, recognizing Don Quixote and Sancho Panza to be Every Man, just as they were.

Fielding's introduction of the mixed comic character into his play and novel inspired by *Don Quixote* points towards his definition of comedy as a mixed genre in the preface to *Joseph Andrews,* a definition based on the visually comic art of his friend and colleague Hogarth. Because the two were such close friends, one can assume that they discussed the topic of the prologue, which thus represents to a certain extent Hogarth's own views.[26] Indeed, Antal argues that Hogarth's well-known print "Characters and Caricatures" (1743), in which he visually layered and contrasted variations on "character" profiles from Raphael's cartoons and "caricature" profiles from Leonardo da Vinci, Annibale Carracci, and Ghezzi, was executed to illustrate Fielding's distinction between the two aesthetic forms.[27] In the preface Fielding differentiates "comic romance," that which treats of the "light and ridiculous" actions of "persons of inferior rank," from "serious romance," that which treats of the "grave and solemn" actions of "the highest."[28] So far Fielding has applied the Aristotelian distinction between tragedy and comedy to prose. But at this point, he newly distinguishes the "comic" manner of writing, which imitates nature, from the "burlesque," which exaggerates nature.[29] Implicit in this emphasis on the mimetic nature of the comedic is his vision of life as humorous, for "life everywhere furnishes an accurate observer with the ridiculous."[30]

Fielding then turns to painting to illustrate better the distinction between the comic and the burlesque, which corresponds to the caricatural in painting:[31]

Let us examine the works of a comic history painter, with those performances which the Italians call caricatura, where we shall find the true excellence of the former to consist in the exactest copying of nature; insomuch that a judicious eye instantly rejects anything *outré,* any liberty which the painter hath taken with the features of that *alma mater,* whereas in the caricatura we allow all licence, – its aim is to exhibit monsters, not men; and all distortions and exaggerations whatever are within its proper province.[32]

With this distinction between the comic and the caricatural, Fielding defends Hogarth from being falsely labelled a burlesque painter according to Dryden's derisive concept of the art of the mob (evidence of middle-class contempt for the art forms of the class below them as well as above them), and thus defines the proper goal of the artist not to be the representation of people's physical features but rather the representation of their inner emotions and thought. Thus, the object of mimesis is no longer visual appearance but psychological motivation and spiritual peace and/or turmoil. The imitation of subjectivity, the fascination with the private being that defines eighteenth-century sentimentalism, was to enter also into the representation of the comic. Thus the public's tears and laughter were to find their source in the same attempt by the observer to understand and sympathize with the interior situation of the characters.[33]

Fielding leaves no doubt concerning the dignity of representing subjectivity, and defends Hogarth's honour for doing so against the vulgarity of those representing the burlesque, artistic vestige of the popular:

He who should call the ingenious Hogarth a burlesque painter, would in my opinion, do him very little honour; for sure it is much easier, much less the subject of admiration, to paint a man with a nose, or any other feature, of a preposterous size, or to expose him in some absurd or monstrous attitude, than to express the affections of men on canvas. It hath been thought a vast commendation of a painter to say his figures seems to breathe; but surely it is a much greater and nobler applause, than they appear to think.[34]

This praise of Hogarth's representation of the thoughts and "affections" of men links him to Vanderbank's markedly psychological approach to *Don Quixote* illustrations, yet here the difference between the classicizing and the comic visions again enters the picture. Vanderbank presents ennobling thoughts, whereas Hogarth, like Fielding, insists on the comical element of Every Man. As Fielding asserts, "The only source of the true ridiculous (as it appears to me) is affectation."[35] According to the novelist, affectation arises from two nearly omnipresent characteristics: vanity and hypocrisy.[36] Don Quixote, once Alonso Quijano, a country gentleman impoverished by his appetite for chivalric romances and maddened enough to proclaim himself a knight errant, provides for the artist an exemplary case of vanity. As such, he is a perfect figure of fun for a bourgeois public, because his aspirations to nobility and his enactment of the ancient, aristocratic chivalric code prove the antiquated nature of the same. At the same time Fielding's and Hogarth's audience was involved in great social climbing, and thus could see itself reflected in the attempt. Therefore, the imitation of affectation, vanity, and hypocrisy in Quixotic figures in Fielding's novels and Hogarth's prints and paintings gave rise to the comic, a form that resided in a middle position between the neoclassical and the burlesque, between the aristocratic and the popular.[37]

HOGARTH'S CONFLATION OF THE HEROIC AND THE COMIC

There can be no doubt of Hogarth's preference for the comical in literary concerns. He refused the invitation to illustrate Samuel Richardson's *Pamela*, and thus must have shared some of Fielding's distaste for sentimental novels. Instead, the reading of "Bunyan, Swift, Defoe, and Butler (with Cervantes) helped importantly in forming Hogarth's world picture."[38] Paulson argues that these same writers, beginning with Cervantes, made possible Hogarth's development of a satirical tradition of historical painting by legitimizing the "comic" as "a concern with the low or commonplace, the unheroic or untragic."[39] One of his first major works was the illustration of Butler's *Hudibras* (ca 1725), a book advertised as the "Don Quixote of this Nation."[40] Hogarth's frontispiece to this edition incorporates allegorical classical figures in order to express the satirical intent of the novel, in a manner similar to Vanderbank's frontispiece to the Carteret *Don Quixote*. According to Paulson's interpretation of the allegorical image, satire triumphantly controls "Hypocrisy, Ignorance, and

Rebellion."[41] In this manner Hogarth presents comic art and literature as extremely serious in its capacity to enlighten and instruct, elevating it as a proper textual source for historical painting. History painting, as based on classical texts and using the visual idiom of classical and Renaissance art, was the preferred genre of neoclassical aestheticians and artists, the primary circle in England being the Burlington School.[42] Thus, Paulson's interpretation of this frontispiece presents it as a visual challenge to this school, for it trumpets the worthiness of the comic genre as a subject of serious art.

In a written commentary to himself Hogarth stated this challenge to the narrow strictures placed upon the material considered suitable for history painting by comparing and contrasting heroic and comic poetry. While illustrating Butler, he wrote in his notebook:

Heroicall Poetry handle's the slightest, and most Impertinent Follys in the world in a formall serious and unnatural way: And Comedy and Burlesque the most Serious in a Frolique and Gay humor which has always been found the more apt to instruct, and instill those Truths with Delight unto men, which they would not indure to heare of any other way ... A Satyr is a Kinde of Knight Errant that goe's upon Adventures, to Relieve the Distressed Damsel Virtue, and Redeeme Honor out of Inchanted Castles, and opprest Truth and Reason out of the Captivity of Gyants or Magitians.[43]

Remarkably, this statement inverts the value of the heroic and epic in contrast to the burlesque and comic by combining the classical image of the satyr with the fantastic image of the knight errant. Whereas neoclassical aestheticians insisted on the elevation of the subject-matter of the heroic epic because it treated of a noble hero such as Achilles involved in the serious adventures of establishing or restoring a cosmic order ordained by the gods, Hogarth saw these actions as insignificant and out-of-place "follies." In turn, the comic, which had been perceived as foolish by these same thinkers, was revalorized by Hogarth as instructive and truthful, the same criteria used by the former to valorize the heroic epic.

Like Mayans y Siscar and the other producers of the 1738 Lord Carteret edition, Hogarth incorporated elements of the neoclassical aesthetics that had condemned *Don Quixote* into his defence of what he saw as the text's genre, the mock-heroic. Yet since Mayans merely drew parallels between Don Quixote and Achilles, Cervantes and Homer, he did not actually question the basic premise valuing the heroic above the comic. Hogarth's inversion of the hierarchy was thus more radical than Mayans' attempt merely to broaden the scope of the heroic within the original hierarchy. The equation of the satyr with the knight errant followed as a revalorization of both the comic element of the mock-heroic and the marvellous hero of chivalric romance rejected by neoclassical aesthetics. Hogarth's use of imagery also echoed and subverted the neoclassical allegory presented in the frontispiece of the Carteret edition. In

Vanderbank's image the satyr hands the mask of the knight errant, Don Quixote, to the classical hero, but the satyr himself is merely a rather perverse muse and the knight errant merely a fictional device (see Figure 13). Hogarth's conflation of the satyr and the knight errant into one figure grants the grotesque, hybrid satyr of the classical tradition a heroic form and presents the beleaguered hero of a fantastic, non-classical tradition in a valorized form. The crucial difference, then, between Vanderbank's allegorical imagery and Hogarth's is that the former retains the preference for the heroic, whereas the latter propounds a newly elevated role for satire as the vehicle of reason and truth. The monsters in both allegories remain the same – the chimeras of the fantastic – even though the hero changes. Yet once again these chimeras of fantastic literature persist, monsters in the closet of the ordered room of reason. The conflation of the satyr and the knight errant bolstered anew the hero of *Don Quixote,* representative to the eighteenth century of the mock-heroic.

BURLESQUE ACTION AND SENTIMENTAL COMEDY: HOGARTH'S ILLUSTRATIONS OF *DON QUIXOTE*

Hogarth's production of the *Don Quixote* illustrations probably followed directly upon the *Hudibras* illustrations between 1726 and 1727, and they were most likely directed in their execution by John Oldfield.[44] Yet, as in the case of Vanderbank, what is more interesting is not the extent of Oldfield's (and, as his agent, Carteret's) control over the imagery but precisely the way the imagery escapes this uncompromisingly neoclassical mold. As Paulson states, "his six illustrations are for the beginning of the book and deal, with one exception, with the same episodes as Vanderbank; but the precise moment and the interpretation are different."[45] In the development of the iconography of *Don Quixote* these differences are important. In his choice and representation of moments Hogarth reveals a vision akin to that of the earlier illustrators, although his engravings give evidence of a more adept hand and his characters a more astute eye for human expression and emotion. Evident in these images is the influence of Coypel, who seems to have been Hogarth's shadow precursor and competitor in much of his early work. Antal states that Hogarth "retained much of Coypel's elegance and certainly remained close to Coypel's narration in general spirit, psychological conception, and his quest for the interesting."[46] Hogarth even directly lifted characters from Coypel's *Don Quixote* illustrations for use in an anti-Masonic print (1724), including Sancho Panza, a butcher, an old woman, and Don Quixote from Coypel's illustration of the mad knight's attack upon the puppet play (see Figure 23; 3:fp181).[47] Hogarth changed the figure of Don Quixote only to show him revering the Masonic mystery, and also adopted a figure from another of Coypel's illustrations, that of the procession of the bearded women at the palace of the Duke and the Duchess. In this manner Hogarth used figures in the interchangeable manner

Fig. 23   Charles Antoine Coypel.
Don Quixote Attacking Maese Pedro's Puppet Play. London.
Department of Special Collections, Kenneth Spencer
Research Library, University of Kansas.

of the craftsman of the popular tradition, and yet deepened the irony of his satire for the alert viewer who might recognize the figure's provenance. Like Fielding a decade later, Hogarth clearly adopted these figures from *Don Quixote* in order to poke fun at a contemporary folly, and underscored the universality of quixotic folly.

Nor did Hogarth spurn violent scenes, as Oldfield and Vanderbank had. For Hogarth, the burlesque joke of the unsuccessful battle provided the perfect visual opposition to the characters' vanity and hypocrisy. His illustration of the combat between Don Quixote and the barber for the barber's basin/Mambrino's helmet (1:21), although rather staid in comparison to his later work, does not lack a satirical jab at the vacuous nature of the protagonist's vision. The deluded knight, surprisingly heroic atop the charging Rocinante, propels his lance towards the empty saddle atop the barber's tranquil mule. The barber himself cowers beside his mount in the right-hand foreground, whereas Mambrino's helmet, clearly a barber's basin, lies in the centre foreground, to be claimed as Don Quixote's hard-won prize. The absence of a worthy opponent in the saddle, necessary for the proof of knightly valour and, indeed, his very adherence to the chivalric code, achieves a comic deflation of Don Quixote's illusions while eschewing the grotesque. In contrast, Vanderbank depends on Sancho Panza's later incredulous comments upon his master's illusions to puncture his delusion. Clearly, Hogarth's illustration presents a more direct, visual deflation, seen also in the illustration entitled, "Don Quixote releases the Galley Slaves"

(1:22). Here the protagonist actually clashes with an opponent, albeit a very unworthy one. Don Quixote's sword has come to rest impotently over the shoulder of the combatant, who is about to lower his own sword against the knight. In the right foreground a horrified Sancho helps a captive out of his handcuffs and chains, while in the midground the rest set each other free. In this image Hogarth used his ability to depict dramatic facial expression, which he considered a vital component of the imitation of life, in order to deflate Don Quixote's pretentious vision of himself as a liberator of the unjustly chained. The malevolence on the face of the captive loosed by Sancho clearly reveals the hypocrisy of his earlier, nobler words, as the shock and naïvité on the face of Don Quixote as he is attacked by the man he freed reveal the vanity of his eager credulity. In contrast, Vanderbank depicts Don Quixote's questioning of the captives, a scene that does not reveal the protagonist's ironic misunderstanding of the prisoners' situation and depends on Sancho's shock to demystify his master's delusion. Hogarth's illustrations, timid as they may seem in contrast to his later work, demonstrate his developing control of visual satirical devices, dependent on the interaction and facial expression of juxtaposed figures, which serve to unmask their interior motives.

Yet, supporting Carteret's assertion that Oldfield was the master of the designs, the two artists represent several scenes with very similar compositions. Hammelmann points to Hogarth's and Vanderbank's respective illustrations of Grisóstomo's funeral, "which correspond so closely in the whole arrangement as to derive plainly from one source, even if only a verbal one" as proof of Oldfield's control.[48] Indeed, both illustrations depict the encounter between Marcela and her accusers around the spurned lover's grave in a manner sympathetic to the woman and her defender, Don Quixote (1:12–13). The main compositional difference is the placement of Marcela atop a cliff in Vanderbank's work, in contrast to her stance on the ground, level with her accusers, in Hogarth's work. Both representations similarly idealize the maiden as she defends her choice of chastity, although Don Quixote's stance and facial expression bespeak much more arrogance in Hogarth's version. In fairness to both illustrators, it must be pointed out that this is one of the few episodes in the novel in which Don Quixote successfully champions an unjustly treated person, and thus appropriate for a more ennobling representation of the character. The decorum and dignity expressed in both illustrations are in keeping with the literary text.

Nevertheless, the text of *Don Quixote* abounds in many indecorous details that the wily illustrator Hogarth could slip into his own representation of a "decorous" scene in order to sharpen the satire. Hammelmann cites the scene in which the innkeeper's wife and daughter attend to the beaten Don Quixote as another example of Oldfield's control.[49] Again, the compositions are remarkably similar, as Sancho Panza and Maritornes confront each other on the margins of the scene (1:16). None the less, the satire bites more deeply in

Hogarth's work. In his image Maritornes holds the candle in the foreground that illuminates the treatment of the wounded Don Quixote by the innkeeper's wife and daughter in the midground, but the grotesque maid's eyes are drawn towards her likeness, Sancho Panza. The equally grotesque Sancho stands in the opposite corner, peering over his shoulder towards her with disgust and fear, even as he turns himself away from her. The mutual attraction and repulsion of the two dwarfish figures mirror the interaction in the midground between Don Quixote and the daughter. Vanderbank ignores this interaction to focus on the less eroticized glance between the wounded knight and the mother. In Hogarth's illustration the daughter stands to the left, her figure tall and dignified, and looks demurely away from Don Quixote's avid gaze as he lies semi-nude on his stomach in the glaring light of the candle. The middle-aged knight is so taken by his vision of the daughter that he ignores the mother's fingers probing his wounds. Through the play of gazes between the characters Hogarth sets up a dynamic series of reactions and reflections that add provocative nuances to a seemingly quiet scene. The sentimental content of the scene – that is to say, the emotional sparks flying between the grotesquely matched pair of Maritornes and Sancho Panza and the grotesquely unmatched pair of Don Quixote and the innkeeper's daughter – uncovers new layers of comedy. In this image one can see Hogarth's talent for stretching the decorous towards the satiric, a talent that would not have been appreciated by Oldfield or Carteret. None the less, his vision of the text expands even the "simplest" or "safest" scenes with its revelations of comic motivation and interaction among all the characters.

THE UNIVERSAL BITE OF SATIRE

Two of Hogarth's illustrations stand out in particular as distinct departures from the decorous vision of the Carteret edition. The first depicts a scene not illustrated by Vanderbank, entitled *The Curate and Barber disguising themselves to convey Don Quixote Home* (see Figure 3; 1:27). The framing device of Sancho Panza and Maritornes remains, although the squire is merely glimpsed drinking from a wine jug through an open door at the left. In the midground the innkeeper's daughter helps the bald priest into his skirt. They both look with condescending smiles towards Maritornes in the right foreground corner, who is doubled in laughter by the sight. Her profile, marked by a lantern jaw, small but pointed nose, and sunken eye framed by a dark, crooked brow, is in itself a source of laughter. That a creature such as she should burst into derisive laughter at the messenger of enlightenment is a sharp jab indeed at the priest's arrogant, even slightly hypocritical mission. In the midright background one glimpses another deflationary mirroring image, an actual mirror. The barber, his face in shadows and his back to the viewer, is reflected in a mirror hanging at an uneasily tilting angle from the back wall. His reflection appears elongated,

as if by a fun-house mirror, and the angles of his face and the room behind
him appear distorted in an almost cubist manner. This distortion actually
creates the optical effect of reflecting a conical "dunce cap" upon the reflection
of his head.

These satirical devices, the presentation of Maritornes' grotesque laughter
and the distorted mirror image, serve to undercut the supposedly noble intentions of the characters in the scene. Most importantly, these grotesque, distorting images do not merely reflect but also reveal what Fielding would call
"affectation," and thus ground the grotesque in the mimetic. According to
Paulson, the representation of the "costuming of these unprepossessing figures,
and the juxtaposition of the antlers above the inn door, the chamber pot on a
shelf, the coat of arms, and the mirror in which the barber regards himself,
broach some of Hogarth's own central themes: these can be summed up as the
comedy of masquerade."[50] This image then uncovers the truth beneath the
charade. The barber and the curate, the seemingly reasonable would-be curers
of Don Quixote's madness, are the objects of Hogarth's most sharply satirical
treatment because they fail to see their own folly in the mirror. According to
Hogarth's vision, Don Quixote's folly is not the only one to be punctured by
Cervantes' satirical barbs. The satirical bite extends beyond the generic parody
of chivalric romances to the content of the novel, beyond its context to its
characters and situations. Hogarth returns to the Every Man of Motteux, in
which the universality of folly and not merely the specific folly of readers of
bad literature is seen as the subject of the satire.[51] This expansion of the satirical
range moves a step beyond the neoclassical reading of the Carteret edition,
which insists above all on the literary satire.

The other distinct print, known as *Sancho's Feast*, illustrates most vividly
Hogarth's view of the universal folly in *Don Quixote*. Paulson assumes the plate
to have been executed around 1724, independently of the plates done for the
Carteret edition, whereas Lindsay considers it another of the unpublished
illustrations.[52] Regardless of the uncertain conditions of its production, this
image seems to have been the most widely known and circulated of the artist's
Don Quixote engravings. It is verbosely captioned "SANCHO at the Magnificent
Feast Prepar'd for him at his government of *Barataria,* is Starved in the midst
of Plenty, *Pedro Rezzio* his Physician, out of great Care for his health ordering
every Dish from the Table before the Governour Tasts it." Paulson considers
this illustration to be "typical of Hogarth in that he takes the plebeian Sancho
as his subject rather than the aristocratic Don Quixote and shows him deluded
into thinking he is the King of Barataria, with his folly being exploited by his
'subjects,' who are starving him."[53] Antal points out the remarkable similarity
between Coypel's illustration of the scene and Hogarth's, stating that "Hogarth
retained the grotesque spirit and lively features of Coypel's representation of
the same subject, carrying it further in individual figures."[54] Indeed, this
illustration is Hogarth's most grotesque representation of *Don Quixote*, particularly

when compared with Vanderbank's illustration of the same scene, in which Sancho gains girth, gravity, and a sense of dignity. In Hogarth's engraving an increase in absurdity accompanies poor Sancho's loss of girth as he is denied food. Sporting a hat that resembles a jester's cap more than a governor's crown, he sits at the table's head. His full face, similar to Maritornes in its snoutish nose and jaw, looks on in wide-eyed stupidity at the doctor who actually takes the fork from his hand. Variously grotesque courtesans and courtiers barely contain their laughter, as one pulls the tablecloth to his mouth to hide or stifle his giggles. This ribald laughter, expressed by a toothless, ragged onlooker, a grotesque lady-in-waiting, with grossly large and over-exposed breasts, as well as the doctor and courtiers, is an extreme use of satire, indecorous by the norms of Carteret and Oldfield. Not only is Sancho the object of satiric laughter but, in turn, those laughing at him are the object of the viewer's laughter. No figure invites the viewer to laugh along, as in Coypel's illustrations, nor would the viewer want to identify with these monstrous humans. None the less, Hogarth used his own likeness to depict Sancho, as his wife revealed to a printer years after his death.[55] Every individual and every sector of society, including the artist, is subject to this derisive, deflating laughter. This more generalized satire is typical of Hogarth and gives rise to the British caricatural tradition, which includes prominent illustrators of *Don Quixote* such as Francis Hayman and the Cruikshank brothers. Along with Vanderbank's sentimental vision, it also sets into motion an interest in the interior characterizations and relationships of the text and an identification with its characters, a crucial step towards the Romantic reading of *Don Quixote*.

SENTIMENT AND SATIRE MEET: SMOLLETT AND HAYMAN'S *DON QUIXOTE*

In 1755 a new edition appeared in London that combined the sentimental and satirical interpretations in both its biography of Cervantes and the illustrations. Published by A. Millar, translated by the novelist Tobias Smollett, and accompanied by a new biography of the author by Smollett and original illustrations by Francis Hayman, this edition encapsulated the satirical, sentimental, and neoclassical traditions initiated by Hogarth and the producers of the 1738 Carteret edition. Vanderbank's illustrations had been republished in the 1742 edition of Frank Jervas's translation and, for this reason, would have been known in Britain. The readers of this edition could also have been familiar with Coypel's illustrations, which continued to be reprinted throughout the century and circulated as independent prints, perhaps accompanied by Hogarth's illustrations. One can state with certainty that Smollett and Hayman followed aesthetically and socially in the footsteps of the older Fielding and Hogarth, whose colleagues and drinking partners they were widely known to be. Clearly, the producers of this edition, unlike those of the Carteret edition,

did not work so ambitiously to establish the authority of Cervantes, either by
allusions to classical literature or by classicizing illustrations. Yet this edition is
still a sumptuous one, printed on high-quality paper with well-executed engravings. Having spent up to six years on the project, Smollett had taken great
pains in the translation, to the point that he included numerous critical
footnotes to the text to explain Spanish customs or the subtleties of translating
certain phrases or words.[56]

One must not make the mistake of taking Smollett's final product too
seriously, for his careful translation is spiced with satire. A lengthy and humorous note describes the debate over the translation of "duelos y quebrantos,"
finally translating the enigmatic phrase, after long-winded scholarly review, as
"pains and breakings" caused by the protagonist's diet rich in fibre.[57] This
footnote exemplifies Smollett's satirical ability and his approach to the text. As
an inheritor of the neoclassical reading of *Don Quixote* initiated by Mayans
and the 1738 Lord Carteret edition, Smollett acknowledged through his satire
the status of the text as a classic, worthy to be thoroughly and critically read
and translated. Yet what he would not sacrifice was the work's humour.
Breaking wind was not decorous, although it certainly was verisimilar and
amusing when referred to in this playful, mocking fashion. In this way, the
comic became established as a middle ground between the high and low
manners of neoclassical aesthetics, where the low discourse of bodily functions
and the elite discourse of literary criticism met. In this footnote one sees the
space opened up by *Don Quixote* for the English satirists, "a text that opened
up the possibility of the mock-text, a way of juxtaposing the heroic, the
romantic, the plainly fictional with the contemporary commonplace."[58]

SMOLLETT'S GOALS AS TRANSLATOR:
SATIRE ELEVATED AND EXTENDED

An anonymous note appended to the introduction, probably written by Smollett himself, states the translator's goals, particularly in the presentation of the
main characters:

The Translator's aim, in this undertaking, was to maintain that ludicrous solemnity
and self-importance by which the inimitable Cervantes has distinguished the character
of Don Quixote, without raising him to the insipid rank of a dry philosopher, or
debasing him to the melancholy circumstances and unentertaining caprice of an
ordinary madman; and to preserve the native humour of Sancho Panza, from degen-
erating into mere proverbial phlegm, or affected buffoonry.[59]

Smollett proposes for himself a middle road upon which to send the wandering
pair, one between the elevated path to Mount Parnassus of the Carteret edition
and the low, earthy path of the earlier burlesque illustrations. The translator

grants Don Quixote his stuffy side, but the very absurdity of his stiffness simultaneously undermines his serious air. In contrast to Mayans, Smollett sees Don Quixote as a comically unified character. His contrasting moments of foolishness and lucidity result not from lapses in decorum committed by a nodding author but from expressions of the incongruous juxtaposition of the elevated and the base essential to humour. Neither is any outside force corrupting the character mentioned, nor is it necessary if the tension exists within Don Quixote's psyche. With respect to Sancho Panza, Smollett also attempts to find a middle ground, this time to preserve his "native humour." Again, the character is accepted as a psychic whole, and thus speculation about or disapproval of the pearls of wisdom scattered throughout the peasant's proverbs and humorous comments is deemed unnecessary. The humour arises simply from the diverse facets of his "native" personality.

Smollett expresses a similar respect for the integrity of the novel on the grounds of satire:

The satire and propriety of many allusions, which had been lost in the change of customs and lapse of time, will be restored in explanatory notes; and the whole conducted with that care and circumspection, which ought to be exerted by every author, who, in attempting to improve upon a task already performed, subjects himself to the most invidious comparison.[60]

Accordingly, the footnotes should function to restore the original satire lost in the passage of time and the passage from one language and culture to another. Although the object of the textual satirical allusions is assumed to be tied to Cervantes' contemporaneous surroundings, the power of perfidious literature is no longer proposed as the overriding satirical object. As seen in the footnote concerning "duelos y quebrantos," Smollett believed that Cervantes was poking fun at his society on many different levels, including the physical. This conception of the broadly satirical text is akin to the satire of Smollett's time, as evidenced in the Hogarth prints *Marriage à la Mode* or Fielding's *Don Quixote in England*, in which every character and element is satirized. At the same time, the satirical text occupied a newly authorized place as didactic literature. As Richard Graves wrote, "I am convinced that *Don Quixote* or *Gil Blas* or *Sir Charles Grandison* will furnish more hints for correcting the follies and regulating the morals of young persons, and impress them more forcibly in their minds, than volumes of severe precepts seriously delivered or dogmatically enforced."[61] Of course, earlier neoclassical critics had stressed literature's didactic function, but to state that satire, rather than heroic epic, was the most effective didactic genre indicated its new elevation and universalization based on its status as a comic, mixed genre. Satire served to critique and correct all vices, not just specific ones such as the addiction to chivalric romances. This universal, comic critique, complemented by its didactic purpose and eighteenth-century emphasis on vices of the subject's sentiments, marked it as a genre revived and repackaged for the middle class.

CERVANTES AS SATIRIST AND ROMANTIC SOUL: SMOLLETT'S BIOGRAPHY

One can imagine, then, how Cervantes as the satirical writer *par excellence* continued to gain stature. This increased appreciation of the author as a man is revealed in Smollett's "Life of Cervantes," a biographical account drawn largely from the author's own writings and the works of Nicolás Antonio, Diego de Haedo, Tomás Tamayo de Vargas, and Francisco de Vergara.[62] Whereas Mayans' "Vida de Cervantes" discourses on the author's writings, Smollett's describes the life of the active man. Smollett recounts Cervantes' captivity in Algeria, and emphasizes his attempted escape and the honour his captor showed him in sparing his life. Smollett also credits Cervantes with reviving Spanish theatre during his service to the Cardinal Acquaviva, a claim scarcely believable now but one that indicates the heroic proportions the figure of Cervantes acquired in the eighteenth century. Cervantes' prison sentence gave evidence of his goodwill and generosity, through which he lost the money in question. Thus, the author appears as a valorous soldier and a man willing to sacrifice himself for others, yet ignored and despised by his own countrymen. Smollett realized that this characterization placed the author of Don Quixote in an ambiguous relationship both to his own country and to his work. With respect to Spain, Smollett writes, "Miguel de Cervantes Saavedra was at once the glory and reproach of Spain; for, if his admirable genius and heroic spirit conduced to the honour of his country, the distress and obscurity which attended his old age, as effectually redounded to her disgrace."[63] Smollett repeatedly mentions the disgrace and distress of Cervantes' old age, when he was either ignored or vilified by his fellow authors and his patrons. In contrast, Mayans manages to avoid projecting this image to such an extent by insisting on the respect Lope de Vega held for the author. None the less, it was Smollett's vision of Cervantes' penury as a prototype of the suffering and alienated artist that would become part of the Romantic legend of *Don Quixote*.[64]

Smollett perceived yet another tension within the person of Cervantes in relation to his country and his work that was far more crucial in the further development of the reception of the novel. Having focused on Cervantes' varied adventures and his valour in the face of hardship, Smollett points to the ambiguous relationship Cervantes may have had with the concept of chivalry and knight errantry:

Notwithstanding all the shafts of ridicule which he hath so successfully levelled against the absurdities of the Spanish romance, we can plainly perceive, from his own writings, that he himself had a turn for chivalry: his life was a chain of extraordinary adventures, his temper was altogether heroic, and all his actions were, without doubt, influenced by the most romantic notions of honour.

Spain has produced a greater number of these characters, than we meet with on record in any other nation; and whether such singularity be the effect of natural or moral causes, or of both combined, I shall not pretend to determine.[65]

He describes these persons, such as Cervantes, as those "who remind us of the characters described by Homer and Plutarch, as patriots sacrificing their lives for their country, and heroes encountering danger, not with indifference and contempt, but, with all the rapture and impetuosity of a passionate admirer."[66] First of all, the allusion to classical authors takes a strange twist, since Smollett does not compare Cervantes to the author Homer but to Homer's heroes, such as Achilles. He admires most in these literary characters their "passion" and "rapture," not their decorum. For Cervantes to satirize the chivalric code by his attack on the romances of knight errantry was to attack a code of passion by which he himself lived and which brought out the finest in himself and his countrymen.[67] To a certain extent Smollett is reworking in Cervantes' favour the old chestnut accusing him of destroying Spain by attacking the nation's code of chivalric honour.[68] None the less, the satirist Smollett expresses a certain respect for this passion and rapture by attributing it to Cervantes himself.

This explicit similarity and sympathy between the chivalric Cervantes and his literary creation, Don Quixote, complicated the issue of authorial intention. For Smollett, Cervantes was not the Herculean author who donned the mask of Don Quixote in the frontispiece to the 1738 Lord Carteret edition but an alienated yet passionate man who expressed his heroic character in his protagonist. As Burton describes Smollett's vision of Cervantes, "Here then is a Cervantes who seems almost to have succeeded, where Don Quixote failed, in being a perfect gentle knight."[69] This sympathy between the author and the character undercut the satirical goal of conquering the fantastic literature of knight errantry and raised the possiblity of more ambiguous interpretations of the character of Don Quixote. He might be more than a tool used merely for the author's satirical intent, perhaps an alter ego. In her book *The Progress of Romance through Times, Countries, and Manners* (1785) the author of Gothic romances Clara Reeve voices this ambiguity:

Compare the times past with the present; and see on which side the balance will turn; in favour of public spirit, or private virtue. Let us suppose the character of *Don Quixote* realized, with all its virtues and absurdities. I would ask, whether such a man is not more respectable, and more amiable, than a human being, wholly immersed in low, groveling, effeminate, or mercenary pursuits, without one grain of private virtue, or public spirit, whose only thoughts, whishes, and desires are absorbed in a worthless self?[70]

Reeve expresses concisely how Don Quixote had been re-evaluated through the course of the English eighteenth century within the new social structure of the bourgeoisie as defined by Habermas.[71] The deluded knight errant, in spite of his madness but certainly through his mad actions, had proven his good intentions in the sentimental realm of "private virtue" and had acted upon them "with public spirit," as a private individual attempting to better the public sphere. When seen through such a lens, Don Quixote began to appear as a positive role model. Ironically, the satirist Smollett, sensitive to the hypocrisies and tensions of the world about him, first signalled the great tension in *Don Quixote*, the sympathetic portrayal of the protagonist, that would burst forth in the Romantic reading.

THE EIGHTEENTH-CENTURY CONCEPT
OF THE ROMANTIC

Since Smollett uses the word "romantic" in his biography of Cervantes, it deserves attention in light of the above observations. The word was first associated with the "Spanish romances," or prose works of chivalric adventures, which were exotic, unusual, even at times fantastic, and in which heroes overcame overwhelming odds to restore honour to the world.[72] Smollett clearly viewed these romances as dangerous:

In the character of Don Quixote, he exhibits a good understanding, perverted by reading romantic stories, which had no foundation in nature or in fact. His intellects are not supposed to have been damaged by the perusal of authentic histories, which recount the exploits of knights and heroes who really existed; but, his madness seems to have flowed from his credulity and a certain wildness of imagination which was captivated by the marvelous representations of dwarfs, giants, negromancers, and other preternatural extravagance.[73]

The distinction Smollett draws between factual and romantic histories – that is, marvellous and fantastic histories – is similar to that drawn by Mayans. Don Quixote, like Mayans' naïve reader, suffered the effects of his uninformed credulity. Perhaps the reference to the worthiness of historical adventurers allows for Cervantes' own chivalric adventures. This use of the term "romantic" to describe literature and persons of a "certain wildness of imagination" appears to have been the standard usage in the eighteenth century, according to the *Oxford English Dictionary*. In fact it is used in just such a way both in Motteux's preface (1700) and in a caption to an illustration in the Cooke edition of *Don Quixote* (London 1774). Yet Smollett describes Cervantes' laudable sense of honour as "romantic." The term had begun to crackle with ambiguous meanings already in 1755. Perhaps a re-evaluation of imagination as a positive mental faculty was already underway. Certainly the sentimental insistence upon sympathy for others depended upon the individual's imagination, and reasserted its importance as a faculty for judging others and creating subjectively compelling literature. Shortly thereafter, writers such as Clara Reeve would reappropriate the romance in the Gothic novel. These changes in literary taste and production at a public level would be as responsible for the Romantic reading of *Don Quixote* as the German Romantic movement – if not more so.

In a reworking of the neoclassical presentation of Cervantes as a learned author Smollett linked his education to the fruitful engagement of his romantic imagination. He argued that Cervantes showed evidence of great training in the classics, history, philosophy, geography, and astrology – in short, a liberal education that had trained him to engage in the "productions of taste and polite literature, which, while they amused his fancy, enlarged, augmented, and improved his ideas, and taught him to set proper bounds to the excursions of his imagination."[74] Thus, Smollett attributed a romantic imagination, prone to fantastic wanderings, to Cervantes as well as to Don Quixote. Of course, Smollett still believed that the imagination must be kept within reasonable bounds through the rational limits of education, but his assumption that the author identified with the protagonist differed greatly from Mayans' assumption of a distanced, critical relationship between author and protagonist. To argue that Cervantes, a man who himself led a heroic, adventurous life, suffered from the same excesses of romantic imagination as his mad protagonist was to argue that Don Quixote represented a facet of the author's own character. This identification of the heroic author with his protagonist was one of the starting points of the Romantic reading because it undercut the authority of the satirical reading and encouraged the reader to sympathize likewise with the protagonist. Yet Smollett refrained from continuing down this path, just as he argued that Cervantes did. According to Smollett, Cervantes' acute powers of observation compensated for the restriction of his wild imagination: "Thus qualified, he could not fail to make pertinent observations in his commerce with mankind: the peculiarities of character could not escape his penetration; whatever he saw became familiar to his judgment and understanding; and every scene he exhibits, is a just, well drawn characteristic picture of human life."[75] Cervantes' restraint of imagination led him to depict life, to create mimetic rather than fantastic literature, and to produce this literature from his interaction with others viewed within the bourgeois framework of commerce. Thus, he served as a precursor to Fielding, Hogarth, and Smollett, all of whom perceived their humorous depictions as faithful to and revealing of the "hypocrisies" and "peculiarities" of life.

The attribution of mimetic intent to Cervantes' novel also began to undermine the emphasis on its parodic intent. *Don Quixote* could be seen as a series of vignettes viewed for pleasurable consumption instead of a book attacking other books, and its subject could be understood as life instead of literature's ill effect on life. As such, the author's satirical intention would transcend the parody of a certain literary genre to address and critique other facets of his contemporary Spain. Smollett's footnotes recognized this same conception of satire's ability to operate at many levels and against many objects as he sought to restore not only the literary but also the social context of Cervantes' work. According to Smollett, Cervantes was packaging a satire of his Spain for reading and discussion by the public. Again, the interpretation of *Don Quixote* opened towards the Romantic interpretations of the novel as a work of social critique on a much wider scale, and/or as a depiction of the customs and manners of exotic Spain. That Smollett initiated this discourse at the same time he restrained it by references to classical literature, liberal arts training, and satirical intention reveals the very real tensions at work beneath the surface of eighteenth-century readings, as literary figures and artists alike attempted to reconcile their growing knowledge of the author's life and their appreciation of his craft with the stated authorial intent of parodying chivalric romances.

SATIRE CRUMBLING:
HAYMAN'S ALLEGORICAL FRONTISPIECE

This 1755 edition, featuring Smollett's translation and Francis Hayman's illustrations, is one of the few in which the interpretations of the novel by all parties involved largely coincide. As Smollett states in the footnote quoted above, he intended the work to provide "entertainment and instruction for our readers." As the same footnote demonstrates, the instructive element is often itself satirized. The satire of the internal elements of the novel, initiated by Hogarth, is developed further in this edition through visual jests at the expense of the characters, the plot, the author, and even the reader. Within the visual component of this edition, which does not contain a portrait of Cervantes, the author – and perhaps his authorial control – is receding in importance. This edition also lacks the framing images of Alonso Quijano reading the chivalric romances and his renunciation of his madness on his deathbed, scenes so crucial to establishing the source of his alter ego's madness and reinforcing its pernicious effect. Instead, the first illustration represents Don Quixote's knighting (1:fp17), and the last Sancho Panza's reunion with his wife and daughter (2:fp458). The allusion to the satirical purification of literature by this work is perhaps satirical itself, conveying the double content of authoritative commentary and the satire of this commentary revealed in Smollett's footnotes. Perhaps nothing should be taken too seriously – or too humorously – in this edition.

That the parody of the literature of knight errantry had receded to become just one of many objects of satiric deflation is manifest in the allegorical frontispiece (see Figure 24). Unlike all the previous frontispieces, excluding the very first one of 1618, no verbal explanation accompanies this image, either in the form of a caption, labels for the figures, or advice to the reader, thus leaving

Fig. 24   Francis Hayman. Frontispiece. London 1755.
Biblioteca Nacional, Madrid.

the allegory open to more ambiguous readings. It would seem that the reading
of the novel as an attack on perfidious, fantastic literature had become a topos
and, therefore, did not require explanation, although a caption was added to
the image in a 1793 edition.[76] Significantly, Cervantes, formerly the Herculean
hero of the 1738 Lord Carteret edition, has been replaced by the heroine
Comedy, evidence perhaps of Fielding's and Hogarth's success in championing
the genre. The content of the frontispiece is predictable, as the feminine
personification of Comedy subdues the crouched dragon of fantastical literature
before a crumbling Oriental edifice. Clearly, her force has both tamed the
dragon and destroyed the fortress before her. In the left midground Minerva,
or Truth, stands before a classical portico and reflects the rays of reason from
her shield as weapons towards her enemies: a hunchbacked dwarf who skulks
away, a four-armed Moor, the shadowy figures of a retreating man and maid,
and another dwarf blowing a warning horn from a crumbling tower. Obviously,
these classical warrioresses are staving off the orientalizing forces of fantasy and

monstrosity with the weapons of reason and Enlightenment. Truth defends a
space of classical decorum and culture while Comedy destroys the fantastic
edifices and tames the grotesque monsters, although the respective spaces of
classical and Oriental culture are impinged upon by Hayman's play with
perspective and optical illusion.

Unlike the frontispiece to the Carteret edition, which was executed to take
part in the serious tradition of baroque allegorical frontispieces, this illustration
may be a visual parody of that very tradition. The artist's use of broken
perspectives and optical distortion, similar to that of Hogarth's *Gin Alley*,
undermines the very structure of this neoclassical allegory. The classical portico
sports a roof very unscientifically foreshortened along the frame. The Oriental
edifice collapses in an extremely visually disorganized manner, as one door falls
into an archway that seems too short to accommodate its height, and another
falls over the moat, only to reveal yet another door. Conflicting light sources
throw confused shadows, as rays clearly beam forth from Minerva's shield, but
a more diffused light seems to fall into the scene from the viewer's space. The
mixture of fantastic and classical literary figures is mirrored in the distortion
of linear perspective and lighting, with the effect of overshadowing, if not
undermining, the image's clearly allegorical content reiterating Cervantes' supposed authorial intention to destroy the chivalric romance. This image may in
fact be an example of the instability of allegory as its forms begin to crumble
within a new intellectual and social context.

DON QUIXOTE'S LUDICROUS SOLEMNITY

Crucial to Hayman's vision of Don Quixote as well as Smollett's is an acute
awareness of the protagonist's dual nature, both ridiculous and appealing in his
serious commitment to an elevated moral code. For example, the illustrations
of the protagonist's knighting (1:fp17) and the capture of Mambrino's helmet
(See Figure 25; 1:fp126) depict Don Quixote's "ludicrous solemnity and self-
importance" without "debasing him to the melancholy circumstances and
unentertaining caprice of an ordinary madman."[77] The ideal of the middle
genre of comedy seen in Fielding's prologue to *Joseph Andrews* has clearly passed
on to shape Smollett and Hayman's aesthetic. In the illustration Don Quixote
bows on one bended knee, his long thin body held stiffly, one bony hand held
to his heart, his head with his large, bony nose and sunken cheeks held high.
Although Francis Hayman was perhaps unfairly criticized by Horace Walpole
as a "strong mannerist, and easily distinguishable by the large noses and
shambling legs of his figures," his style was particularly apt for capturing the
solemnity and absurdity of Don Quixote.[78] This solemnity, indeed ludicrous
in such a shambling figure, is not, however, openly derided by the onlookers.
The innkeeper and maids look amused and amazed by the madman rather
than derisive. There are no open smiles, except for the boy holding the taper,

Fig. 25   Francis Hayman.
Don Quixote with Mambrino's Helmet. London 1755.
Biblioteca Nacional, Madrid.

who shields his smile with the back of his hand. A sentimental condescension towards the madman, very different from the bawdy laughter of seventeenth-century readers, has crept into the picture, the result of the Augustan disapproval of the "small, ungenerous man who laughs at others' unavoidable defects."[79] And yet the illustration itself is humorous to the viewer.

The illustration showing Don Quixote admiring his newly won barber's basin/helmet demonstrates well this new, gentler humour, which focuses more on the relationship between the characters than on the physical humour and ridiculous folly. Seated to the right, his own helmet removed to reveal his balding head, he holds the helmet high as he proudly points to his spoils with his long, bony index finger. His admiration of what is clearly a barber's basin is stressed and satirized by the figure of the barber fleeing in the right midground, seen by the viewer underneath Rocinante's long neck. At the left stands Sancho Panza, holding his own index finger towards his mouth to stifle a laugh. Interestingly, the gestures of Don Quixote's and Sancho Panza's left and right hands, respectively, are mirror images, the former viewed from the back of the hand, the latter from the palm. This use of a mirror image, the one to point towards an absurdity, the other to stifle a reasonable peal of laughter, resembles Hogarth's use of mirror images to reveal illusion and delusion. Thus, Hayman presents and undercuts Don Quixote's mistaken identification of the barber's basin as the helmet of a giant through the contrasting gestures of the two protagonists.

Fig. 26   Francis Hayman. *Midnight Fight with Maritornes.*
London 1755. Biblioteca Nacional, Madrid.

HAYMAN'S DRAMA OF THE SENTIMENTS

The subtler representation of folly through visually significant, and at times contrasting gestures leads to several different visual results. The vivid representation of characters as individuals in relationship to each other achieves a new sort of drama that depends less on the tumbles and beatings suffered by Don Quixote and Sancho Panza than on their sentimental anguish and distress. The illustration of the midnight fight in the inn with Maritornes (see Figure 26; 1:fp92), in itself an extremely physical episode, reveals Smollett's theatrical expressiveness. This print, designed by Hayman and engraved by J.S. Müller, contains many of the bawdy elements of earlier illustrations. The image focuses on the fight as Maritornes crouches above the prone Sancho, the bed collapses underneath them, and the grotesque swineherd grabs the hapless squire from behind. In the fray, Maritornes' loose gown falls away to reveal one breast, while one leg is left bare. Yet more striking than her grotesque nudity is her expression as Sancho grabs her by the hair. Her broad nostrils flare, her eyes roll upwards into her head, and her mouth grimaces in a look of pain and tenacity. The action is neither a matter of frolicsome play nor burlesque violence, but serious distress. The figure of Don Quixote, who lies in the shadows of the left background, accentuates the tension. His bare shoulders contort in agony as he throws back his head, his eyes shut and his mouth parted in pain. His anguish exacerbates the desperation of the three fighting figures. What first appears to be a funny picture seems more sombre on closer inspection, particularly once one's eyes move to the prone Don Quixote and back.[80] The effect of Hayman's experience with the theatrical world as a set painter is clear. Not only had he mastered dramatic expression, as seen in his illustration to Le Brun's *Treatise on the Passions* (used by David Garrick to improve contemporary acting), but he had also learned much from the staging, grouping, and interaction of characters.[81] This theatrical attention to parallel relationships and the interaction of characters ties Hayman to the tradition of Hogarth despite his almost rococo manner.[82] Its result is the increased depth of interpretation it begins to add to the scenes.

The interpretive depth is largely composed of a new sentimentality. Hayman collaborated with the French artist Gravelot on the illustration of Richardson's *Pamela* (1742), on images that combine "highly dramatic scenes" with the gloss of rococo grace and delicacy.[83] The configuration of the illustrations to Volume 2 of *Don Quixote* reveals the new sentimental conception of the work's drama:

> *The Enchantment of Dulcinea* (see Figure 27; fp54)
> *The Unmasking of the Knight of the Mirrors and His Squire* (fp80)
> *The Wedding of Camacho* (fp127)
> *The Attack on the Puppet Play* (fp163)
> *Don Quixote Meets the Duchess* (see Figure 28; fp187)
> *Sancho Panza and Doña Rodríguez Tussle After He Asks Her to Tend His Mount* (fp189)
> *The Priest Denounces Don Quixote at Dinner* (fp194)
> *The Doctor Bans Food from Governor Sancho's Table* (fp284)
> *The Midnight Rendezvous of Don Quixote and Doña Rodríguez* (see Figure 29; fp296)
> *The Girl Disguised as a Boy Is Led to Sancho Panza* (fp305)
> *Teresa Panza Receives the Envoy from Sancho Panza* (see Figure 30; fp311)
> *Don Quixote Asks the Talking Head about Dulcinea's Disenchantment* (see Figure 31; fp400)
> *Don Quixote Stops Sancho Panza's Beating* (see Figure 32; fp449)
> *Sancho Panza Is Reunited with Teresa Panza and Daughter* (see Figure 33; fp458)

The first four scenes are often illustrated in all eras. For example, the enchantment of Dulcinea by Sancho Panza is the basis for most of the plot thereafter, and is particularly suited to the extra emphasis given it by an illustration. The

Fig. 27   Francis Hayman. *Enchantment of Dulcinea.*
London 1755. Biblioteca Nacional, Madrid.

following three are all masterful episodes exploring and revealing varying facets of enchantment and disenchantment, folly and Enlightenment, to use eighteenth-century terms. Illustrators of these episodes focus on the moments of greatest deception: when Quiteria marries Basilio; when Don Quixote, maddened by the play in progress, attacks the stage; and when Don Quixote refuses to believe his eyes and chooses to believe that enchanters have altered the face of the Knight of the Mirrors to appear as the face of Bachelor Samson Carrasco. Perhaps showing these moments serves the enlightened purpose of highlighting Don Quixote's folly. Yet the representation of these scenes, charming in their execution of the plot twists and devoid of direct explanation of Don Quixote's folly, probably serves more to entertain than to instruct.

THE REASONABLE DEFLATION OF FOLLIES

The other episodes illustrated provide an odd panorama of Book 2, particularly when one takes into account the attention paid in earlier editions to the scenes in the Duke and Duchess's palace and of Sancho Panza's governorship in

Fig. 28 Francis Hayman. *Don Quixote's First Meeting with the Duchess.* London 1755. Biblioteca Nacional, Madrid.

Barataria. None of the spectacles arranged by the Duke and Duchess to exploit Don Quixote's and Sancho's folly further is depicted. Instead, Hayman represents moments emphasizing the falsity behind the elegant façade of this cruel castle of marvels. With the exception of the scene in Barataria, in which Sancho's common sense shines, the scenes involving Sancho Panza show his degradation at the hands of the Duke and Duchess. The very first episode depicted, that of Don Quixote's meeting with the two aristocrats, shows Sancho lying flat on the ground, his foot caught in the halter around Rucio's neck (see Figure 28). His feet flail helplessly while, grimacing, he attempts to lift his weighty body off the ground with his arms. In the centre, as they look down upon the knight and ignore the squire, the Duke and the Duchess cordially receive the bowing Don Quixote. Sancho's degradation continues in the next illustration, when Doña Rodríguez refuses to care for his mount (2:31). Having been influenced by his master, Sancho claims that his ass deserves to be attended by the maids-in-waiting, as was Lancelot's horse. Smollett's translation renders the exchange in very earthy language:

"Heark ye, friend, replied the duenna, if you are a jack-pudding, keep your jokes for a proper place, where they may turn to account: from me you'll get nothing but a fig for them." "Very well, said the squire, I'll answer for its ripeness: your ladyship won't lose your game by a short reckoning." "You whoreson, cried the duenna, in a violent rage, whether I am old or not, I must render an account to God, and not to such a garlic-eating rascal as you."[84]

The representation of this most indecorous moment when two characters confront each other in a battle of vulgar insults is not seen in the neoclassically informed 1738 Lord Carteret edition. The standards of decorum appear to have changed considerably. Clearly, there is no Dr Oldfield overseeing this edition. Although Doña Rodríguez's words are harsh, they are also ones of Enlightenment to the extent that they deflate Sancho Panza's pretensions to inhabit the world of chivalric romance. Nor does the illustrator Hayman eschew the violence of the clash, as he depicts Sancho Panza and the lady-in-waiting actually grappling with each other, their faces distorted with hate. The satiric deflation of Sancho Panza is extremely corporal, linking these illustrations, despite their more refined execution and greater attention to the characters, to the earlier burlesque illustrations.

In the following illustration Hayman depicts Don Quixote's debasement by the ecclesiastic, another harsh speaker of the truth (2:31–2). He leaves the Duchess's table in disgust at the knight's foolishness in pursuing his "ridiculous conceit of ... being a knight-errant" and at the squire's delusion in following his master at the expense of his family's well-being.[85] The illustration shows the cleric as he steps away from the table with his arms outstretched and arched in distaste to prove his point. Don Quixote merely looks coolly back at the cleric, while the Duke and Sancho Panza attempt to suppress their amusement. Of course, Don Quixote has an eloquent reply in store for the cleric, but that is not the moment illustrated. What is illustrated are both moments when the two protagonists get their come-uppance.

But how does one interpret these illustrations? Perhaps it is evidence of enlightened sympathy for the characters to depict moments of verbal attack and deflation rather than Don Quixote's defeat by the Knight of the White Moon or Sancho Panza's fall into the cave. Or perhaps it is evidence of a new middle-class sensibility that shuns looking directly upon defeated, desperate beings. However comical or grotesque the ecclesiastic and Doña Rodríguez may appear to the reader, in the illustrations their role as the voice of reason, or perhaps common sense, is represented and, to wit, emphasized. It is particularly interesting that the cleric, as represented by Hayman, attacks not only Don Quixote but also the Duke and Duchess. He would seem to represent the English man of sentiment, authorized by his superior sensibility and morality to chastise the decadent aristocracy for their cruel pastimes. The tone of sentimentality creeps even into this rather dramatically satirical edition, a reminder that this voice of satire has ambitions to reshape society in order to establish and safeguard a respectable place for the middle class, including artists and authors. With respect to the Duke and the Duchess, the illustrations of

Vanderbank and Hayman, despite their sharply different tone, converge upon a critique of their shameless manipulations.

SANCHO PANZA STRENGTHENED

Hayman, like Vanderbank before him in the Carteret edition, sets up at this point in the narrative a series of parallel illustrations of the separate adventures of Don Quixote and Sancho Panza in which Sancho's character gains strength. In the Smollett edition the parallels between the scenes depicted are clear. Don Quixote is greeted by the Duchess; Sancho Panza is not so kindly greeted by Doña Rodríguez. Don Quixote is upbraided by the cleric at dinner for his spiritual malnutrition in the intake of excessive fantasy; Sancho Panza is upbraided at dinner for his physical malnutrition in the intake of excessive food. Don Quixote has a midnight encounter with Doña Rodríguez, whom he helps; Sancho Panza has a midnight encounter with Diego de la Llana's unnamed daughter in disguise, whom he helps. Of course, this alternation of characters and episodes is true to the text at this point. None the less, the choice of these episodes reveals a clear emphasis not just on switching from one protagonist to the other but on placing them in juxtaposition to each other. Don Quixote is mocked just as Sancho Panza is, only under the Duchess's breath; Don Quixote is scolded for his mental folly just as Sancho Panza is for his physical excesses; Don Quixote in good faith aids a woman, just as Sancho Panza does. The use of mirroring and paralleling now extends beyond the frames of the single illustrations and demonstrates well how the illustrations begin to operate as a narrative in their own right.

As in Vanderbank's illustrations, Sancho Panza's character gains dignity and strength towards the end of the series. This process begins in the pair of illustrations depicting the protagonists' encounters with the women in distress (2:48–9). Hayman's illustration of the meeting of Don Quixote and Doña Rodríguez epitomizes the mixture of sentimentality and satire typical of this edition (see Figure 29). Doña Rodríguez, with broad, wrinkled face, broad smile, and round spectacles, beams at the chaste knight as he gingerly takes her hand, a gesture set off by the candlelight. Don Quixote, modestly clutching a blanket to his chest, leans back from her hesitantly and cautiously, his back arching in a graceful S-curve reminiscent of Hogarth's favourite shape (which the latter found for himself in Coypel's *Don Quixote* illustrations). The large, unmade bed awaits behind them. As Smollett's translation of the text reads, "Here Cide Hamet, in a parenthesis, swears by Mahomet, that to have seen these two originals thus linked, and walking from the door to the bed, he would have given the best of his two jackets."[86] To see this illustration is almost worth that much, for here Don Quixote's vulnerability, accentuated by the bandage around his jaw, and generosity appear at their most humorous and charming. This image stands in marked contrast to Sancho's gravity and authority as night watchmen lead a girl disguised as a boy caught roaming the streets of Barataria at night

Fig. 29   Francis Hayman. *Don Quixote and Doña Rodríguez's Midnight Encounter.*
London 1755. Biblioteca Nacional, Madrid.

towards him. She is the one who shields herself in modesty, this time from the light of the candle held to her face. He stands proudly, hands hooked in the sash about his waist, as he gazes at the girl in august judgment tempered by gentleness. The parallel between the two figures is striking, not so much for its satirical effect as for its exploration of the two characters' psyches. Don Quixote's restrained behaviour appears particularly gentlemanly when contrasted with the sordid midnight rape and near-rape scenes of Richardson's novels. If one adopts Eric Ziolkowski's view of Don Quixote as a "good man" according to latitudinarian theology, his behaviour at this moment gives evidence of both charity and chastity.[87] This image comes closest to Skinner's characterization of the eighteenth-century English Don Quixote as a "benevolent eccentric, thwarted melancholic, yet a man of exquisite feeling withal."[88]

DON QUIXOTE AND SANCHO PANZA: THE CONFLICT OF SENTIMENT AND GOOD SENSE

In the closing illustrations of this edition, both characters gain dignity through their virtuous actions according to eighteenth-century bourgeois standards. Don Quixote becomes a man of sentiment in his treatment of his servant, and Sancho Panza becomes the bourgeois family man in his return to the responsibility of home. By means of the illustrations, *Don Quixote* is transformed from a satire to a *Bildungsroman*. Whereas Don Quixote's character has softened from that of a stuffy, arrogant Spanish country gentleman into a gentle and somewhat passive man of sentiment, Sancho's character has strengthened into that of a robust man of action and judgment. Nor does Hayman avoid depicting the conflict that arises as the master and squire grow to change places. The final four illustrations depict the resolution of their relationship. In the first of these (2:50), a page dropping humbly to his knees offers Teresa Panza the letter from her husband (see Figure 30). In the second Don Quixote and Sancho Panza confront each other about the self-inflicted whipping of Sancho required for the disenchantment of Dulcinea (see Figure 31). On opposite sides of Don Antonio's talking bust, Sancho Panza reacts in terror and Don Quixote leans forward eagerly as the head repeats the requirement (2:62). Delineated with deeper, darker lines than the other characters, who seem to fade away, master and squire occupy centre stage in their conflict. In the third illustration Don Quixote rushes forward, laying his hands upon Sancho's bare shoulders to stop the whipping (see Figure 32). The master's figure, clothed in loose garments rather than armour, seems diminished. Although Sancho's wrinkled brow still discloses anger, the illustration's focus centres on Don Quixote's release of his squire from his obligation. The wrestling match between the two, in which Sancho declares his independence, is notably *not* shown (2:71). Hayman has transformed Don Quixote into a man of sentiment who is finally moved by his servant's physical pain to act magnanimously.

Fig. 30   Francis Hayman. *Page Delivers Sancho's Letter to Teresa
Panza.* London 1755. Biblioteca Nacional, Madrid.

Sancho Panza gains dignity not through his open defiance of his tormentors
but through his sensible decision to attend to his family. This edition's very
last illustration does not show Don Quixote's death but Sancho's reunion with
his family (see Figure 33). In this illustration Sancho Panza, converted into a
storyteller as he recounts his adventures, proudly walks home, joined by his
eager wife and daughter as the dog leaps up to greet him (2:73). His hands
gesture widely, and his face is full of the gravity of the story to be told, the
bitterness of the end of the journey, and the sweetness of reunion. Sancho
Panza has heeded the advice of the ecclesiastic and returned home to tend to
his own. A new moral emerges from the story, particularly since this edition's
producers have decided not to illustrate Alonso Quijano's death but rather to
focus on Sancho Panza's good sense.[89] Throughout this edition the author's
parodic intent, his desire to castigate bad literature, has been underplayed to
the benefit of a more universal satiric thrust and a sentimental approach to the

Fig. 31 Francis Hayman.
The Talking Head of Don Antonio. London 1755.
Biblioteca Nacional, Madrid.

characters. Smollett and Hayman introduce both sentimental and satirical elements to broaden the novel's critical scope to encompass the decadence of the aristocracy, the sensibility of the moral man, and the responsibility of the family man. They educate Don Quixote and Sancho Panza, and by extension their readers, towards their proper social roles, rather than educate readers at the protagonists' expense.

IDENTIFICATION WITH DON QUIXOTE AND SANCHO PANZA

The doubled and simultaneous movements seen in Vanderbank's, Hogarth's, and Hayman's depiction of *Don Quixote* towards a more encompassing reading of the novel's satirical thrust and a more sympathetic representation of the novel's protagonists were largely based on a new understanding of the novel as mimetic. Already in 1700 Motteux saw in Don Quixote the reflection of "Every Man," made foolish by whatever darling hobbyhorse of his heart. William Hogarth used his own likeness to depict Sancho, as the artist's wife revealed to a printer years after his death,[90] just as Hayman used his for Sancho's corpulent counterpart in English literature, Falstaff. Certainly the stolid Sancho, defending his mastery of his own self against the elevated rhetoric and social position

Fig. 32   Francis Hayman. *Don Quixote Stops Sancho Panza's
Whipping*. London 1755. Biblioteca Nacional, Madrid.

of Don Quixote, mirrored Hogarth's confrontation with the neoclassical and
aristocratic artists and aestheticians of the time as he discovered a new middle-
class public for his art. By so doing, he defined a new middle ground for the
comic. Samuel Johnson stated most explicitly the emergent identification with
the inner world of Don Quixote:

Very few readers, amidst their mirth or pity, can deny that they have admitted visions
of the same kind; though they have not, perhaps, expected events equally strange, or
by means equally inadequate. When we pity him, we reflect on our own disappoint-
ments; and when we laugh, our hearts inform us that he is not more ridiculous than
ourselves, except that he tells us what we have only thought.[91]

Johnson took Motteux's Every Man to be every man, saw Don Quixote as his
mirror image, and acknowledged the doubled movement of sympathy with the

Fig. 33   Francis Hayman. *Sancho Panza Reunited with his Family.*
London 1755. Biblioteca Nacional, Madrid.

madman and laughter at his foolishness. This double reaction was, of course, typical of the later Romantic interpretation. But its emergence in the eighteenth century was not associated so much with idealist philosophy or wild imagination as with a new sentimental code of manners adopted by the members of the emergent middle class (who employed it as a ticket to spiritual elevation, if not social), and a new understanding of comedy, not as a low genre but as a mimetic genre fit for the new public. The comic, according to Fielding and Hogarth, imitated life; and *Don Quixote*, as a definitive work of this mixed genre, imitated life as well as literature's effect upon life.

"El Quixote ilustrado":
Illustration and Enlightenment
in the Real Academia Edition

CADALSO'S HINT OF HIDDEN MEANING

At the end of the eighteenth century in Spain, the fortune of the errant *Don Quixote* took a turn for the better as the novel was finally acclaimed a classic in its own land. This new appreciation of the novel and its characters grew from the assumption that the work did, indeed, contain deeper meanings, satirical or otherwise. The young writer José Cadalso, known now for his proto-Romantic interest in the lugubrious and the sentimental, discerned new depths in the old work. "In this nation there is a book highly applauded by all the rest. I have read it, and doubtlessly liked it; but I can't help being mortified by the suspicion that the literary sense is one thing, and the true meaning another."[1] This cryptic statement, enveloped within the letter of a young Moroccan traveller in Spain relating the country's strange customs to his mentor (a voice that echoes the accent of Cide Hamete Benengeli) in the *Cartas marruecas*, has escaped the attention of many scholars who have written on the reception of *Don Quixote* in eighteenth-century Spain.[2] None the less, the brief paragraph devoted to the novel succinctly refers to the various debates surrounding Cervantes' work at the time. The first sentence simply and uncannily sums up the fact around which Spanish response to the novel would subsequently take form: *Don Quixote* had been recognized as a classic first in England and France. The publication in England of Mayans y Siscar's biography of Cervantes and analysis of the novel, contained within the first de luxe edition, was later cause for a national debate, if not necessarily disgrace, among the elite lettered classes fostered by the court of Charles III. Yet the debate was fundamentally nationalistic, for at stake was not merely the literary honour of Spain but the legitimacy of its culture, the importance of its place in Europe, and the manner in which eighteenth-century Spaniards understood their past glory, contemporary decline, and possible future.[3]

To a large degree the aesthetic debate surrounding *Don Quixote* in Spain – its value as a satirical work, the neoclassical comparison of Cervantes to Homer, etc. – vanished in the maelstrom as Spanish intellectuals either defended their culture from overt and perceived attacks from without or adopted outside critiques in order to reform their culture from within. The attempt by the court leaders to introduce Spain to what they perceived to be the European values of the eighteenth century, based on the development of industry, commerce, and rational analysis, largely failed.[4] From a socio-economic point of view these reforms were ineffective because the society itself did not create a new stratum of the bourgeois public. The fact that the king sponsored the establishment of academies and the promotion of technological enterprises, such as the development of the publishing and textile industries, reveals that the split between the public sphere and the state – crucial for the emergence of an independent middle class – did not occur.[5] The various popular riots, such as that in Madrid in 1766 against Charles III's Italian adviser, Squillace, also indicate that the populace recognized the introduction of these reforms from above (and outside). Their discontent probably arose from their sense of mass impotence and rage rather than public engagement and debate. Certain intellectuals indeed aligned themselves with the *pueblo* in a conservative defence of the traditional Spanish valorization of military strength and Catholic orthodoxy above industry, commerce, and critical debate. They battered the court intellectuals, many young and/or foreign, with continuous accusations of national treachery and betrayal. Too often literary critics have accepted without question the mutually exclusive camps into which the eighteenth-century participants divided themselves, the *afrancesados* who sought reform and the *nacionalistas* who fought to preserve traditional society. As understood at the time, the "Frenchified" reformers adopted neoclassical literary ideals as well as Enlightenment ideas to the exclusion of the Spanish literary heritage, whereas the latter defended the same heritage to the exclusion of any possible external influence.

Yet, as will become evident in the case of *Don Quixote*, this neat dichotomy often fails to describe the actual conflicts and controversies of the time. For example, Cadalso's *Cartas marruecas* was clearly inspired by Montesquieu's *Lettres persanes,* which contained harshly unfair observations of Spanish culture. Subsequently, Cadalso's work served as a simultaneous apology for and critique of his nation's culture.[6] His brief observations on *Don Quixote* functioned in a similar manner: he acknowledged the foreign reception, offered the standard apologetic for the work as a satire, and then confessed his mortification that there might be more meaning hidden beneath the surface narrative. Of course, one can read this mortification ironically, taking into account the Spanish literary topos of the Moorish liar, exploited by Cervantes in his use of the narrator Cide Hamete Benengeli in *Don Quixote.*[7] Yet the possibility that the tale of a madman may indeed disclose deep truths could be mortifying *and* tantalizing for an *ilustrado*, particularly for one such as Cadalso, whose drama *Noches lúgubres* hints at a permeable boundary between reason and madness.[8] Cadalso's speaker continues to comment on *Don Quixote* by referring to a dictionary that reveals the true, hidden meanings of words: "No other work needs more than this one Nuño's dictionary: what one reads is a series of extravagances of a mad man, who believes that giants, enchanters, etc., exist; some proverbs in the mouth of a fool, and many well-critiqued scenes of life; but there is beneath this surface, to my mind, a mixture of profound and important matters."[9] Cadalso's language, despite his attempt to hide the implications in this concise, oblique statment, reveals that he had glimpsed the conflict of the literal/the truthful, or appearance/profundity, around which so many later interpretations and representations of the novel revolve.

Nor was Cadalso the only eighteenth-century Spaniard to peer into the darkness beyond the light of reason. Paul Ilie has noted a parallel between Cadalso's *Cartas marruecas* and Goya's *Caprichos* in the conception of the mimetic power of dementia. If society as it exists is nonsensical according to the light of reason, then dementia alone has the power to view and reflect it, and, by so doing, achieves *mimesis*.[10] The Spanish *ilustrado*, alienated from a larger social stratum, unlike his English contemporaries, could not enjoy the "self-evidence" of reason representing the interests of the dominant as worked out in public debate. As Habermas writes of the "'domination' of the public," "Public debate was supposed to transform *voluntas* into a *ratio* that in the public competition of private arguments came into being as the consensus about what was practically necessary in the interest of all."[11] The opinion of the Spanish people, as expressed in mob demonstrations as well as by conservative thinkers, did not support the authority of reason above that of tradition and religion. On account of this isolation from the larger populace, the Spanish *ilustrado* compromised his critical stance by aligning himself with an institution – in the case of the late eighteenth century, the court of Charles III – in order to effect the desired reforms of society.[12] By the same token, given the absence of a sizeable, economically powerful, and well-educated middle class, no buffering stratum of society existed to adopt and defend the Enlightenment ideals espoused by the Spanish court. The Spanish *ilustrado* found himself confronted by a society of the people that at best disregarded his thought as foreign and anti-Catholic and at worst exploded from class resentment in mob reaction to his reforms. The isolation of the *ilustrado* from a public society outside the protected and inaccessible spaces of the court and academy could not help but reveal to the Spanish populace the element of class interest inherent in his ideals. At the same time, as seen from his own perspective, this alienation also clothed the enlightened thinker's efforts to combat the enchantment of superstition and irrationality in the guise of a noble, but probably doomed, heroic struggle.

For the Spanish *ilustrado* no work was so engaged with the enchantment and disenchantment of the world as *Don Quixote*, whose protagonist, enchanted by literary myths, saw the dusty, violent world about him as enchanted by evil forces. In its resistance to his heroic efforts to reform it, his environment proved to the protagonist the veracity of his deluded vision, until he himself was disenchanted by reason on his deathbed. For Cadalso, the satire appeared superficial, masking deeper truths behind its opaque clarity. For Goya the boundary between reason and madness consumed itself in shadows. As will be shown in this chapter, the publishers and illustrators of the 1771 Ibarra and 1780 Real Academia (also published by Ibarra) editions of Don Quixote prepared the ground for these more revolutionary readers both by displaying the contradictions basic to the enlightened satirical reading and also by revealing its burlesque underpinning. In eighteenth-century Spain no middle ground existed to buffer the elite, rational reading from the popular, slapstick one. José Camarón's illustrations and the anonymous dedication to Don Quixote in the 1771 edition exploited this bawdy play with the mock-heroic, in its burlesque form mindless of possible didactic lessons, by combining it with more refined visual and literary idioms. The frontispieces and vignettes to the 1780 Real Academia edition continued to poke fun at the elevated forms through the introduction of popular and parodic imagery into the very edition that was intended to canonize Don Quixote as a foundational work of Spanish literature. In this way elements of burlesque humour contributed to a mock-"classic" reading of the novel, indicative of popular distance from the enlightened reading in Spain, supported by a court elite rather than a middle class. In addition, the two contributors to the edition who took Don Quixote seriously, the illustrator José del Castillo and the critic Vicente de los Ríos, occasionally cast beams of light upon episodes, characters, and characteristics of the text left in shadows by the dominant neoclassical aesthetic by using the very tools of the Enlightenment: composition (visual order) and reasoned analysis. At the moment of its official sanctioning in Spain, the enlightened, satirical interpretation of Don Quixote would be undercut by burlesque humour, and then opened to a serious Romantic reading by the very logic of its canonizing endeavour.

THE RECONSTRUCTION OF CERVANTES' BIOGRAPHY

Following the brief intellectual skirmish of the 1730s over the comparative worth of Cervantes' and Avellaneda's Don Quixotes, in which Cervantes' work had emerged the loser due to its "indecorous" characters, the next battle concerned not the novel but Cervantes' supposed critique of Lope's theatre in the Canon of Toledo's discourse on proper theatre in chapter 49 of the first part of Don Quixote and his own theatrical works.[13] Considering the Aristotelian content of the Canon's critique, it is less surprising that the very same Blas Antonio Nasarre who championed Avellaneda later extolled Cervantes in a 1748 edition of the latter's theatrical writings. As the central circle of critics in Madrid gradually appropriated the figure of Cervantes, his biography became of interest to them as part of their effort to restore Spain's lost cultural legacy in their own time of decadence.[14] Ignacio Henares Cuéllar has described the founding of the Spanish academies and the subsequent construction of a Spanish artistic canon fuelled by what he calls the «perspectiva Decadencia/Restauración».»[15] Although he writes of historians and critics of the visual arts, his observations are just as applicable to literary historians and critics:

History is conceived as a progressive and cyclical movement within the frame of the nation itself. Concerning the sense of Europe, nationalist history orients itself as much inwards as outwards towards other countries. Turned inwards, the idea of decadence forms part, as a reaction, of the consciousness of backwardness that the *ilustrados* feel upon comparing their national reality with that of Europe. By the same token, restoration implies the recovery of the rational aspect of culture conceived as a unitary and cyclical whole: flowering of the arts in antiquity; decadence in the Middle Ages; restoration in the Renaissance; and again decadence in the Baroque period.[16]

The loss of information about Cervantes' life a mere 150 years after his death served as evidence of the new decadence of the Baroque period for the *ilustrados*. Just as Antonio Ponz travelled throughout Spain in order to uncover architectural treasures, various literary historians journeyed to provincial archives to unearth documentation of the writer's life, to establish the skeletal time-line of his biography.[17] Nasarre rushed to Alcázar de San Juan in La Mancha to search for the coveted birth certificate, but the document was found in 1752 in Alcalá de Henares, thanks to Padre Martín Sarmiento's inspiration and either Agustín Montiano's or Manuel Martínez Pingarrón's footwork.[18] Nevertheless, few new analyses of the novel were undertaken at the time. A discourse read by Cándido M. Trigueros to the members of the Real Academia Sevillana de Buenas Letras in May 1761 rehashed the supposed satirical intent of the author: "Cervantes ridicules, treads on, annihilates, undoes everything that composes chivalric mania, boasting, and ridiculous honour; that was his goal."[19] Yet Trigueros did note the psychological integrity of the characters of Don Quixote and Sancho Panza, and thus refuted the earlier neoclassical charge that the latter, in particular, was indecorous.[20] Despite the lull in critical interaction with the work, it is safe to assume with Paolo Cherchi that the number of readers grew between 1750 and 1787, since eighteen new editions of *Don Quixote* appeared.[21]

THE 1771 IBARRA EDITION: THE BURLESQUE AND THE DYNAMIC INTERTWINED

In 1771 the renowned publisher Joaquín de Ibarra, commissioned by the Real Compañía de Impresores y Libreros del Reino, issued a new edition of *Don Quixote* accompanied by Mayans y Siscar's *Vida de Cervantes*, with illustrations designed by José Camarón and engraved in copper plates by Manuel Monforte.[22] The type and paper are of excellent quality, distinguishing this as the finest edition yet to be printed in Spain. Likewise, the illustrations, although still largely influenced in conception by the Bouttats illustrations, are also indebted to Coypel in their superior technical quality and flowing elegance. Because of this mixture of a popular, burlesque content and a more sophisticated, accomplished execution, the illustrations capture and make visible the change from the earlier burlesque reading to the enlightened, satirical reading in Spain. This transformation enjoys a transition that might seem organic, as the rough laughter enjoyed at Don Quixote's expense cedes to a more refined titter with the stated aim of instruction in the illustrations for this edition. None the less, certain biographical details reveal that José Camarón Boronat (1731–1803) enjoyed a rise in his own status as a result of Charles III's efforts to renew Spanish art and technology. Having been trained in his father's workshop in Segorbe, he moved from the old popular system of artistic production as a family business to become a *director supernumerario* of painting in the academy in Seville and an *académico de mérito* in the Real Academia de Bellas Artes in Madrid.[23] The artist's ascent, propelled not by the commercial creation of a middle class but by royal patronage, paralleled the rise of *Don Quixote,* also so favoured by the court, from popular joke book to national classic.

Camarón's depiction of the battle with the Basque and the battle of the windmills (1:8) in the same image illustrates well the aesthetic results of this transition, in which the humorous elements become stylized (see Figure 34; 1:fp75). Most notably, the artist has conflated the two episodes into one frame, employing the technique of simultaneous narration typical of popular prints yet shunned by serious historical painters for centuries. Indeed, the same compositional format seen in Bouttats' seventeenth-century image is used: in the foreground the Basque and Don Quixote freeze in combat; in the right-hand midground the women sit in the carriage watching; in the background the small figure of the mounted Don Quixote charges towards the windmills. Camarón's illustration differs from Bouttats' largely in the longer, more swaying motion of the two combatants, evidence, perhaps, of the influence of Coypel's willowy elegance. In fact the two figures form parallel contours as the Basque, with pillow flung back to protect himself, leans into Don Quixote, who arches backward with sword flung forward. This stylization of Bouttats' compositions lends them a refined, rococo elegance in the flowing lines, and yet conserves the basic burlesque emphasis on physical humour in its choice of subject-matter and its parallel presentation of the two combatants by emphasizing the basically defensive posture of the knight in reaction to the aggressive knave. The image reveals both the impact Bouttats' illustrations still had in Spain and the growing distance from the openly, even raucously burlesque readings of the past. Action still takes precedence over characterization, but the body in action is no longer merely a puppet to contort and twist for bawdy theatrics; rather, it has become

Fig. 34   José Camarón. *The Battle*
with the Basque. Madrid 1771.
Biblioteca Nacional, Madrid.

an abstract design element with which to play. The novel's humour seen as a
literary element experienced the same abstraction in the satirical reading; it no
longer existed for the sake of eliciting simple laughter, but rather referred to
an overriding didactic message.

Another example of this stylization of the burlesque tradition is the treatment
of the body in its carnivalesque facets, in which the physical functions of the
lower body are indulged.[24] Camarón did not illustrate the adventure of the
fulling mills (1:20), even though depictions of this most unexemplary adventure,
in which Sancho's bowels move from fear, continued to appear into the middle
of the century. In one roughly executed illustration published by Sanz in Madrid
in 1735, excrement actually spews from Sancho Panza's buttocks (1:fp210). Camarón's illustration does preserve the paddling of Doña Rodríguez at the hands of
the Duchess's maids (2:48), her full buttocks bared to the reader (see Figure 35;
4:fp124). Shadows obscure her face, stereotypically composed of the small
mouth, nose, and eyes perfunctory in female figures of the period. In contrast,
the artist and engraver have more carefully revealed and engraved her lower
body. Her full buttocks are rounded with hatch strokes; her legs, one propped
upon a chair, are slender, well-formed, and lent a certain elegance by her high
heels. Camarón renders her burlesque lower body erotic, distancing the reader
to the perspective of a voyeur, the same position occupied by Coypel's viewer.

Fig. 35   José Camarón.
The Paddling of Doña Rodríguez. Madrid 1771.
Biblioteca Nacional, Madrid.

These illustrations have assimilated to Bouttats' burlesque style the elegant eroticism of the French rococo artist, whose illustrations experienced success in
Spain as well as in the rest of Europe. One finds further evidence of Coypel's
artistic influence in the figures of the two maids, who, instead of paddling the
elder woman in a burlesque frenzy, mirror each other concavely in a surprisingly
delicate curve moving away from the centre, reminiscent of the curves so
admired by Hogarth in Coypel's illustrations.[25] Don Quixote himself recedes in
the face of such abundant feminine grace and eroticism as he sits up in his bed
in the right midground. The excited ridges and valleys of the curtains and
blanket of his bed are actually more animated than he is.

   Although the figures themselves are stock and inexpressive, the vivacity
attributed to the setting's inanimate elements reveals the introduction of the
norms of history painting to the content of *Don Quixote*. The crazed protagonist appears young and lanky, devoid even of madness, frustration, or fatigue
until the very end. Sancho Panza is small and boyish, never really acquiring a
personality of his own. The psychological superficiality of these illustrations

Fig. 36   José Camarón.
The Battle with Cardenio. Madrid 1771.
Biblioteca Nacional, Madrid.

stands in sharp contrast to Vanderbank's probingly sensitive portrayals or even Hayman's satirically biting crowd scenes. Again, these figures bear much more resemblance in their generic flatness to Bouttats, despite their elegant lines. Yet the trees, the light, and the shadows take on life. One dramatic example of this animation is the depiction of Cardenio's tussle with Don Quixote and Sancho Panza (see Figure 36; 1:fp347). An energetically spiralling composition, well befitting the fight, is achieved with the visual support of a twisted tree behind the contorted figures of Cardenio and a goatherd. In the centre Cardenio stands with one foot atop the fallen Sancho Panza. Approaching him from behind, the straight figure of the goatherd stabilizes the dynamism of Cardenio's figure. The tree twisting immediately behind them echoes Cardenio's posture and starts again the swirling effect. Don Quixote, whose flurry of feet further destabilizes and agitates the composition, falls to the side, legs flailing in the air. The image's dynamism is powerful, and the same composition will be used by the illustrators of the 1780 Ibarra edition for a far different effect. As one sees so vividly here, the setting and composition begin to express the mood of the scene, heightening or deepening its effect as it reveals Camarón's knowledge of history painting, a high, academic form of art.[26]

As Camarón's assimilation of elements from Bouttats' and Coypel's illustrations shows, the burning desire of so many Spaniards to reclaim *Don Quixote* as their own began, by necessity, with an engagement with these previous foreign interpreters. Their illustrations were already too widely known and favoured within Spain to be ignored by a Spanish illustrator. To some extent this edition, published almost a decade before the monumental undertaking of the Real Academia de la Lengua to forge an authentic, and therefore Spanish *Don Quixote*, gives the lie to the attempt by the academicians to give critical precedence to a chauvinistic interpretation of the novel as the foundational text of the national literature. These illustrations manifest the roots of the novel's popularity as a seventeenth-century parodic romp through the clichéed wastelands of the European genre of chivalric literature, as seen in both the earlier illustrations and the literary adaptations of the text, rather than through the parched, abandoned lands of sixteenth-century La Mancha, the setting favoured by a more nationalistic interpretation in both illustrations and criticism. As a parody of the pan-European taste for chivalric romance, the novel enjoyed international popularity and began to spawn the illustrations and interpretations that would keep it alive through the century of critical neglect at home. Later, the academic canonization of *Don Quixote* was required by the norms of neoclassicism in order to stress the universal, instructional content of the novel, supposed to be Cervantes' attempt to eradicate the spell of fantastic literature from the minds of his readers. This interpretive manoeuvre, in reality a very strong one, sought to harness the popular laughter elicited by the physical humour and broad parody of the work, as read in the seventeenth century, to a didactic purpose. Yet in eighteenth-century Spain, unlike eighteenth-century England, the popular humour could not be so easily absorbed into a reading of the novel. No middle class existed to redefine the genre as one mediating between the high art of the court and the low art of the carnival.

THE ACADEMY BURLESQUED:
"CIDE HAMETE BENENGELI'S" DEDICATION TO
DON QUIXOTE IN THE 1771 IBARRA EDITION

The facetious dedication written by Cide Hamete Benengeli to Don Quixote, published in the 1771 Ibarra edition, expressed yet again the humorous delight at the expense of the novel and its protagonist that still underlay the novel's popularity. The writer, adopting the mock-heroic voice of Cervantes' Arabic narrator, who so richly parodied the hyperbolic language of the chivalric romances, reiterates the adventures of Don Quixote. For example, the anonymous writer exclaims: "Because you avenged the unjust beatings you saw rain on Rocinante, the cruel mare herders clobbered you with their staffs. Because you resisted the amorous advances of Maritornes, an Asturian beat you silly, and a teamster pasted you with oil and candle drippings. For defending Sancho's expert and resounding brays, a cloud of rocks was unleashed on your ribs."[27] The writer conflates into these short sentences the lofty language and intentions of Don Quixote and the very humbling physical beatings the same loftiness inspired. The humour depends upon the collapsing of the ideal and the real worlds of the novel, perceived respectively as the ethic of knight errantry and the rough violence of the Manchegan countryside. The author is so aware of the game he plays that he quotes that well-known conflation of contradictions, describing the romances themselves in chapter 1 of the first part of *Don Quixote*: "The reason of the unreason that afflicts my reason, in such a manner weakens my reason that I with reason lament me of your comeliness."[28]

Just as humour often lies ambiguously in the cleft between two positions, this short, tongue-in-cheek piece itself shares the space between the ideal code of the knight errant and the rough and ruthless world of the sixteenth-century Spanish road and inn within *Don Quixote*. Yet there is also evidence that this dedication occupied a position between two critical strategies for reading the novel. The neoclassical critic Mayans y Siscar, whose biography of Cervantes accompanied this same edition, exemplified the first by approaching the work as a repository of knowledge and wisdom. The anonymous writer of this dedication quite clearly pokes fun at the attempt to transform the novel and its protagonist into a font of useful maxims and facts as well as pleasant digression: "If one then looks for clear understanding, love of books, and news of the principal arts in you, all will be found in perfection, because you were blessed with an understanding, not only clear, but *lucid*: you knew like the back of your hand all the books of knight errantry that were, are, and shall be, and you were and are more well-read than any other man in the world. You knew music like a crow, spoke about politics like a thrush, discoursed on mathematics like a butterfly, disputed like a parrot."[29] Don Quixote, like the neoclassical critic, used literature as an encyclopedia of knowledge. Yet this writer, through his use of oxymoronic compliments concerning the character's erudition (acquired through reading chivalric romances), calls into question this reading strategy. Knowledge gained from reading, particularly the reading of this genre, transforms the would-be erudite into a fool who merely parrots ill-founded opinion. This short, satirical essay reminds us that Cervantes' literary satire against the genre of knight errantry was still effective, even when removed by at least a century from the height of the genre's popularity.[30] But it also underlines the continued reception of the novel as a funny book about the sayings and misadventures of the fool – with a notable change. Don Quixote appears to be an enlightened fool, seen from below to lack the common sense necessary to counterbalance book learning.

Nevertheless, the author subscribes to the reading of the satire as universal, extending beyond the merely literary realm of undiscerning readers of fantastic literature to the larger social realm of foolishly deluded fanatics of all types:

Inherited nobility is so old in your quixotic lineage, that already in Adam's time it wandered naked through the Oriental mountains, as a bag of bones from sheer age: and thus we know that a jaw bone [*quixada*] was found in the company of Cain in the first bloody massacre the world knew. And because glory of the most fertile extension followed from such a brilliant origin, Providence has permitted that there have always been and always will be QUIXOTES forever, like raindrops; and thus one sees now, to my great pleasure, a QUIXOTE in every corner, and one hundred in each village; but so much to their pleasure, that it is the same to identify oneself as a son of your house, as to take possession of all the privileges of your QUIXOTERIA.[31]

This belief in the universality of quixotic folly, in which the follies were varied and the deluded Don Quixotes legion, was obviously so widespread in eighteenth-century Europe that it joins here with the burlesque humour typical of a popular rather than an erudite reading. Once again, the producers of this 1771 edition proved to be participants in an international reading of the novel rather than contributors to the strongly nationalistic reappropriation of *Don Quixote* as a distinctly Spanish work seen in the 1780 Real Academia de la Lengua edition. None the less, the specifically Spanish slant they brought to the novel was the wedding of the burlesque with the satirical in a mock-satirical tone, allowing for no moderating concept of comedy as both serious and funny such as that put forth by Fielding.

There is yet one other current of interpretation, or perhaps more appropriately an ambiguity, that informs this parodic dedication to Don Quixote. Most eighteenth-century interpretations of *Don Quixote* insisted upon the satirical distance between the mystifying language of chivalric romance and the disillusioning language of reason or common sense – that is, the distance between the language of the character, Don Quixote, and the author, Cervantes. By recognizing this distance, the reader glimpsed the danger of folly, and thus experienced Enlightenment. The critical voice carefully distinguished itself from the protagonist and aligned itself with the author. In this piece the writer speaks through the voice of the narrator, Cide Hamete Benengeli, and places himself between the deluded Don Quixote and the rational Cervantes. Cide Hamete does give voice to Don Quixote, the hero within the novel, an identification the parodist's prose reflects in its florid and erudite apostrophes and flourishes. In general, of course, one can clearly discern the voice of reason in the novel through the parodic conflation of the lofty with the base. None the less, a neoclassical critic such as Mayans y Siscar did not allow this playful baseness to the "enlightened" Cervantes, whose voice must always be erudite and didactic – in short, authoritative. By adopting the voice of Cide Hamete

Benengeli, however, the anonymous author of this dedication allows the old voice of the burlesque to sound again, as the authoritative voice of Cervantes cedes before the mock-heroic voice of the narrator, whose voice parodies within the novel serious, erudite discourse as much as fantastic literature. Typical of this strain of humour are the dedicatory poems and the foolish student who suggests Don Quixote's adventure in the Cave of Montesinos. Remarkably, the novel carries within itself, in the voice of Cide Hamete, a parody of its own canonization. The writer of this dedication to the 1771 Ibarra edition astutely mimics that mockingly erudite voice.

In parallel fashion the playful loftiness also lets another censored voice sneak in, the mock-heroic, which parodically uses the hyperbolic figures of speech and overblown exposition of the glorious deeds of the hero essential to the literature of knight errantry. As "Cide Hamete Benengeli" proclaims in the 1771 dedication:

Truthfully (most celebrated Don Quixote) you were without equal in your deeds, and in your toil; and Orlando spoke very well when he said:

"If you are not a Peer, neither have you had one,
For you could be a Peer among a thousand Peers:
There cannot be one where you are to be found,
Unconquered conqueror, never overcome."[32]

It would clearly be mistaken to assume that this brief, laudatory verse is not parodic. Indeed, it is one of the novel's parodic verses written by Cervantes in the voices of various romance heroes. Unlike other eighteenth-century contributors to editions of the novel, this writer allows mock-heroic discourse to enter again into the apparatus surrounding the text, and even lets it stand alone without the normal didactic explanation of its satiric intent. The neoclassical critic rarely trusted the reader's capacity to discern such parody without his erudite assistance, and therefore reinforced the superiority of his interpretive status. This anonymous writer, however, aligns himself with the popular reading, and thus does not attempt to control authority but rather plays with it. Once critical authority had been even more questioned and loosened, just such mock-heroic discourse would accompany the Romantic vision of a heroic Don Quixote. Even Vicente de los Ríos's discussion of Don Quixote as the hero of a burlesque epic in the 1780 Real Academia edition raised problems concerning sympathy with rather than derision of the deluded madman within the context of the neoclassical literary aesthetic of the heroic.

A MONUMENT TO THE AUTHOR: THE 1780 REAL ACADEMIA DE LA LENGUA EDITION

In sharp contrast to the mocking tone of the 1771 edition, the 1780 edition, also published by Ibarra, finally presented *Don Quixote* as a classical work of prose acclaimed by the Spanish intelligentsia and arbiters of taste. The Real Academia de la Lengua commissioned and supervised the production of this edition as definitive and scholarly. The "Prologue of the Academy" stated as a given the recognition of the work as a classic, thus obscuring the debate that still lingered around the novel in Spain. "It would be an abuse of the readers' patience, and a useless waste of time, to detain ourselves in this prologue recommending a work, that through the long span of almost two centuries has always circulated with the greatest applause and esteem among cultured nations, having merited from them all very great words of praise."[33] The writer of this prologue sidestepped the debate in Spain by referring to the supposedly unanimous acclaim of the text among the "cultured nations." This characterization of those countries where *Don Quixote* had already been hailed a classic implied that the work must likewise be proclaimed a classic within the peninsula as well as beyond the Pyrenees in order to establish and defend Spain's own culture. The tension between cultural decadence and restoration signalled by Henares Cuéllar appeared once again, as the court endeavoured to restore Spain's glory through proclaiming *Don Quixote* a national treasure.

The motto, that of the Real Academia de la Lengua gracing a vignette at the top of the first page of the prologue, states most concisely the academy's editorial intention upon publishing *Don Quixote*: "Clean, fix, and grant splendour."[34] In fact, this motto could describe much of the intellectual enterprise undertaken by scholars in the reign of Charles III (1759–88). This activity ranged from Antonio Ponz's *Viaje de España*, in which he recorded and studied the architectural monuments and artistic artifacts of the small towns and countryside of Spain, to Juan Sempere y Guarino's *Ensayo de una biblioteca española de los mejores escritores del reynado de Carlos III*, in which he defended his contemporaries from the disdain of both foreign and Spanish critics. Reflecting their own political stances, scholars have generally attributed this flurry of activity either to a nationalistic defence of Spain's honour in response to the French challenges or, more recently, to absolutist political stratagems to control Spanish society on all levels. Nevertheless, eighteenth-century Spain had fallen into a state of social and economic ruin, and was urgently in need of reform.[35] The academy found the text of *Don Quixote* and the biography of its author in a similar state of disrepair:

Those who know this work's merit, and know how to appreciate the purity, elegance and cultivation of its language, will not wonder that a Body, whose principal institution is to cultivate and promote the study of the Castilian language, has resolved to publish one of its best texts and models: particularly when, among the many editions that have been made of *Don Quixote* within and without the kingdom, it can truthfully be said, that there is none that does not have substantial defects, having arrived at such a point as to alter and corrupt the work's very title. Whereas Cervantes had entitled it with much propriety and knowledge: THE INGENIOUS GENTLEMAN DON QUIXOTE DE LA MANCHA, in almost all the editions later than the very earliest they have put: *The Life*

and Deeds of the Ingenious Gentleman Don Quixote de la Mancha: a title as improper
and as alien to this story, as if one were to call Homer's *Odyssey* the *Life and Deeds of
the Prudent Ulysses.*[36]

The academy thus envisaged theirs as a work of restoration in its attempt both
to restore the original text and to frame the work in an edition physically more
appropriate to its status as a classic.[37] Their canonization of the novel depended
upon two interpretive strategies. First, they overlooked *Don Quixote's* rather
dubious lineage as a parody of a popular romance genre in order to focus on
the merit of its language. Its content, earlier maligned as indecorous by
neoclassical critics, receded with the new focus on its style and form. Secondly,
they compared Cervantes' mock-epic work to Homer's in order to establish the
former as the patriarch of Spanish literature. This comparison, which seems so
unlikely to the twentieth-century critic, was actually the crux upon which the
academy could appropriate the "universal" values of a neoclassical aesthetic to
the glorification of a nationalistic aesthetic and national literature.

Therefore, this edition was monumental in an explicitly metaphorical sense:
it erected the work of a founding author of Spanish literature as a national
monument. As the writer of the academy's prologue points out, the paper was
specially made in the factory of Joseph Llorens, a new typeface designed by
Gerónimo Gil, and the printing undertaken by Ibarra; this edition, made of
the best and by the best, was physically a completely Spanish monument to
the author. The physical presentation of the text was to be of the finest quality,
and indeed it is. The portrait of Cervantes, for example, exemplifies the process
by which the author was recast in heroic terms (see Figure 37). In relationship
to earlier portraits, this one, designed by José del Castillo and engraved by
Manuel Salvador del Carmona, shares much in common with the depiction of
the face seen in Kent's portrait from the 1738 Carteret edition.[38] In the Kent
portrait, with its soulful resemblance to many of the Pope and Dryden portraits
of the time, Cervantes appears with the attributes of both soldier and writer,
with sword and plume (see Figure 14). In Castillo's image the author of *Don
Quixote* appears as the classical man of letters, shown in a three-quarters-profile
portrait bust set within a monumental architectural frame. The tradition of
portraying an author in a frontispiece by a bust dated back at least to the 1660
Rouen edition of Corneille's works, appropriately enough, according to David
Piper, since he was "the most severely classical of all French tragedians."[39] Stone
wreathing surrounds the roundel in which the bust is set, and two stone laurel
wreaths hang over his head, granting him heroic status. The entire effect is to
memorialize the man, or perhaps to leave him the memorial his contemporaries
failed to erect. In fact, one can consider this stone monument an emblem of
the edition itself, for, like its counterpart designed by Kent, it elevates Cervantes
to the rank of a classical author.

At the base of the monument Castillo has placed the attributes of a Greek
comic mask, a lyre, an inkwell with plumes, and a pile of books, all typical of

Fig. 37   José del Castillo. *Portrait of Cervantes.*
Madrid 1780. Biblioteca Nacional, Madrid.

seventeenth-century classicizing frontispieces and portraits of authors.[40] The artist then links Cervantes with three of the classical arts, comedy, poetry, and music. As stated earlier, Cervantes' theatrical writings enjoyed the approbation of neoclassical critics at the time, but he was certainly not a musician. Yet within this context the lyre links him not only to the muses but also to Orpheus. In his allegorical frontispiece to the 1738 Lord Carteret edition John Vanderbank had cast Cervantes as the classical figure of Hercules, the muscular, semi-nude figure marching up Mount Parnassus to expel the fantastic monsters of the literature of knight errantry (see Figure 13). In turn, Kent's portrait of the author had revealed a man both physically active and creatively gifted through the attributes of both the sword and the pen. But in Castillo's portrait no sword appears, therefore limiting Cervantes to his poetic, Orphic persona. Indeed, Vicente de los Ríos, in his Cervantine biography published in this same edition, presents the author sinking to hellish spaces in which he displays his sensitivity and creates his art, such as the cave of his captivity or the jail cell in La Mancha, rather than his heroic struggle to attain the mountaintops of fame and excellence. More strikingly, however, Castillo's portrait of Cervantes resembles the same artist's depiction of Don Quixote in its mouth and facial structure, but particularly the eyes. Cervantes' eyes are large, almond-shaped, and full of the depth and sensitivity of a dreamer. In fact, they appear as the sane counterparts of the reading Alonso Quijano's maddened eye (see Figure 2). The eyes of the author bespeak a knowledge of the sentiments and sympathy for mankind. Cervantes the hero now manifests himself as a sentimental visionary rather than a satirical reformer.

Nor was the cult of sentimentality so prevalent beyond the Pyrenees foreign to the thinkers of the Spanish Enlightenment. Although Rousseau's works were forbidden by the Spanish Index of 1764, they nevertheless penetrated the Pyrenees to enjoy considerable influence in the peninsula.[41] Likewise, Locke's ideas entered, although at times filtered, as seen in Feijoo's "Descubrimiento de una nueva facultad, ó potencia sensitiva en el hombre, á un philósofo."[42] In this article Feijoo announced his belief in a sixth sense, known as "sensitive" or "perceptive," which allowed knowledge of the emotions and sentiments of others. Although the breast most strongly expresses this extra sense, the eyes also reveal its presence, as seen in Castillo's portrait of Cervantes. The noble but vulnerable author, having been stripped of his sword, is left to depend upon his sensitivity and perception. The visual resemblance between Cervantes and Don Quixote emphasizes even more the author's worldly impotence. In light of the nineteenth- and twentieth-century image of Cervantes as an alienated, impotent genius, it is helpful to bear in mind the link between the sentimental hero and the Romantic tortured genius. As R.F. Brissenden has shown, "The myth of the unloved, misunderstood, agonised and alienated artist is a romantic myth; and it is intimately related to, is in part perhaps a variant of, the myth of the virtuous but impotent man of sentiment. Both grow out of the conviction that it is either impossible or immensely difficult to bridge the gap between innocence and experience, to bring about the marriage of heaven and hell."[43] The neoclassical conmemoration of the learned and poetic author likewise inched towards the Romantic celebration of the alienated genius through the introduction of these sentimental elements into this edition's literary and visual portraits of Cervantes.

CERVANTES AS SENTIMENTALIST AND *ILUSTRADO* IN RIOS'S ANALYSIS OF *DON QUIXOTE*

Vicente de los Ríos's *Análisis del Quixote*, which includes a biography of Cervantes, illustrates well the strategies and tension involved in both the neoclassical elevation of the novel to the status of a classic and the subsequent cracks in the monument's foundation. In the terminology of neoclassical literary criticism, Don Quixote is the hero of the novel, the protagonist whose central characteristic, madness, unifies the plot and acts as an example, albeit a negative one, for the instruction of the reader. This Spaniard's insistent conception of *Don Quixote* as a burlesque epic, of Cervantes as the literary counterpart of Homer, and of the novel's protagonist as the comic counterpart of Achilles has led Anthony Close to comment that Ríos's "principles of criticism are unswervingly neo-classical."[44] If so, then his text reveals tensions in the neoclassical canonization of the author and the novel that appear to be the seams of the Romantic rupture in interpretation signalled by Close. Most problematic for a neoclassical interpretation is the characterization of both author and protagonist as heroes, for the one was a half-forgotten writer afflicted by a lifetime of failure, and the other a deluded madman. To a degree, then, the tensions apparent in Castillo's portrait of Cervantes as the classical yet sentimental author are repeated in Ríos's analysis.

Vicente de los Ríos, a captain in the royal artillery company, offers a surprisingly mystified view of Cervantes' experience as a soldier. Downplaying Cervantes' prowess with the sword, he calls attention to his literary vocation, paralleling the change in emphasis evident in the absence of the sword from Castillo's portrait. Of course, as an earnest biographer, the captain mentions the details of Cervantes' escapades in captivity, then known thanks to the archival work of others. Yet as Ríos recounts the tales, he voices a certain tension regarding the inverisimilitude of the heroic events:

This situation, capable of prostrating and conquering any man of spirit, had the opposite effect in Cervantes. His heroic soul, bent under the yoke of such violent slavery, fought with greater vigor and doubled force to escape from his oppression. It is difficult to persuade oneself that a slave was capable of attempting such extraordinary and risky enterprises in the sight of a barbarous and bloodthirsty owner; but success proved that Cervantes owed the preservation of his life to the firmness and daring with which he always persisted, although in vain, to escape from captivity.[45]

Ríos sets up the situation as a conflict between the heroic slave, a man of *spirit*, and the barbarous master, a cruel man of *blood* ("sanguinaria"). As such, the master had at hand all the means to beat down the slave not only physically but also emotionally and spiritually. An insurmountable obstacle provided by a cruel, barbaric enemy confronted the heroic Cervantes, which he overcame emotionally and spiritually – in the realm of the sentiments – instead of merely physically. In fact, he triumphed through his strength of character, for he refused to give up even though his active efforts never actually succeeded. One sees in eighteenth-century sentimental literature that a moral victory was the mark of virtue, since actual victory so often implied complicity and compromise with the world. As John Mullan has written, "In the [sentimental] novels themselves, benevolence belongs to the 'simple,' the 'innocent,' the 'sensible' – those who have had to retreat from a world which maligns or abuses their feelings."[46] For Ríos this moral victory over evil was difficult to believe, and thus stretched the bounds of what we would call psychological verisimilitude as Cervantes survived these trials in a heroic, almost superhuman fashion – but this was history.

Thus, Ríos cast Cervantes' bold actions into the model of sentimental triumphs of the spirit over the physical world, and transformed the author into a hero of sentiment, not the sword. The ultimate proof of his heroic virtue is the effect his example worked on the heart of his barbarous captor: "Doubtlessly, it appears to be a marvellous thing that Cervantes escaped without punishment in the midst of these attempts, and could walk out unharmed from among owners so tyrannous and inimical to humanity; but solid valor and heroic, extraordinary spirit are recommendable talents, respected even by the barbarians themselves."[47] Ríos uses the archetypal plot of the sentimental novel, in which the virtuous hero/ine survived intact from the advances and/or violence of a barbaric superior on account of his/her virtue, to remold the tale of Cervantes' captivity. According to the new paradigm, the captive transcended his vulnerable position, compromised by the threat to integrity of spirit and body posed by a debauched master, through a pure spirit that in turn converted the master.

The ultimate fruit of Cervantes' heroic virtue, the spirit that refused to be crushed, was not merely the preservation of his body but the creation of his literary masterpiece, asserted by Ríos to be *Don Quixote*. Referring to Cervantes' imprisonment in Argamasilla, the biographer deems it to have been crucial to the inception of the novel, a product of the author's sentimental strength and resiliency:

He had lived in La Mancha, and observed carefully its particularities, such as Ruydera's lagoons and Montesino's cave, the situation of the fulling mills, Puerto Lápice and the other parts that he later made the theatre of Don Quixote's adventures, when, as a result of a commission he had, the inhabitants of the place where he was commissioned denounced, mistreated, and put him in jail. Amidst the abandonment and discomfort of this sad situation, he composed, with no other assistance than that of his marvellous wit this discreet fable, whose difficult execution, which requires much space, mature reflection, and continuous work, shows that he stayed in prison a long time.[48]

Although Ríos's restrained prose emphasizes the difficulties of Cervantes' imprisonment less than his virtuous use of the isolation and empty time, he does refer to the injustice of the author's treatment by the "inhabitants" and his "abandonment" from human company. It was this alienated situation that provided Cervantes the time and space in which to write. Although this concept of the *artiste maudit* appears to be quintessentially Romantic, Ignacio Henares Cuéllar has noted its appearance already in the *Elogio de Don Ventura Rodríguez*, read by Jovellanos in 1788 to the Sociedad Económica de Madrid.[49] He attributes this early characterization of the artist as alienated from society to the isolation in which the Spanish *ilustrados*, despite their reformist intentions, found themselves in a nation with no mercantile middle class. As he has written, "the paradox, the limitation of the Enlightenment spirit, appears from the moment in which the enlightened elite assumes its isolation in the bosom of a society where the very idea of reform lacks meaning and makes it a question of honour to hope for nothing that is not connected to its own development."[50]

Although a version of this biography was read before the Real Academia de la Lengua on 4 March 1773, with the final version handed over to the body on 28 March 1776[51] (thus dating it from a supposedly more optimistic period in the history of the Spanish Enlightenment thinkers), it certainly presents Cervantes in the image of the *ilustrados*. Central to this image is the perception of Cervantes as a thinker alienated from his own time. In his biography of the author written fifty years earlier, Mayans y Siscar had made much of Cervantes' lack of renown among his contemporaries, but only as evidence of his mistreatment. In contrast, Ríos highlights Cervantes' reformist intentions towards a whole array of social ills, let alone the literature of knight errantry.[52] He interprets *Don Quixote* as a critique of the decadent aristocracy, of the individual gentlemen who refused to subject themselves to the reasonable laws of the Crown and the Church, of the lack of "good breeding" (*buena crianza)* among the children of the aristocracy and the peasants (*pueblo*) alike, and of the superstition and lack of religious training among the common people. In short, Ríos read *Don Quixote* as a manifesto expressing the social criticism and reform efforts of the *ilustrados* themselves. In his support of this agenda, in particular his opposition to superstition, he characterizes Cervantes as a man *not* of his own age: "Here one sees that Cervantes was free of the worries of his century, and that he knew how to recognize them, make them public, and find fault with them with the tact and circumspection those times required: for which he deserves more glory than some writers of our century, because much earlier and without having the same liberty as they, he corrected the same abuses."[53] Ríos presents Cervantes as a model for eighteenth-century men of reason as well as heart, many of whom he surpassed in his own enlightenment.

The *ilustrado* even placed Cervantes within the same social position, as a critic of the old aristocracy, representatives of traditional authority against reason, and as a would-be reformer of the society of the common people. Indeed, according to the biographer, the aristocrat's lack of regard for Enlightenment and the common man's lack of education created Cervantes' alienated situation, caught between the upper and the lower classes, similar to that in which the eighteenth-century Spanish *ilustrados* found themselves: "The slight dedication of the powerful to the sciences, and the ignorance of the masses caused men capable of enlightening the nation with their literary writings to abandon it, and to dedicate themselves to things that, by appealing to the public's taste, could put food on their tables. Therefore, Lope de Vega devoted himself to the composition of bad comedies, even though he knew how to write good ones. Thus, Cervantes makes the situation known in the quoted discourse of the Canon of Toledo, and so Lope himself also admitted it."[54] Ríos returned to the interpretation of the Canon of Toledo's neo-Aristotelian censure of the *comedia* as evidence of Cervantes' own enlightened view of literature. By the same token, the eighteenth-century biographer deemed Cervantes, unlike the prolific and popular playwright Lope de Vega, to have taken the moral higher ground and to have duly suffered for his rational standards. Thus, the popular success of Cervantes' *Don Quixote* was absorbed into the neoclassical mythology of the work as a classic by presenting it purely as a didactic work of social and literary satire.

A HEROIC DON QUIXOTE?
RIOS'S ANALYSIS OF THE NOVEL

In the *Análisis del Quixote,* Vicente de los Ríos also undertook a similar re-evaluation of Cervantes' protagonist, Don Quixote, according to eighteenth-century values that would, in turn, point towards the nineteenth-century reclamation of the deluded man as a hero. First, Ríos finally states what some illustrations had already manifested, the felicitous "happy ending" to the novel: "Don Quixote, having been restored to his old self, Alonso Quijano the Good, recognized his errant ways, detested his madness and the books that had caused it, and died in the bosom of Christian peace and tranquility ..., and thus this character ended up with all the happiness imaginable, and the fable ended with the most opportune and proper instruction of the end for which it was composed."[55] This interpretation of Don Quixote's death clearly supports Ríos's assertion of the novel's satirical intent. Nevertheless, his analysis of the character he terms the "hero" goes far beyond a simplistic identification of allegorical relationships between elements of the novel and corresponding social or literary ills. Most strikingly, as Etienvre has pointed out, this neoclassical critic discovered Cervantes' "perspectivism."[56] Ríos observes that "the reader experiences a secret pleasure upon first seeing these objects as they are in themselves, and contemplating afterwards the extraordinary mode by which Don Quixote apprehends them, and the humorous disguises with which his fantasy dresses them."[57] What was this secret pleasure felt by the reader? According to Ríos, within satire "we find two pleasures, that of seeing the absurdity of vices, and that of seeing ridicule directed at another person."[58] This laughter causes the reader to want to differ from the protagonist rather than imitate him, thus resulting in a negative act of identification in which the satiric protagonist functions as a foolish alter ego. As seen in various illustrations, the reader then identifies positively with the chastened but reasonable Alonso Quijano who emerges from the delusions of Don Quixote at the novel's close.

None the less, this negative identification with Don Quixote could give way to a positive one, in which the hero's madness is not merely ridiculed but also pitied. Like Mayans y Siscar, Ríos valued the protagonist's moments of lucidity, such as the discourse on the lost Golden Age (1:11), which renders the character "amable"/"loveable."[59] Yet the critic's recognition of Don Quixote's exemplarity passes beyond praise of the character's rational side to hint at the possibility that his insanity could also be laudable. At the very least, his discussion of the play of perspectives in the text verifies the pleasure felt by sharing the madman's vision: "This is the principal merit of Cervantes: those deeds which seen as they are in themselves make Don Quixote ridiculous and worthy of laughter, those same deeds looked at with the lens of this Hero's madness, represent him as a valiant and fortunate knight. Only this author's discretion could have discovered such an ingenious medium by which Don Quixote's adventures ridicule his action in reality, and make them plausible in his imagination."[60] According to Ríos's neoclassical analysis, this doubled perspective renders Don Quixote's madness plausible, thus verisimilar. If Don Quixote had not seen his adventures as noble, then his madness would not be psychologically credible. As in the case of the plausibility of Cervantes' valour during captivity, the test of verisimilitude hinges upon the integrity of an individual's personality rather than the propriety of his actions with respect to his social position. The standards for verisimilitude had changed to such an extent that they freed Cervantes' Sancho from the taint of indecorousness noted by earlier critics and opened up the possibility of interpreting the same author's Don Quixote in a more sympathetic light. By accounting for the character's madness, this description begins to take on the overtones of an apology for the protagonist's madness and the author's genius in creating this psychologically plausible personality. That Don Quixote's madness would require an apology was unthinkable within a purely neoclassical reading of the text as satire, for the madness was the motor of the satire. The cult of sentimentality, though, had begun to render the laughter aimed at others uncomfortable,[61] since a character such as Don Quixote still possessed a heart.

Although Ríos attributes his apology for the character of Cervantes' protagonist to the demands of verisimilitude, a growing cultural discomfort with madness also underlay his thought. He argues that in the representation of the Duke and Duchess's excessively cruel treatment of Don Quixote and Sancho Panza, Cervantes satirized the people who went to insane asylums to laugh at the inhabitants: "What is most remarkable in this case, is that many people, who are naturally tender and compassionate, nevertheless are used to enjoying such barbarous recreation, which proceeds doubtlessly from not considering the crazy as sick, and believing that because they laugh, eat, and feel no pain, they do not merit our pity: an error that arises, like many others, from the false ideas they receive from childhood."[62] Ríos's assumption that madness was an involuntary illness differs greatly from the earlier belief that the insane chose to be irrational of their own volition, and corresponds well to a similar change in attitudes in eighteenth-century France.[63] According to George Rosen, this change grew out of a Rousseauian view of civilization, in which the mad were seen as symptomatic of an insane culture.[64]

More germane to the problem of madness for Ríos was the ambiguous nature of laughter at the insane. He writes that the reader must laugh at Don Quixote in order to learn from the satire, yet he criticizes the Duke and the Duchess for laughing cruelly without the exemplary lesson of the character's folly in mind. The concept of laughter Ríos employs parallels that developed by earlier English thinkers such as Dryden, Addison, Steele, and Fielding, who stressed that laughter must be based on something other than mere pride in order not to be small-minded.[65] Their rejection of bawdy laughter, based on derision of those lesser than oneself, owed a debt, in turn, to Lord Shaftesbury's vindication of those deceived by their senses into irrational thinking as neither wicked nor unjust.[66] A sympathetic, albeit condescending perspective upon the deluded Don Quixote grew from this new conception of insanity, as the eighteenth-century reader viewed both his mad actions and his befuddled evaluation of sensory input. "There but for the grace of God go I" seems to have been the sentimental reaction of Ríos and his implicit reader towards the protagonist's madness.

This recognition of a doubled perspective, that of the sane narrator and reader accompanied by that of the deluded protagonist, corresponds to a newly conceived concept of Don Quixote and Sancho Panza as complementary characters, doubling each other:

Don Quixote is a naturally discreet, rational, and educated gentleman, who works and speaks as such except when dealing with knight errantry. Sancho is a greedy peasant, but sly by nature and simple by his breeding and condition. It results that these two characters have a doubled character, which varies the dialogue and plot, and pleasantly entertains the reader, representing Don Quixote at times as wise, other times as crazy, and manifesting Sancho successively as ingenuous and malicious. These characters are never untrue to themselves. Don Quixote conserves within his very madness glimpses of wisdom, and in affairs not concerning him, he always picks up the thread of discourse from the viewpoint of his mania, or at last ends up in it.[67]

Ríos discusses two levels of "duplicity," or doubling, one in which each character has a dual character himself, discerning and mad, innocent and malicious, and the other in which the characters double and complement each other in their dialogue and their actions. Thus, the two characters escaped from being merely allegorical types, the one crazy and the other simple, to become complex psychological entities reacting to and acting upon each other. Sancho's wisdom as a governor (2:45–53), so criticized by earlier neoclassical critics, and Don Quixote's reasonable discourses, a source of wonder to the same, no longer represented lapses in decorum but rather appeared as entertaining and instructive variations within the plot and the characters. Ríos's approval of this phenomenon extends to the doubling of Don Quixote's nag Rocinante and Sancho Panza's donkey Rucio, "according to his ridiculous character."[68] The protagonists on their respective mounts appear in reciprocal relationship to each other, just as they appear on a dusty Manchegan road in a very important illustration to this edition by José del Castillo (see Figure 4).

THE CONTROVERSY SURROUNDING THE ILLUSTRATIONS TO THE 1780 REAL ACADEMIA EDITION

Vicente de los Ríos's analysis of *Don Quixote* and biography of its author enjoyed the full approval of the Real Academia Española de la Lengua. Working from the minutes of the academy, Cotarelo Valledor notes that it was received as a work of "great merit" from its first presentation as a short discourse.[69] In fact, the captain's preliminary work inspired the academy to undertake the publication of an edition "correct and magnificent ... , adding the work of Mr. Ríos, because it will serve to reveal the work's perfections and to illustrate various passages from the author's life."[70] The illustrations, however, proved to be much more troublesome for the academy. Although included in order to employ the nation's artists, as seen in Charles III's letter approving the endeavour,[71] the illustrations also met the demand of the public, as noted in the edition itself: "The prints, head pieces, and end pieces could have been omitted without causing the Work to lack anything essential. But the Academy, without being worried by the increased payments it was necessary to make, has desired that it not lack these ornaments, according to the wishes of the public, and with the object of contributing simultaneously to giving occupation to the professors of the arts."[72] Of course, the eighteenth-century public expected illustrations in an edition of this calibre.[73] By insisting that the public demand was basically for an ornament inessential to the work, this anonymous member of the academy both gave priority to the literary text – to be expected from a literary critic – and acted as an arbiter of public taste. Although its demand would be met in the marketplace, this academician implied that the public did not necessarily understand the priority of the text. The academy merely stooped magnanimously to please it, rather than being at the mercy of its demand. Here the writer simultaneously distanced the academy from responsibility for the illustrations, downgraded their value in relation to the text, and relegated them to the status of mere ornaments.

This reticence alerts us to a controversy between the Royal Academy of the Language and that of the Fine Arts (Real Academia de San Fernando de Bellas Artes) recorded in a series of letters to the Conde de Floridablanca concerning the former academy's claim that the other had overseen and approved the images.[74] The minutes of the literary academy reveal the production of the illustrations to have been burdensome from the beginning, in part due to the delays and overriding pecuniary interests of the artists, particularly Castillo.[75] On 15 June 1773 it was recorded in the minutes that the academy decided not to trust the "free flight of fantasy" of the artists; instead they issued specific instructions concerning the content of the images, chose thirty-three from the sixty-six passages copied from the text by Ríos to be depicted, and named a committee of three members to oversee the execution of the illustrations.[76] In addition, the artists were to copy arms and armour from the collection of the Royal Armory and examples of physiognomy from clay models of "popular heads of la Mancha" in order to assure the greatest verisimilitude.

Three years later, however, only four more illustrations had been completed, inciting the Royal Academy of the Language to request that their sister academy, Fine Arts, take over the project, with Pedro de Silva and Ignacio de Hermosilla, engravers and members of both academies, serving as go-betweens.[77] A paragraph in the prologue published with the edition attests to the same transfer of responsibility for the production of the illustrations. In a letter dated 11 February 1781 Antonio Ponz, secretary of the Academy of Fine Arts, objected to the statement in the prologue of the *Don Quixote* edition and claimed that his academy had seen none of the illustrations. Furthermore, he complained that this incorrect assertion "could be the cause of the public's criticism targeted against the Academy itself, and if defects were found in the prints, they would be attributed to the lack of experience of that body, and that would be unjust."[78] A letter concerning the complaint was dispatched by Floridablanca's office to Manuel de Lardizábal y Uribe, secretary of the Royal Academy of the Language, who responded the same day, reasserting the original statement. Finally, in response to Floridablanca's continued insistence, the institution agreed to remove the offending paragraph, which at that point meant removing and replacing pages from the already bound volumes.[79] The new paragraph stated simply that the artists attempted to reproduce more accurately sixteenth-century Spanish clothing and settings, including the use of actual armour as models, and that "they have chosen the most important adventures as the subjects for the prints, being careful to represent them at that point, or action, which distinguishes and characterizes them best."[80]

Unfortunately, the existing letters provide no clue concerning the reason both academies apparently feared so much the public's disapproval of the illustrations. One illustration had to be corrected since it showed Sancho Panza, who serves as the voice of reason in the scene, rather than his donkey, Rucio, wearing a dunce cap (see Figure 38). With this exception, the illustrations were remarkably loyal to the passages of text depicted. In fact, in his introduction to the 1797 Sancha edition Pellicer praised this set of illustrations for having corrected the anachronistic clothing and character types of the earlier foreign editions and having rendered them more properly Spanish.[81] In addition, these prints exercised great influence over later illustrations, in particular those of the 1797 Sancha and Imprenta Real editions, the Spanish editions printed in Leipzig, 1800 and 1818, and the Paris/London edition, 1814, for which the images were engraved anew.[82] The reasons for which the Academy of Fine Arts washed its

Fig. 38   Gregorio Ferro. *Bad Omens on
the Road Home.* Madrid 1780.
Biblioteca Nacional, Madrid.

hands of any responsibility for the illustrations seem not to have stemmed from
disapproval of the technical quality of the illustrations, particularly since the
two main illustrators, José del Castillo and Antonio Carnicero, were promising
young artists. Castillo had received a stipend from the institution to study in
Rome and, in the 1770s, worked under Mengs, alongside Goya, designing
tapestry cartoons for the royal palace in Madrid.[83] Antonio Carnicero belonged
to an established family of artists and was the brother of one of the later
secretaries of the same academy, Isidro Carnicero.[84] It is perhaps easier to
speculate concerning the literary academy's displeasure. Like John Oldfield, the
author of the explanatory notes for the illustrations in the 1738 Lord Carteret
edition, the members of the Academy of the Language perhaps distrusted the
effect of visual representations upon the imagination of naïve readers. Indeed,
this distrust of the visual image may account even more for that body's
defensive stance towards the illustrations, as indicated by the complete instructions issued to the artists in order to prevent excessive licence in the illustration
of episodes. None the less, this edition's illustrations began to offer a new
interpretation of Don Quixote and Sancho Panza as psychologically complex
characters in relationship with each other rather than as satirical types func-
tioning as the allegorical figures of folly and material self-interest. As already
noted, Vicente de los Ríos, with the academy's complete approbation, had also
proposed a similar vision of the main characters based on a new concept of
psychological verisimilitude and a sentimental understanding of insanity. Some

clues to the controversy may be revealed by a study of the vignettes, to follow immediately, and Goya's rejected submissions, with which this study closes.

THE MARGINALIZATION OF THE BURLESQUE: THE VIGNETTES

The vignettes, the visual element perhaps least likely to attract attention due to their reduced size, marginal placement, and minor content, nevertheless strike the reader's eye in the 1780 Real Academia edition. Small images placed at the bottom or top of pages of text or adorning illuminated capitals, vignettes became quite common in the nineteenth century, although they were still rare in 1780. Two exemplary Romantic illustrators of *Don Quixote*, Tony Johannot and Gustave Doré, made great use of them, yet they first appeared in this edition of the novel. Printed only at the beginning and end of volumes, tables of contents, critical commentaries, appendices, and the first illuminated capitals of each volume, their number is limited in the academy's edition. Many of them are simply architectural friezes with greenery or bunting shown as if carved in relief. Others are groups of elements already granted emblematic meaning in relation to the text or other illustrations. For example, Cupid armed with an arrow appears at the end of the first prologue, and refers to Don Quixote's love for Dulcinea. The vignettes adorning the first pages of the first and second parts in each volume actually illustrate scenes, such as the whipping of Andrés or Don Quixote telling Samson Carrasco goodbye as he leaves on his third sally. In the most salient cases, however, the vignettes contain scenes or images that are truly marginal.

The most provocative vignettes accompany the second part and depict grotesque and fantastic material that would certainly have been deemed indecorous by some. Designed by Isidro Carnicero and engraved by F.S. (most likely Fernando Selma), the image atop the first page of Cervantes' prologue to the second book depicts a dog having wind blown into his belly through a cane stuck up his anus as children and a couple watch (see Figure 39; 3:vii).[85] Cervantes himself uses this image as metaphor for writing a book. According to the narrator of the prologue to the second part, a crazy man in Seville did just this, explaining his action to the onlookers in this way: "'Do your Worships think, then, that it is so easy a thing to inflate a dog?' So you might ask, 'Does your Grace think that it is so easy a thing to write a book?'"[86] At first glance one would assume that such a scene, with its carnivalesque overtones, would be considered unacceptable according to neoclassical norms of decorum, and thus would not even be included.[87] The vignette at the end of the prologue illustrates another textual reference to writing (see Figure 40; 3:xii). Devils in hell bat about copies of Avellaneda's apocryphal *Don Quixote*. Attributing this conceit to Cervantes' wounded pride, Vicente de los Ríos specifically objected

PRÓLOGO

AL LECTOR.

Válame Dios , y con quanta gana debes de estar esperando ahora , lector ilustre , ó quier plebeyo , este prólogo , creyendo hallar en él venganzas , riñas y vituperios del autor del segundo Don Quixote , digo de aquel que dicen , que se engendró en Tordesíllas , y nació en Tarragona. Pues en verdad que no te he de dar este contento , que puesto que los agravios despiertan la cólera en los mas humildes pechos , en el mio ha de padecer excepcion esta regla. Quisieras tú que lo diera del asno , del mentecato y del atrevido ; pero no me pasa por el pensamiento : castíguele su pecado , con su pan se lo coma , y allá se lo haya. Lo que no he podido dexar de sentir , es , que me note de viejo , y de manco , como si hubiera sido en mi mano haber detenido el tiempo , que no pasase por mí , ó si mi manquedad hubiera nacido en alguna taberna , sino en la mas alta ocasion que viéron los siglos pasados , los presentes , ni esperan ver los venideros. Si mis heridas no resplandecen en los ojos de quien las

TOM. III.   B

Fig. 39   Isidro Carnicero. Vignette to the Prologue to the Second Book of *Don Quixote*. Boys blowing up a dog. Madrid 1780. Biblioteca Nacional.

to this episode as an offence against verisimilitude, originating as it does in Altisidora's reported experiences of the underworld. However, if this episode really is so indecorous, one must explain why it was depicted at all, since the censure of an image usually leads to its expulsion from an edition rather than its marginalization. Of course, the image of Avellaneda's *Don Quixote* being volleyed by demons in hell was a damning satirical blow on the part of Cervantes to the pretensions of his imitator. From this point of view one could argue that the representation of this conceit constituted a blow against the earlier champions of Avellaneda. Similarly, the tale of the man who blows up the dog could also prick the balloon of Avellaneda's spurious undertaking. The vignettes may have been understood, then, within the climate of eighteenth-century literary circles, in which satirical attacks upon literary enemies, such as Iriarte's *Fábulas literarias* and Forner's *El asno erudito,* were common. In this manner the producers of this edition could attack Avellaneda's advocates

Fig. 40   Isidro Carnicero. Vignette to the Prologue to the Second Book of *Don Quixote*.
Devils bat about Avellaneda's continuation of Don Quixote. Madrid 1780.
Biblioteca Nacional.

obliquely, since the debate that the writer of the academy's prologue refused to discuss reappeared in the marginalized space of the vignette. A non-academic explanation for the depiction of these grotesqueries remains. Given the continuous conflicts recorded in the literary academy's minutes – between that body and the artists over the contents of the illustrations, the timetable for their delivery, and their monetary value – it is possible that the artists chose the image of the dog in particular as a way to thumb their noses at their employers.[88] The point of Cervantes' tale, after all, was that the making of a book is very difficult indeed.

The use of marginal spaces to express the grotesque, fantastic, and insulting is certainly not unique to this edition, as the marginalia of many medieval manuscripts testify. None the less, these vignettes correspond to this edition's full-page illustrations in a manner typical of the late eighteenth century. An interesting thematic and organizational parallel to the relation between the vignettes and the full-size images exists in the tapestries based on Goya's cartoons created for the dining-room of the palace El Pardo. On 25 January 1778 Goya delivered four cartoons for weaving, two dealing with adult activities, *The Kite* and *The Card Players*, and two with children's games, *Boys Inflating a Bladder* and *Boys Picking Fruit*.[89] According to Janis A. Tomlinson, who refers to the northern European tradition of genre scenes, all these images represented allegorically *vanitas*.[90] In addition, the two scenes of children, executed in a reduced format, occupied the spaces above the doorways of the dining-hall, as they also did in two other rooms of the palace. Explaining the significance of the juxtaposition, Tomlinson notes, "Intended as counterpoint to the adult activities portrayed in the larger cartoons, the children's blatant pursuit of ephemeral gratification reveals the futility of adult concerns."[91] Within the iconographical composition of this palace, the images in the marginalized spaces over the doors echoed in miniature, both physically and thematically, and subverted or satirized the larger images placed in the central spaces.

The same compositional ordering of elements pertains to this edition of *Don Quixote*. As noted with reference to the 1738 Lord Carteret edition, these monumental de luxe editions that represent an attempt to canonize the text purport to offer a totalizing presentation of the novel; that is to say, they are to be physical vehicles for the literary work worthy of a classic in all aspects. Through their emblematic representation of the vanity involved in the production of a book, the marginalized images of the dog and the demons serve as satirical counterpoints to the editorial intent of memorializing the novel. Even the blowing up of a bladder balloon as a sign of vanity resembles the blowing up of the dog as a sign of the vanity of Avellaneda's undertaking. The devil's (or demon's) advocate could offer an interpretation of Goya's tapestry cartoon of the overdoors and these vignettes as evidence of the enlightened satirical vision and a totalizing attention to the whole appropriate to such enterprises in the *ilustrado* court of Charles III. Yet, even when viewed within such an argument, these images carry with them dangerously supplementary overtones, as shown by Vicente de los Ríos's objection to the flouting of verisimilitude in the demonic tennis game. In the case of Goya's tapestry cartoons, one sees that the slightly grotesque character of the overdoors, rather than the more mimetic local colour of the genre scenes, grew into the artist's most powerful and mature work, such as the *Caprichos*. The neoclassical aesthetic, with all its touting of the satirical, actually attempted to restrain its more extreme manifestations within the bonds or bounds of decorum. It was no accident that Mayans y Siscar and Ríos compared Cervantes to Homer rather than Juvenal. In the case of later illustrations of *Don Quixote*, one sees that Robert Smirke (1818) preferred to depict the protagonist's fantastic adventure in the Cave of Montesinos (see Figure 41; 3:fp278), or that Gustave Doré (1863) chose to depict the ominous dead horse in the Sierra Morena rather than the deflationary beatings suffered in reparation for his folly on the road, in the inn, and within the palace (see Figure 42; 1:fp170). What occurred was a historical shift of the marginal to the centre, in which the material of the vignette moved centre stage to the space of the full-page illustration.

Fig. 41   Robert Smirke. *The Tomb of Durandarte*.
London 1818. Biblioteca Nacional, Madrid.

Fig. 42   Gustave Doré. *Ils trouvèrent au bord d'un
ruisseau le cadavre d'une mule*. Paris 1863. University
of Illinois Library, Urbana-Champaign.

Fig. 43   Antonio Carnicero. Frontispiece, Vol. 1.
Madrid 1780. Biblioteca Nacional, Madrid.

ALLEGORY SATIRIZED: THE FRONTISPIECES

The same tone of satirical self-consciousness, a propensity to play with the serious conventions of the book conceived as a monument to a classic, informs the frontispieces, central to any neoclassical presentation of the text, as well as the marginalized vignettes. In this manner, a parodic, mock-"classical" approach to the novel, already glimpsed in the burlesque dedicatory piece to Don Quixote in the 1771 Ibarra edition, reasserted the novel's humorous character by subverting the erudite visual and literary apparatus with which it was canonized. Designed by Antonio Carnicero and engraved by Fernando Selma, the frontispiece to Volumes 1 and 2 draws on the allegorical images from earlier editions that presented the novel as an enlightened work of satire. Don Quixote is led astray by Folly, who holds a picture of Dulcinea towards the rather vapid hero, and Cupid, who hovers over him with a wreath of roses in his hand and a quiver of arrows on his back (see Figure 43). To the side a satyr sets fire to a pile of books, clearly identified as *El cavallero de la cruz*, *Amadís de Grecia*, and *Olivarte de Laura*, all popular sixteenth-century chivalric romances consigned to the bonfire in the scrutiny of Don Quixote's library (1:6). The standard elements of the satirical frontispiece are present, including an allusion to Don Quixote's foolish delusion and Cervantes' expressed intent to satirize chivalric literature through his protagonist's negative example. The lion at his feet, referring to his epithet as the Knight of the Lions, renders this rather doltish character even more grotesque by contrast. Following the main diagonal line of the composition from the lion in the lower right-hand corner to the upper left-hand corner, the viewer discovers that the lion and a castle frame the allegorical figures. It is hard *not* to think of the shield of Castilla/León when faced by such a juxtaposition. Thus, the foolish knight Don Quixote, rather than the wise author Cervantes, is framed by the symbols of the Spanish nation and her monarch.

Allegorical representations of this sort were used not merely for book frontispieces to ennoble authors and protagonists in neoclassical terms but also to ennoble aristocrats and monarchs. In 1763 Manuel Salvador Carmona, Fernando Selma's teacher, presented an allegorical print honoring Carlos III to the monarch.[92] In recompense, he received a prize for his work. The allegory, engraved after the model of Francesco Solimena's painting *Allegory of Louis XIV* (ca 1700), enjoyed general praise as an example of the improving fortune of Spanish engraving and entered the collection of the Royal Academy of Fine Arts.[93] Carnicero's satirical allegory of Don Quixote incorporates and inverts certain elements from this print. The allegory unfolds against a similar backdrop of monumental architecture receding on a diagonal line towards a castle perched on a distant horizon.[94] Carnicero replaces the Hydra representing the vices and Envy eating an apple in Carmona's print with the satyr burning books. The medallion representing the profile of Dulcinea held aloft by Folly replaces that representing the profile of Charles III held up by Religion and Prudence. Cupid, granting Don Quixote a laurel wreath, replaces the three *putti* crowning the king with the wreath of Eternity. The similarities between the two prints are certainly numerous enough to show the roots of these allegorical frontispieces in the "high art" designed to monumentalize the sovereign. To replace a sovereign with the figure of the foolish Don Quixote would surely uncrown the latter's ambition through a visual exaggeration of his deluded self-importance, but would also uncrown the king's elevated status through its subtle exploitation of the elements of high art. Thus, the allegory of sovereign power could escape the frame of interpretation binding the image's meaning, a danger evidenced by the need to circulate an explanatory text accompanying the print dedicated to Charles III.[95]

Allegory continues to prove itself to be a slippery genre in the frontispiece to Volumes 3 and 4, designed by Pedro Arnal and engraved by Juan de la Cruz (see Figure 44).[96] A monumental tomb inscribed "El Ingenioso Hidalgo Don Quixote de la Mancha" and bearing his profile in relief dominates the image. His face is craggy as usual, but he gazes up at the sky intently. Two female

Fig. 44   Pedro Arnal. Frontispiece, Vol. 3. Madrid 1780.
Biblioteca Nacional, Madrid.

statues flank the sepulchre itself. On the left stands Reason, in the form of
Minerva, holding a shield with a lion upon it, but also Mercury's caduceus,
which traditionally refers to reason and eloquence.[97] To the right Folly, clad in
bells and bearing a jester's staff, leans against the tomb, looks down despon-
dently, and rubs her eyes. The victory obviously belongs to the triumphantly
smiling Reason. Yet, strangely enough, her shield bears a lion, the symbol of
the Knight of the Lions, Don Quixote. In addition, the entombed character
celebrated by such a monument is Don Quixote, not Alonso Quijano, for it
is the foolish character and not the sane one who is notably the hero of this
allegory. The sharp distinction between the sane Alonso Quijano the Good
and the mad Don Quixote de la Mancha essential to the Enlightenment
interpretation of the novel as an allegory is lost in this image. The allegory
opens itself to the non-sanctioned interpretation of the protagonist as hero as
the image of Don Quixote slides into the serious milieu of "high," meaningful
art. This elevation of the literary character in the guise of the fool, albeit
satirical, very soon began to yield to his serious elevation to the status of a
noble hero at the end of the eighteenth century. None the less, in these prints,

Fig. 45　Antonio Carnicero. *The Capture of*
Mambrino's Helmet. Madrid 1780.
Biblioteca Nacional, Madrid.

regardless of stated editorial or artistic intention, the elevated visual idiom of
the memorial allegory recedes before the appearance of various elements that
make possible a parodic reading of the image. This monument to Cervantes
and the novel read as a classic carries within itself images mocking the very
enterprise through the reintroduction of burlesque parody.

INTERPRETIVE STABILITY VERSUS DYNAMISM: THE ILLUSTRATIONS

Of the full-page illustrations published in the edition, eighteen are designed
by Antonio Carnicero, six by José del Castillo, two by Bernardo Barranco, one
by José Brunete, one by Gerónimo Gil (who also designed the typeface), and
one by Gregorio Ferro.[98] Of most importance are the illustrations by Carnicero
and Castillo, especially since they stand in revealing contrast to each other.
Carnicero's compositions are very stable, his settings stock, the action stiff, and
the characters one-dimensional. In other words, his illustrations are derivative
of other eighteenth-century depictions of the novel, although they lack Coypel's
rococo refinement or Hayman's satirical punch. Carnicero's illustration of the
moment when Don Quixote tries on Mambrino's helmet indicates how this
depiction has become standard within the novel's eighteenth-century iconography (see Figure 45; 1:fp184). In the foreground Don Quixote, with one arm

bent at an impossible angle, gingerly places Mambrino's helmet on his head. His gaunt face, with its aquiline nose and fixed eyes, clearly reveals his foolish pride in his trophy. A stout Sancho Panza, in contrast, smiles in glee as he places his spoils, the saddle, on Rucio's back. The emotions represented by this depiction are typical of a satirizing interpretation of the episode: Don Quixote's face reveals his foolish delusion, Sancho Panza's his materialistic self-interest. As Vicente de los Ríos asserts in his analysis of the novel accompanying this edition, "Cervantes deduced the plot of his fable from this so well-chosen subject, Don Quixote's madness,"[99] and "Sancho's character is to be neither simple nor clever, brave nor cowardly, but to be selfish, and to be so in such a way that this selfishness makes him appear in different forms, depending on the amount of effort required to accomplish his goal."[100] In order to clarify the actual origin of the "baciyelmo" (barber's basin/helmet), the artist shows the barber fleeing in the distance. Careful attention to the rain, which caused the basin to gleam in the distance as the barber wore it to cover his head, requires a storm to be represented in the background. Everything is quite logically, clearly, and solidly depicted. The same faithfulness to the realistic presentation of Don Quixote's continual deception is manifest in the illustration of the enchantment of Dulcinea by Sancho Panza (3:fp80). Dulcinea is clearly a peasant, with a figure, gaze, and ruddy complexion similar to Sancho Panza's. No previous artist had depicted such an ugly Dulcinea, before whose visage Don Quixote's face falls in dismay. No romanticizing of these images takes place.

The illustrations designed by José del Castillo stand in contrast to their companion pieces by Carnicero on account of their more innovative composition and subsequently subtler interpretation of the episodes and the relationship of the characters depicted therein. Known mainly for his tapestry designs, particularly a series of genre scenes of contemporary Madrid street life, Castillo earned recognition for his introduction of local Madrid types such as the *petimetre,* or dandy, and the *maja,* an attractive young girl from the working class, into a genre and artistic environment heavily influenced – perhaps even stifled – by Dutch and French traditions.[101] As Tomlinson remarks, "easily recognized by contemporary viewers, these types embody an awakening national consciousness reflected by historical events, as diverse as the 1766 uprising against Squillace or the Spaniards' attempt twenty years later to oust the Flemish Vandergotens from the directorship of the tapestry factory."[102] Therefore, Castillo would seem to be a perfectly appropriate contributor to this Spanish monument to the new national hero, Cervantes, creator of the two most famous Spanish *types*: Don Quixote and Sancho Panza, seen as representatives of the upper and lower classes unreconciled in Spain by a middle class and its sentimental values.

Castillo originated one of the most durable and functional conventions of the novel's iconography, the scene of Don Quixote and Sancho Panza chatting as they ride along a barren Spanish road (see Figure 4; 1:fp50). Rarely before had this scene been depicted, once in an image possibly unavailable to the Spaniard, the first visual representation of the pair in the 1618 Paris/1620 London frontispiece. In Castillo's illustration the two ride side by side on Rocinante and Rucio across a rocky ridge, offset by an almost cloudless sky and dropping away to the left to reveal a small village in the valley below. Don Quixote sits erect, sternly squinting down his aquiline nose towards Sancho Panza. The peasant, short and squat with a naturalistic paunch, holds one hand earnestly to his chest, the other extended outward, as he gazes up towards his master. A certain tension exists in the empty space between the haughty master and the obsequious squire, for the two seem to be struggling for a balance of power. The opposition of Rocinante and Rucio represents most clearly the nature of this conflict, for beneath the armour and arrogance of one stumbles along a haggard nag, whereas beneath the simplicity and girth of the other walks a sturdy donkey. The gaze between the two men is, however, crucial for interpreting the dynamics of their relationship. For the first time an illustrator of *Don Quixote* centres a composition around a gaze shared between the two protagonists, although history painters from the Renaissance on had used the gaze quite powerfully to depict relationships between individuals. Previously, exchanged looks between Don Quixote and Sancho Panza were few and subordinate to the action. Contrasts between the two were drawn, but in relation to their reactions to a third element or party. In this image Castillo draws a contrast between the two in their relationship to each other, elevating it as worthy of expression in the visual language of history painting. The effects of the neoclassical training offered by Anton Raphael Mengs, teacher of Castillo, and Manuel Salvador Carmona, teacher of the engravers of these illustrations, now enter into the representation of *Don Quixote*, granting the novel the iconographic language of the high arts based on gestures and gazes. Not only does the gaze attribute new depth to the depiction of the two characters' relationship, but it also manifests Castillo's recognition of the social distance between an *hidalgo* (gentleman) and a *labrador* (labourer). The artist plays again with social types (play that lays the ground for social satire), just as he does in his Madrid genre scenes. Yet the figures's respective social status and the elevating element of the shared gaze are undercut by their mounts, since the gentleman appears atop a broken-down nag and the peasant atop a sturdy donkey. This juxtaposition of the pair as a duality, replete with its tensions and paradoxes, echoes Vicente de los Ríos's observation of the novel's *duplicidad* (doubling), in which the two contrast with and complement each other. Castillo sets Don Quixote and Sancho Panza well on the road towards the Romantic reading of the duo as complementary opposites.

Another visual element operates in this image to render the relationship dynamic: a circular object central to the composition, Don Quixote's shield. In almost all of Castillo's illustrations of the novel, with the exception of the protagonist's attack on the monk and the appraisal of Mambrino's helmet and saddle at the inn, a circular element functions as the centre of the composition. In this depiction of Don Quixote's and Sancho Panza's shared gaze, the would-be knight holds the shield parallel to the picture plane, thus directly in front of the viewer. The shield is engraved with concentric, circular lines, darker and fuller at the top than towards the right and bottom, giving it the illusion of spinning movement. Don Quixote's eyes are almost directly above the vortex of the shield. In this manner the lines of the shield propel his gaze towards Sancho, whose own gaze is pulled back by centripetal force as the shield continues circulating the shared look. Since the reader's eye repeatedly moves from one character to the other, the gazes seem to acquire depth. In fact, this depth is due in part to the creation of an ellipse, perpendicular to the circular shield, that moves from one character's eyes to the other's, propelled by the vortices of the engraved concentric circles of the shield, animating thus the shared look. The tilt of Rucio's outstretched ears delineates and accentuates this ellipse. Unlike the circle, which has only one centre such as that clearly seen in the shield, the ellipse has two foci around which its arcs move. In this ellipse one focal point lies near Don Quixote, the other near Sancho Panza. The psychologist of art Rudolf Arnheim has observed, "compositionally the ellipse is the format of choice for the presentation of a duet or dialogue, two antagonists or partners – or, more abstractly, two centers of energy coping with each other ... The ellipse can be perceived as the result of interaction between two spheres of forces."[103] The ellipse has the power to enliven the relationship of these partners (and at times antagonists) by moving their mutual gaze. By identifying the two characters with two focal points of an ellipse, Castillo develops visually their mutually complementary and oppositional relationship. Indeed, this ellipse demonstrates the power of the neoclassical aesthetic for history painting taught to the young artist by his master Mengs, who emphasized the work of the artist as one of conceptual abstraction.[104]

Castillo's illustration of Don Quixote's fight with the mare herders (1:15) uses once again the central circular shape of the shield, this time in opposition to a strong vertical element, in order to heighten the protagonist's strength of character evidenced in the battle (see Figure 46; 1:fp116). The scene from this episode illustrated most often in the eighteenth century depicts the aftermath of the battle, when Sancho checks his master's mouth for dislodged teeth. Clearly, such a scene presents Don Quixote at his most ridiculous. Castillo, however, represents him fallen in battle, holding his shield up to protect himself from the blows of two large herdsmen. Once again, the artist uses the shield in the centre, this time as a base upon which to establish a strong diagonal axis resistant to the blows of the mare herders. The engraving of the shield has a chain-like, locked pattern, darkening at the top and the bottom to emphasize its convexity. Don Quixote grips a strap in the centre of the shield, making his figure the stabilizing force of the curve centreed around the shield and

Fig. 46   José del Castillo. *Fight with the Mare
Herders*. Madrid 1780. Biblioteca Nacional, Madrid.

formed by the windswept tree immediately behind the attackers and the
protagonist's own fallen body. This curve dominates the composition, lending
the image a dynamic effect similar to that achieved by Camarón in several of
his compositions for the 1771 Ibarra edition. The foremost herdsman stands
straight in relation to the curve based on the shield and serves as an opposing
force, both literally and compositionally. Yet the curve continues to sweep
towards Don Quixote, highlighting his force as he hangs valiantly on to the
shield and the fight. The fallen man's gaze is indeed strengthened by this
struggle, as his face is ennobled. His profile is strong but not gaunt, his hair
flowing from the fight but not stringy, his eyes and mouth set in admirable
determination despite his fall. The contrast between Castillo's courageously
noble Don Quixote and Carnicero's foolishly arrogant Don Quixote is
immense. As a further means by which to accentuate his unjust fate and deepen
the reader's sympathy for the protagonist in the centre, Sancho Panza's beating
in the right midground mirrors his master's. Perhaps Castillo merely wishes to
grant these Spanish "types" some dignity and sympathy, but Don Quixote's
noble face and Sancho's undeserved suffering indicate that they are more than

fools. Like his English predecessor Vanderbank, Castillo uses a visual language that comes directly from history painting and thus places the novel's protagonists within an elevated iconographic tradition. In this manner Don Quixote once again takes on the countenance of noble suffering. But the revolutions of the shield point towards even greater changes in interpretation.

In addition to establishing the depiction of Don Quixote and Sancho Panza in dialogue, Castillo makes an important contribution to the iconography of the scene of the protagonist reading (see Figure 2; 1:fp4). Vanderbank first illustrated this scene for the 1738 Lord Carteret edition, in which it served as a frame to ground the root of Don Quixote's madness in his excessive reading of novels of knight errantry. The significance of the book in male portraiture changed during the course of the eighteenth century, as it became a companion in solitude to the reader.[105] In Castillo's illustration, the reader bears the marks of solitary madness upon his own person. Illustrators up to this point had depicted the foolish, deluded *actions* of Don Quixote, incongruous with the physical world around them, but little in the figure itself, if it were set in another context, would indicate that the man was mad. Insanity was not perceived as an inherent, interior quality but rather as a maladjustment (at times wilful) to the exterior world. In this illustration of the character reading the books of chivalry, Castillo uses as the centre of the composition, the point so powerfully dynamic in his images, one eye of the reading gentleman's profile. The setting is quite bare and simple, composed of an empty room with a lance and a sword hanging on the wall, a wooden table and chair piled about with books, including *Amadís de Gaula*, and a small dog wagging his tail at his master.[106] The overwhelming presence in this stark room belongs to the reading Alonso Quijano/Don Quixote. His eye, wide with troubled fantasy and depicted frontally within his profile, becomes the centre of his being. Castillo then draws the corner of the eye into an upward curve to render this reader's transport even more delirious, mysterious, and dangerous. The lines of his wrinkles and features quite literally swirl around it. For example, his eyebrow follows the same twist as his eye, rising a little bit higher in the corner. The folds and wrinkles of his turban follow the same pattern, all turning upwards as they appear to rotate about its corner. Below, the lines of his face curve down in the opposite direction, rotating on the eye's other corner. Finally, his dark moustache emphasizes again the curve of the eye and the brow.

All of this repetition and revolution causes the eye to become the vortex of the composition and grants it a powerful, almost devouring quality. Even the arms seem swept up by its force, as one rises up in the air in a broad gesture in reaction to this reading (or his madness), whereas the other grips the arm of the chair with excitement. Alonso Quijano seems ready to catapult himself from the chair – and, indeed, he is about to catapult himself from the fictional world of the chivalric romance to the dusty roads of La Mancha. The energy contained in his movements and posture are fine examples of how an artist could actually realize the academic ideal of expressing interior affect through physical gesture.[107] Yet in this illustration the eye is the central motor of the dynamic movement representing the turbulence of his mind – and ironically so, since the eye/sight, "noblest of the senses," is the perceiver of light, "formal reason," in the neoplatonic words of an early *ilustrado*, Antonio Palomino de Castro y Velasco.[108] This mad eye renders problematic the enlightened presentation of Don Quixote's madness by distorting, almost caricaturing, the sense of vision in a madman's eye, for vision serves as the metaphorical underpinning of the concept of Enlightenment. Castillo's use of the centre in this illustration actually serves to de-centre the faculty of reason in an episode typically used to highlight the protagonist's folly in Enlightenment Don Quixote iconography. By the same token, books, the companion of the sentimental man in eighteenth-century iconography, become the motor of the reader's madness. The dynamism of Castillo's vision propels his images beyond the Enlightenment tradition from which they spring towards an ironic, doubling vision of the novel, epitomized by Goya's interaction with the work.

Carnicero's stolid illustration of the death of Alonso Quijano, with its use of a circular, central element, serves to highlight by contrast the strength of Castillo's vision (see Figure 47; 4:fp338). Like Castillo, Carnicero represents a staple image from the eighteenth-century reading of the novel, the moment before his death when Alonso Quijano enjoys enlightenment and renounces his deeds as Don Quixote. This image also participates in another iconographic tradition, that of the deathbed scene. As Robert Rosenblum writes of the eighteenth century, the motif of the "deathbed surrounded by mourners … is so prevalent from the mid century on that examples may well run into the thousands."[109] Most of these depictions represent classical death scenes and somberly function as *exempla virtutis*. Describing Gavin Hamilton's *Andromache Bewailing the Death of Hector*, painted in 1761 and reproduced in an engraving by Domenico Cunego in 1764, he writes: "A distant Homeric world of noble deeds and simple, powerful passions is created by a staid, gravity-bound composition in which the strong horizontal accent of the deathbed, in parallel alignment to the picture plane, is offset by the chorus of standing and seated mourners who demonstrate their grief with academic rhetoric."[110] Carnicero's illustration of Don Quixote's death echoes this static, grave composition, although his mourners are even more restrained than Hamilton's. In his typically straightforward, logical manner the artist places the notary, who transcribes the dying man's renunciation of his deeds as Don Quixote, at a desk in the left foreground. The dying man sits on his bed, his eyes wide and almond-shaped, but here still and even empty – perhaps peaceful. The others line up behind the deathbed, as Sancho Panza, Don Quixote's niece, and his housekeeper express varying degrees of overt sorrow. In the centre of the composition stand two candles, placed on the notary's table, putting forth a perfectly round circle of light, represented as opaquely white. Short lines radiate

Fig. 47   Antonio Carnicero. *The Death of Don
Quixote*. Madrid 1780. Biblioteca Nacional, Madrid.

at the edges, forming a slight sunburst. The light itself, however, has no
compositional relationship to the lines or the figures around it. Carnicero uses
a central circular element for an emblematic rather than a compositional
purpose. The light functions in a static, allegorical manner, as it suggests the
rational enlightenment taking place as the formerly deluded man regains his
sanity.

Whether or not the viewer chooses to accept the interpretation of the novel's
ending implicit in this circle of light, its use clearly points to the difference
between the typical eighteenth-century Enlightenment representation and
Castillo's more dynamic and ambivalent readings of the characters. The former
is emblematic, the latter dynamic and relational in its understanding of the
elements of the text. The former always looks beyond the text towards an
abstract conflict of folly versus reason, which can be generalized as a universal
human trait, thus giving rise to spiritual *Don Quixotes* and *Schwärmer*, foolish
enthusiasts. The latter also looks beyond the text for external meanings to
explain it, but less in a simple one-to-one relationship, in which one textual

element clearly refers to one universal element. Instead, clues to the larger "meaning" are to be found within the text itself, beneath the surface.

ILLUSTRATION AND DOUBLED MEANING IN
DON QUIXOTE

It was the perception of a *duplicidad* within *Don Quixote*, glimpsed by José Cadalso, Vicente de los Ríos, and José del Castillo, that characterized the Romantic reading of the novel. This belief in a possible layer of meaning beneath the string of burlesque beatings has been attributed to an original rupture with earlier interpretations begun by the German Romantics. Traces of this "duplicity" of meaning are already visible in Vanderbank's sentimental Don Quixote, in Hogarth's sharp satire, in Castillo's pairing of Don Quixote and Sancho Panza, and even in Ríos's recognition of the levels of narrative perception and interpretation of Don Quixote's misbegotten adventures. One of the reasons the visual interpretations of the illustrators tended towards a more ambivalent, whether satirical or sentimental, interpretation of the text than that of their critical counterparts was the nature of book illustration as an act of representation. The artists engaged in a re-creation of the narrative and thus dealt with chosen moments of episodes in narrative sequence. They saw and made seen the changing fortunes of the two principal characters throughout both books of *Don Quixote*. By the same token, these changes in station were rendered acceptable, even laudable, rather than laughable within the eighteenth-century social context of the emerging middle class in England, the court effort to reform traditional society in Spain, and the pan-European cult of sentimentality. Don Quixote and Sancho Panza, seen through these lenses, could rise in spirit and in life, and began to represent positive rather than negative models to their readers.

At the same time, the eighteenth-century literary critic applied the Aristotelian model of the epic or the neoclassical model of satire based on the primacy of authorial intention, and rearranged the characters and events to fit these ideal forms. The abstract model of decorum, in which the character should not only fit his situation but also his own character as stated from the outset of the text, insisted on the character's continuous identity with himself. In so doing, it censured any deviations from this original identity. Obviously, this interdiction against changing a character's station or allowing characters of different stations to fraternize improperly had a base in a conservative ideology seeking to bolster the traditional split between upper and lower classes. The neoclassical model eschewed the concept of a narrative that involved growth and change within the character, favouring instead a chain of logical events springing from the character's traits but never changing them (of course, many writers themselves never fell into the logical trap of decorum). These same critics perceived the power of representation to depict change in identity and to challenge a simple allegorical relation between figure and meaning, and thus sought to censure, if not censor, the visual imagery based on *Don Quixote*. They also sought to change its status from that of a popular novel to an elite one and, by so doing, inaugurated a fundamentally problematic endeavour to recast the work's humour into a serious mold. John Oldfield, involved in the production of the 1738 Lord Carteret edition, and the members of the Real Academia de la Lengua, publishers of the 1780 academy edition, strove mightily, but with only partial success, to control the artists' choice of episodes and use of "fantasy" (imagination). For these thinkers the English connotation of false-hood linked to the word "duplicity" would have been very appropriate, for they saw non-allegorical or non-satirical interpretations as false depictions of the text. None the less, their efforts to control interpretation were doomed to failure because of the structure of allegory, the tool of the neoclassical critic. As Angus Fletcher insightfully notes, allegory, the means by which meaning is read into a narrative, involves a doubling of levels, the literal and the allegorical.[111] The doubled structure of allegorical interpretation, which posits a literal layer of meaning and a symbolic layer, opens the text up to interpretations because it raises the possibility of meaning beneath the surface.

The German Romantics, who discovered the novel during their experimental years as rebellious young students and writers in Jena, were capable of embracing the duplicitousness of doubled meaning in *Don Quixote* because of their fondness for fragmentation, multiplicity, and irony. A similar impetuosity, coupled with a taste for English Gothic literature, animated Cadalso, who glimpsed the duplicity of *Don Quixote* almost two decades earlier.[112] Nor was he alone, for many of the Spanish *ilustrados* of the 1770s, although involved in the court or in practical schemes of reform, constituted a generation of young upstarts, reading forbidden books, questioning traditional institutions and artistic conventions, and critiquing the society around them from a stance alienated from the lower classes and the institutions of the church and university. Although Cadalso's *Cartas marruecas* was not published for decades, it was read and well-received in the *tertulia de San Sebastián* in Madrid.[113] The members of this discussion group included Moratín, Iriarte, and even Vicente de los Ríos. It is not so surprising, then, to see Cadalso's glimpsed "duplicidad" straining through the cracks in the neoclassical aesthetic espoused by the academics in the 1780 Real Academia edition. That edition, a monument to the newly won status of *Don Quixote* as a classic, bears witness both to the "universal" aesthetic criteria by which the novel could be considered a classic and to the claims of the particular, especially in its use as a foundational work of a Spanish national literature and the introduction of a psychological treatment of character, which would develop into the Romantic reading.

Conclusion:
Goya and the Romantic Reading of
Don Quixote

The 1780 Real Academia edition appeared on the cusp of an interpretive change in the history of the reception of *Don Quixote* commonly called "Romantic," attributed to the literary movement from which it derived its name. Literary historians have viewed this moment as one of rupture, and either implied that the subsequent change in reading constituted a critical advance or more openly derided it as anachronistic.[1] According to studies done up to the present, the transformation of Don Quixote from a madman to a hero, the reinterpretation of the text as novelistic (involved with psychological development and philosophical issues) rather than satirical, and the new vision of Cervantes as a man of heart and sentiment all mark nineteenth-century readings as distinct from earlier ones.[2] One of the goals of this study has been to question the novelty of the Romantic reading of *Don Quixote* through a re-evaluation of the earlier interpretive strategies themselves. The examination of the illustrations along with the literary commentaries within editions respects the context of the commentaries and offers a method by which to assess more fully the eighteenth-century reader's experience of the novel in concrete and conceptual spaces created by the book. This study reveals the coexistence of hermeneutic traditions that came together like tributaries to meet in a given point, the edition, therein to commingle and contrast, only to flow out again separate but changed. These interpretive approaches to the text did not exist in an aesthetic vacuum but participated in and grew from various social and technological contexts, ranging from the interests of the eighteenth-century Spanish court to conserve and glorify their national culture in an elite, neoclassical form to the power of print technology to subvert an elite culture by granting a literate middle class access to the same.

The four interpretive practices isolated by this study consist of the burlesque and the satiric, focusing on the humour of the novel's premise, characters, and action; and the sentimental and the classicizing, focusing on the serious aspects of the same. The burlesque, unquestionably the earliest of readings, simply delights in the folly and pratfalls of the novel's main characters. Although it is very difficult to measure the extent of its dissemination, it is certain that this approach to the text reflects a non-elite reading in its embracing of carnivalesque and theatrical traditions typical of popular culture. The satiric differs from the burlesque in its elevation of the humour for a didactic purpose, which thus renders the humour acceptable for an educated, if not necessarily elite audience. The sentimental ennobles the author and protagonists as heroes of the heart by reflecting the eighteenth-century middle-class interest in an aristocracy of spirit accessible to the bourgeoisie. By contrast, the classicizing makes a hero of the author for his literary and cultural achievement, according to the standards of a classically educated elite. Obviously, these strains of interpretation meet and blend at certain points, making the precise differentiation of the satirical from the classicizing in the 1738 Lord Carteret edition, for example, difficult. Very often the difference lies in the idiom, visual or literary, used by the interpreter. The satirical prints of Hogarth depend on his personal iconography of visual puns and his sharply mimetic depiction of human life, whereas Vanderbank's neoclassical frontispiece of Hercules ascending Mount Parnassus depends on classical mythology and the idealized forms of history painting.

This study does not deny the existence of the Romantic reading as defined by earlier critics, but rather seeks to explore its headwaters. Neither does it seek to accuse it of anachronistically forgetting the novel's bawdy humour, nor of radically departing from a satirical appreciation of the author's literary parody of a fantastic, florid literary genre. What distinguished the Romantic reading was its capacity to absorb the four hermeneutic traditions of the burlesque, satiric, sentimental, and classicizing without obliterating them.[3] This tolerance of, indeed, joy in the fragmentary, ironic, inconclusive, and contradictory marked the German Romantic movement in particular. Friedrich Schlegel, like most of the German Romantics, read *Don Quixote* in such a way that laughter and tears coexist in an ironic tension. Likewise, illustrators drew from the existent iconographic traditions, both burlesque and elevated, satirical and sentimental. For example, the Cruikshank brothers, Robert (1828) and George (1833), further explored the mirroring, grotesque exaggeration, and unmasking used by Hogarth, but tempered their predecessor's unrelenting bite with sympathetic depictions of the character's suffering, thus establishing a caricatural iconography for *Don Quixote*.

Three other important nineteenth-century illustrators, Robert Smirke (1812), Tony Johannot (1836), and Gustave Doré (1863), all worked primarily within the sentimental tradition. Smirke and Johannot produced a stream of many fanciful, fantastic images, as well as burlesque, through their profuse vignettes. In order to increase the reader's sympathy for his unabashedly noble lover, Don Quixote, Smirke broke the theatrical frame of the image through figures standing with their backs turned towards the reader. This extended the space of action towards the reader to focus the reaction through the character. Yet Smirke never stopped illustrating the burlesque scenes of physical humour and deflation. Johannot's most innovative vignettes explored the text's verbal rather than physical play, illustrating turns of speech and multiple narrative levels, ambiguities, and even voices, such as that of Cide Hamete Benengeli. More than any other illustrator Johannot exploded the strict separation between page and text for wry humorous effect, as in his depiction of Sancho Panza's signature, a rough X. Many of the chuckles elicited by Johannot's vignettes arose, then, from these visual puns and their ironic attention to the ambiguities of the text rather than from Don Quixote's misadventures. The humour remained, but had been recast into a new mold. In contrast, Doré indulged his sympathy with Don Quixote to such an extent that the deluded fool appeared to be the hero of a chivalric romance rather than the protagonist of a parodic novel. The knight bravely confronted mysterious, threatening land-scapes and suffered cruel torment and ridicule by grotesque persecutors. In his reappropriation of romance Doré returned to the eighteenth-century definition of the romantic as the exotic and sentimental, an aspect rarely seen in *Don Quixote* illustrations of that century. Only with Doré did the tears drown the laughter, for subsequent illustrators reincorporated burlesque and satirical elements in tension with the sentimental.

THE TRANSFORMATION OF SATIRE

Nevertheless, in the case of *Don Quixote* two eighteenth-century Spaniards, Luis Cañuelo and Francisco Goya, exemplified first and best the inflowing and intermingling of hermeneutic traditions from which the Romantic reading grows. Luis Cañuelo, self-proclaimed imitator of Addison and Steele, announced the return to publication of his satirical periodical in 1785 with a flourish of the pen by proclaiming himself an imitator of Don Quixote, not of Cervantes. "Yes, gentlemen, the *Censor* is very similar to a Don Quixote of the philosophical world (something he considers very honourable), that travels everywhere seeking adventures, managing to undo errors of all kinds, and righting wrongs and follies of all types, regardless of the type to which they pertain. This is his mania."[4] He had offended conservative clerical and political figures through his efforts to enlighten the Spanish people with the sword of satire guided by reason, thus placing himself fully within the Enlightenment tradition. Truth was his idol; he was "in love with his most chaste Dulcinea, whom he calls Truth,"[5] for whom he set out on his quixotic mission to critique and reform. The price he paid for his devotion was the silencing of his newspaper *El Censor* in 1784, returned to publication in 1785 by order of the Conde de Floridablanca. Upon this, his "third sally," Cañuelo was fully aware of the vulnerability of his position as the champion of truth as revealed by reason. His weapons were weak – "some little satire as fragile as a straw."[6] He identified himself with Don Quixote, who was likewise vulnerable and weak, but more heroic, since "his valour was never seen to flag in the slightest."[7] That an Enlightenment journalist would identify himself positively with Don Quixote, the exemplar of foolishness and deluded zealotry, must have startled his readers.[8]

Indeed, Cañuelo opened his article with a statement that turned on its head the established Enlightenment reading of *Don Quixote*: "Despite all that Mr Ríos explains in his excellent *Analysis of Don Quixote*, I have never been able to pardon Cervantes for having made the subject of his immortal work the burlesque of a such a madness as that of this fabulous hero."[9] Cervantes was no longer seen by this critic as a hero using Don Quixote as a satiric mask, but as an abuser who targets his literary creation with ridicule. The protagonist had taken on an identity independent of the role assigned to him by the author. Central to that character was his heroically unfaltering stance as "a crazy man, but at the core a truthful man of integrity, full of probity and honour, incapable of saying or doing anything that to his mind would be vile: a lover of glory, sober in abundance, generous in poverty, valiant on all occasions, compassionate, merciful, gracious to all; in a word, a complete and perfect man, in spite of that upset suffered by his imagination."[10] Cañuelo inverted the neoclassical characterization of Don Quixote as a fool to one much closer to the Romantic depiction of Don Quixote as a heroic madman. The character became an ideal model for the brave champion of a noble but lost cause. Cañuelo's cause did prove to be lost once he found himself broke, silenced, censured by the Inquisition, and crazed. Shortly after his death in 1802, his brother described him thus: "marginalized (to our misfortune), he has just died the most painful and sad death, his senses confused, believing that nothing was left to him but begging for his very sustenance."[11]

Already in 1781 Cañuelo recognized the futility of his defence of truth through reason, his Dulcinea, for he identified himself as a "martyr of reason" in the very first issue of *El Censor*.[12] His situation must be taken seriously, for it reveals two important things about the reception of *Don Quixote* (things likely more important in relationship to the larger political and social problems of the period). First, when faced by the growing disillusionment concerning the power of reason to reform society, the Spanish Enlightenment thinker found himself alienated from the resistantly unreasonable society around him. No burgeoning middle class arose about him to support and extend the ideologies of sentimentalism and public, rational debate. This placed him in a position to identify and sympathize with the alienated Don Quixote. Secondly, the satirical critique of society undertaken by an enlightened thinker was conceived by him to be heroic, and could lead to sacrifice and defeat. In this manner the satirical coexisted with, and depended upon, the heroic and utopian belief in the possibility of an enlightened world. Other European men of letters faced a similar disillusionment with the supposedly "self-evident" ideology of Enlightenment in the following generations, as revolutions failed and society proved itself stubbornly resistant to reason.[13] The difference between an Enlightenment and a Romantic thinker may be merely the passage of one or two generations.

THE JANUS FACE OF GOYA

The work of Francisco Goya, the only Spanish artist whose *œuvre* truly spanned both the Enlightenment and Romanticism, has challenged all the attempts of critics and art historians to pigeonhole it as belonging completely to either epoch. André Malraux and José Camón Aznar, two proponents of the Romantic Goya, both dare to face the monstrous forms that gradually devour the nightscapes of the artist's work. Aznar distinguishes this grotesque vision from the caricatural vision of Hogarth. "For the sensibility of Goya, the world is a chaos in which each bestiality can set out on adventure with the security of finding countless victims. But this pitiless vision of reality does not suppose, as in Hogarth, a moralizing intention, nor as in Gross a social subversion. Goya does not qualify. He signals in brief synthesis the abnormalities and the demons that palpitate in the rage of men and the insinuations of women, even managing at times to conceal his sympathy for the sacrificed."[14] Malraux names this "pitiless" vision Saturn, the god who devoured his children, revealed by Goya's "instinct that everything sacred … rested on *awareness* of the other world, that it had been obscured by the passionate eagerness of humanity to arrange the world to suit itself."[15] The espousal of the god Saturn, whom Goya depicted grotesquely devouring his own child in one of the famous black paintings, required him to reject the classicizing imperative (which Malraux labels Italian) to "rescue man from his condition by reducing him to his perfection."[16]

This vision of Goya as the priest of Saturn, the artist of the inhumanly grotesque rather than humanistic perfection, stands in sharp contrast to the vision of Goya as a Spanish Hogarth, the enlightened caricaturist who sought to instruct men towards reform. The producers of the seminal exhibition "Goya y el espíritu de la Ilustración," in particular Eleanor Sayre, have most actively promoted Goya as the priest of reason. Sayre argues for the enlightened Goya through a comparison of his *Caprichos* with the visual context of his time, a problematic approach given Goya's unquestionable tendency to subvert artistic if not social convention.[17] To further the depiction of Goya as an enlightened satirist, Reva Wolf asserts that Goya's work paralleled Hogarth's in concept, since "both endeavored to produce satirical art that would transcend specifics of time and place."[18] She continues to assert that Goya was even influenced by the English tradition of caricatural prints.

Edith Helman takes a more successful approach through a comparison of the *Caprichos* with the literary work of Goya's contemporaries, including Cadalso's *Cartas marruecas*: "The most significant aspect of Cadalso's 'caprice of some demented painter,' what most affected Goya, is that of a purely aesthetic precept, he made a moral and social doctrine with which he could censure a theory so absurd as that of hereditary nobility."[19] Paul Ilie also develops the comparison between Cadalso and Goya by pointing out the similarity in the use of madness to reflect the insanity of social conventions in the work of both. For Ilie, Goya represents the "final step" of "irrationalistic skepticism within the Spanish Enlightenment" because he finally substituted "cognition through dream in the place of cognition through waking reality, sensorial or otherwise."[20] Thus, the interpretation of Goya's work has been complicated by his liminal position between two aesthetics and ideologies.

THE EPISODE OF THE BRAYING ASSES

Appropriately, this Janus-faced artist, both critic and champion of the irrational, guides us towards the dualistic reception of *Don Quixote* at the turn of the nineteenth century. Goya produced a drawing of the episode of the brayers (2:27), actually engraved by J. Joaquín Fabregat but rejected for publication in the 1780 Real Academia edition, perhaps due to its flouting of neoclassical standards.[21] The presentation of the episode is none the less conventional in the manner of much of Goya's early work (see Figure 48). According to the classicizing rules of history painting, he represented the moment of climactic action. A stable pyramid, formed by the figures of the angry mounted Don Quixote at the left, the peasant knocking Sancho Panza off Rucio to the right, and the mounted townspeople framed by the large banner of the brayers, firmly roots the composition. The triangular composition is in fact that recommended by Goya's neoclassical teacher, Anton Raphael Mengs, as the best manner by which to create a solidly grounded but rounded formation of figures.[22] The only dynamic element is the falling Sancho Panza, who clutches his cheek in pain. The figures themselves are standard.

The material that the publishers found offensive would seem to be the content of the print rather than its style, although the Real Academia de la Lengua must have initially chosen this episode as suitable for depiction. Eighteenth-century illustrators generally overlooked this episode, perhaps since the folly depicted belonged to neither Don Quixote nor Sancho Panza. The conflict stemmed instead from a case of communal folly, in which one town had offended another through mocking its vanity in its inhabitants' expertise at braying. One easily sees how the episode would interest Goya as an example of the ridiculous nature of communal local pride and the dehumanizing violence resulting from it. A comparison of this print with Goya's later works affirms the interpretation of this image as a satire aimed at the values of the *pueblo* rather than at Don Quixote or Sancho Panza. Significantly, in the *Caprichos* Goya used asses to portray many of the follies of contemporary Spain, in particular when representing important men: the ass showing off his lineage

Fig. 48   Francisco de Goya. *The Battle of the Brayers.*
Biblioteca Nacional, Madrid.

in *Even up to his grandfather / Hasta su abuelo*; the asses masquerading as doctors
in *Witches disguised in common physiques / Brujas disfrazadas en físicos comunes*;
or those in *From what ill will he die? / ¿De qué mal morirá?*. Edith Helman
suggests that his *asnería* series was inspired by a satirical attack on the academies, published under the title *Memorias de la insigne Academia Asnal*, written
by Doctor de Ballesteros in 1792.[23] Yet this illustration shows that Goya's use
of the imagery of asses to ridicule human delusions and vanities predated the
Caprichos and that the class targeted by this device was not only the educated
elite or nobility. Like Cervantes, Goya probably drew from the carnivalesque
traditions of representing human follies with animals, in addition to classical
sources such as Lucian and Apuleius. Nevertheless, he did *not* view the people
and their carnivalesque language as "the only possible voice for an endeavour
of public opinion to attain the liberty of expressing a moral judgment without
compromise,"[24] contrary to Teresa Lorenzo de Márquez's opinion.

Instead, Goya used the voice of the people to demonstrate the restrictive
effect of the *sensus communis* upon individual freedom and tolerance, an effect
he criticized most clearly in his painting *The Burial of the Sardine / El entierro*

de la sardina (1812–19). This painting, much sharper in its satiric bite, depicts a community procession, expanding upon the same triangular base used in the brayers' illustration. Three figures form a triangle as they dance with their arms thrown stiffly up in revelry, yet the celebration is a result of the "triumph of disorder."[25] Behind this triangle rises a banner representing a grotesquely grinning face, similar to the banner of the brayers, which proclaims their grotesque slogan that the two mayors did not bray in vain. Clarifying his satirical intent for the image of the brayers, Goya used his earlier rejected illustration as the basis for this later, much more clearly satirical attack on the *pueblo*. In this critique of popular culture Goya concurred with some of his contemporaries. As Helman writes: "He had represented the superstitous lower class as Moratín and Jovellanos had conceived them, as a mass made idiotic by fear and ignorance and, above all, as a depersonalized mass, much earlier, finally, than the word 'mass' was used in Spanish with this meaning."[26]

But the question remains unanswered: why does it appear that this illustration was rejected, particularly if it represented a critique of popular culture shared by some of the *ilustrados*? It must be kept in mind that the Royal Academy of the Language attempted to control the content of the illustrations by dictating the passages to be depicted. Perhaps the use of any carnivalesque thematic content, even if satirized, in a full-page illustration, once actually made visible, was deemed too daring for the conservative neoclassical aesthetic that shaped the academy's intention upon publishing the edition. Perhaps the representation of Don Quixote and Sancho Panza as the victims of the folly of others was too alien to the neoclassical reading of the novel, in which the opinion of the people around Don Quixote constituted the *sensus communis*, indeed common sense, and the protagonist's vision constituted folly. Goya inverted the equation by showing common sense to be foolish as he unmasked the beast behind the human and the irrational behind the conventional. This rational critique extended beyond the *pueblo* in several *Caprichos* to the *asnos* of knowledge, the doctors, politicians, and critics, who were also unmasked as asses. Goya's all-encompassing satiric vision reminds one of Hogarth, whose illustrations were also rejected from the classicizing 1738 edition. Unlike Hogarth, Goya seems to have lost faith in the possibility of effective instruction through satire.

CRACKS IN THE EDIFICE OF REASON: ALONSO QUIJANO READING

The analysis of the previous chapter has, to a large extent, focused on what was *not* neoclassical in the classicizing eighteenth-century editions of *Don Quixote*, particularly the 1780 Real Academia de la Lengua edition. Cracks in this systematically reasonable interpretation of the novel as a satirical work appeared in the sentimental representation of Don Quixote as a man of heart, in the enthronement of Cervantes as a hero of the sentiments, and in the illustration of the development of the characters of Don Quixote and Sancho Panza. Goya actually made manifest the threatening creatures behind the fissures of reason in a drawing of Alonso Quixano (or perhaps Don Quixote – the distinction blurs at this point; see Figure 49). Through a study of the paper and the numbering of the original drawing Gassier has proved that the drawing belongs to Goya's Sepia Album, executed between 1812 and 1823.[27] This image might have been intended as the frontispiece for a series of etchings based on the novel entitled *Visiones de Don Quixote,* to have been published in a format similar to the *Caprichos.*[28] The image did not appear publicly, however, until Félix Bracquemond published an etching of the drawing in Paris in 1860.

In many ways this drawing grows out of both Goya's series of grotesquely satirical etchings, the *Caprichos,* and the traditional iconography of the novel. Similar to the *Caprichos* in its acerbic lines and sharp visual wit, it represents a satiric vision of Don Quixote through the use of fantastic imagery. Such a marriage surely could not have been imagined or foreseen by the publishers of the 1780 Real Academia edition, let alone John Oldfield of the 1738 Lord Carteret edition. The typical attributes of the image are present: the reader seated at a table with a pile of books, the ravenous greyhound, a sword leaning against the chair, and the edge of a shield protruding through the frame of the image. The depiction of the sword reveals, however, the paradox central to the image as a whole. The sword gleams naturalistically, given the very flat style of Goya's drawing, as light reflects off its three-dimensional hilt. It leans against the chair, as indicated by the angle of the blade and the shadow thrown beneath it, yet no point of contact appears. Indeed, the arm of the chair, upon which Don Quixote supports his elbow and the sword leans, does not appear at all. The laws of rationally illusionistic pictorial depiction are suspended, even as they appear to be mimicked. Goya thus moved beyond the rational web of eighteenth-century engraving, in which the evenly spaced lines illusionistically defied their own two-dimensional quality to portray depth,[29] to use the viewer's own tendency to fill in the blanks.

Subsequently, the manner of Goya's drawing (and Bracquemond's etching) echoes the transgression of the boundary between the real and the imagined presented pictorially by the fantastic creatures of Don Quixote's imagination. These strange figures defiantly penetrate the frontier between "fiction" and "reality" as they swirl about the reading gentleman, threatening and seducing him. The person of Alonso Quijano/Don Quixote himself begins to undergo a metamorphosis, as he becomes a liminal character partaking in both realms. In his excitement he falls to one knee, points to a passage of his open book, and looks directly at the viewer. His body is substantial, but his hair defies the laws of gravity as it stands straight on end, "as if an electric current shot out of his sick cranium."[30] The lines of his face are small and quick, and thus lend

Fig. 49 Félix Bracquemond, after a drawing by Francisco de Goya. *Don Quixote Reading*.
Biblioteca Nacional, Madrid.

a melting impression to all his features except his large phallic nose and his sentimental eyes creased at the corners in sadness. These eyes preserve for Don Quixote a softened, humane aspect, particularly in contrast to the grotesque, frenetic creatures emanating from (or are they attacking?) his excited mind. Givanel Mas and "Gaziel" assume these phantasmata to be characters from the novel itself, such as the Duke and Duchess in the upper right-hand corner.[31] None the less, the identification of these figures with specific characters is problematic due to their fluidly grotesque forms.

The identity of the phantasmagorical creatures is much more richly multi-valent when set within both the iconographic tradition of *Don Quixote* and Goya's own iconography of satyrs, witches, and flying creatures escaped from nightmares.[32] The erect penis of the trollish creature with donkey's ears to the left defines it as a satyr and links it iconographically to the satyr tossing up a man in an emblematic allusion to lust in Capricho 56, *Rise and Fall / Subir y bajar.*[33] Goya, then, employs the satyr, symbol of Cervantes' satirical attack on decadent literature in eighteenth-century frontispieces (although without the erection), to introduce a supplemental interpretation of Don Quixote's madness as sexually motivated as well as literarily rooted. Bracquemond heightens this sexual allusion in the etching by delineating more deeply the satyr's penis as it points right towards the protagonist's overwrought mind. A satyr also appears in Capricho 70, *Devout profession / Devota profesión*, which depicts either the heretical use of sacred texts by ecclesiastics, according to the Ayala manuscript, or the initiation of a witch, according to the Prado manuscript.[34] On his shoulders he supports a young initiate with donkey's ears, who reads from a text supported on the wings of a huge, black bird of prey and held open with pincers by witches dressed in ecclesiastical robes and mitres.[35] A similarly winged, carnivorous creature, although larger, darker, and more menacing due to its wolf's head, bears the entire coven of phantasmata to Don Quixote through the text he reads. The satirical commentary on the incorrect, harmful, and even heretical reading of texts is not lost in this image of Don Quixote but rather is made darker, even diabolical. Folly does not accompany Satire but joins a witch wielding strange keys and the carnivorous flying creatures, figures Goya frequently employs to represent irrationality in conflict with reason.[36] Although Goya may indeed have been championing reason and truth, it is no longer clear in these images that the forces of Enlightenment would triumph.

In the nightmarish insistency and consistency of these menacing figures, Goya represented the path satire takes in its most daring journeys to the extremes of human folly: fanaticism, voracious desire, and inhumanity. This image of Don Quixote reading should be compared to the ambiguous frontis-piece of the *Caprichos, The Sleep (or Dream) of Reason / Sueño de la razón.*[37] A telling slip in the extremely meticulous care with which Gassier studies Goya's works indicates how Goya's image subverted the iconographic tradition of *Don*

Quixote to the point where the Enlightenment reading converged with the Romantic one. Gassier and Wilson write in reference to the *Sueño de la razón* and *Don Quixote reading*, that "the two compositions in effect show the author assailed by the creatures of his dreams and visions."[38] Of course, in the *Sueño de la razón* it is most likely Goya, the author/artist, who is assaulted by the creatures of his dreams, especially since he depicts his own face emanating from the sleeping man's mind in a preparatory drawing. But it is not the author, Cervantes, who is assaulted in the image of Don Quixote reading, but rather the protagonist. Nevertheless, Cervantes and Don Quixote are conflated in this image to a certain degree. In the eighteenth-century iconographic tradition Cervantes looks out at the reader with soulful, sentimental eyes, surrounded by the attributes of the shield and sword as soldier and the books and plume as author. In the only image in which Don Quixote trespasses the fourth wall between the reader and himself through eye contact (José del Castillo's illustration for the 1780 Real Academia edition), madness clearly ravages his mind and enrages his eyes (see Figure 2). Still, in Castillo's image Don Quixote appears as a sensitive man, weakened by a constant onslaught of trials and temptations but perhaps heroically resisting them as he appeals to the reader. Goya clearly places his Don Quixote into the eighteenth-century model of Cervantes as sentimental hero. He then combines the image of the suffering author with the satirical allegory emphasizing the author's heroic fight against decadence. Goya forces his viewer to face a Don Quixote assailed not only by bad literature but by physical desire, obsession, fanaticism, and the dark creatures of our nightmares. This Don Quixote is not merely Every Man but ourselves, as he both shares the seat of creative excess with Goya and looks to the viewer in appeal.

RARA PENITENCIA

Another drawing from the Journal Album, 1803–24, appears to be inspired by the novel (see Figure 50). Entitled *Strange penitence / Rara penitencia*, this drawing has largely escaped the notice of art historians, who have not identified its iconographic content. The drawing shows a crazed man with his arms clutched protectively about his chest, standing with his pants dropped around his ankles. There is no setting to speak of except a horizon line, a blob of shadow about the man's feet, and an object on the ground to the left that resembles nothing so much as an upturned barber's basin, or Mambrino's helmet (1:21). Goya scarcely defines his face, except for his large phallic nose and a strangely incongruous expression of self-contained ecstasy, in which his mouth breaks into a large grin and his eyelids hood his downcast eyes. His figure is certainly not thin and attenuated as is customary in the depiction of Don Quixote, nor is his face sufficiently long. None the less, given the title, the object that looks like a barber's basin, and the strange subject itself, the

Rara penitencia

Fig. 50   Joaquín Fabregat, after a drawing by Francisco de Goya.
Rara penitencia / Strange Penitence. © Padro Museum, Madrid.

identification of this figure as Don Quixote inflicting penance upon himself in the Sierra Morena merits consideration. If so, then Goya is portraying a Don Quixote never seen before this time, a fool enveloped in what Gassier calls a "state of primitive bliss."[39] Eric Ziolkowski claims that the affinities between Don Quixote and a holy fool were central to Dostoyevsky's assimilation of the Spanish gentleman to his own fool, Prince Myshkin. As he writes: "There is a natural affinity between the kenotic ideal and the *Quixote*, which is a virtual epic of humiliation. From being trampled by various herds of farm animals to being transported in a cage on a cart, from being beaten and stoned to being victimized by practical jokesters, Don Quixote is subjected to constant humiliation and hence might appear as a kenotic figure – or a parody of one."[40] The other possibility is that Goya is depicting Sancho Panza, his pants dropped around his ankles as he prepared to lash himself in order to disenchant Dulcinea. In this case the body would more appropriately represent the robust peasant, and his smile would indicate his glee at fooling his master. Whether this be Don Quixote or Sancho, the character is clearly a fool.

It does not seem warranted to suggest that Goya had the ideal of a holy fool in mind as he executed this portrait of either Don Quixote or Sancho Panza. Yet Goya repeatedly portrayed fools and madmen throughout his career – for example, in his painting *Corral of Madmen / Corral de locos* (1793–94), executed immediately after his own mysterious illness and breakdown, and in a series of drawings done in the last years of his life in Bordeaux (1824–28). As Manuela Mena Marqués writes of these later drawings: "The artist doubtlessly shared the philanthropic opinions of his enlightened friends about insanity or the treatment the insane deserved, but in his images he seems to advance intuitively towards the discoveries of modern psychology and thus to denounce the deeply rooted traditional and popular ideas about the diseases of the mind."[41] Goya's depiction of madness appears to be more advanced than his contemporaries' interpretation of insanity – and of Don Quixote or Sancho Panza as madmen – precisely because he might have glimpsed the madness in all minds, and the very creative power of that madness. In this image, *Rara penitencia*, the satirical heightening of folly, achieved through the caricatural reduction of the character to his foolishness and the grotesque exaggeration of his eyes and nose, veils the vulnerably bare-legged figure in a blissful transcendence that Goya rarely granted his figures. Of course, the figure's dropped pants hint at a physical, sexual cause for the transport, thus linking this image to the artist's earlier drawing of Don Quixote reading. The satirical tradition of Don Quixote as fool and the sentimental tradition of Don Quixote as suffering hero meet in this ambiguous image, hidden until now in Goya's private treasury of images.

This departure from the discussion of illustrations in the public space of the editions of *Don Quixote* has brought to light the point of conjunction of the satirical and the sentimental in Goya's private œuvre. The first illustration was probably rejected from the 1780 Real Academia edition, whereas the later images were withheld from public view by Goya himself in his lifelong – and largely well-justified – habit of self-censorship. One wonders and rues that he did not realize his plans to create and publish his *Visions of Don Quixote*. Nevertheless, his acute visual combination and re-creation of previous iconographic traditions disclose the two traditions composing the Romantic reading of *Don Quixote*: the caricatural, growing out of the burlesque and satirical traditions, and the idealizing, growing out of the sentimental and neoclassical traditions. The caricatural and the idealizing oppose and offset each other in a continuously fluctuating tension that creates the irony central to the Romantic reading. Among the nineteenth-century artists to follow in Goya's wake were masters of the caricatural tradition, such as Daniel Chodowiecki and George Cruikshank, three major artists of the idealizing tradition – Robert Smirke, Tony Johannot, and Gustave Doré – and the only other artist of that century to recombine the two iconographic threads, Honoré Daumier.

Notes

1 Cervantes, *Don Quixote de la Mancha*, trans. Putnam, 2:898. The Spanish reads, "tratar de las cosas del gran Quijote" (2:970).

2 Cervantes, *Don Quixote*, 2:898. "Retráteme el que quisiere, pero no me maltrate" (2:970).

3 Elizabeth L. Eisenstein, *The Printing Press as an Agent of Change*.

4 Roger Chartier, *The Cultural Uses of Print in Early Modern France*, 100.

5 The prologue to the first book is in fact a parody of prologues. The author sits at his desk stymied by writer's block because he cannot supply learned citations or marginal notes until a friend comes by to suggest to him how to write a prologue. The friend states, "This is especially true in view of the fact that your book stands in no need of all these things whose absence you lament; for the entire work is an attack upon the books of chivalry of which Aristotle never dreamed, of which St. Basil has nothing to say, and of which Cicero had no knowledge; nor do the fine points of truth or the observations of astrology have anything to do with its fanciful absurdities" (Cervantes, *Don Quixote*, 1:15) / "Cuanto más que, si bien caigo en la cuenta, este vuestro libro no tiene necesidad de ninguna cosa de aquellas que vos decís que le falta, porque todo él es una invectiva contra los libros de caballerías, de quien nunca se acordó Aristóteles, ni dijo nada San Basilio, ni alcanzó Cicerón, ni caen debajo de la cuenta de sus fabulosos disparates las puntualidades de la verdad, ni las observaciones de la astrología" (1:24). The speaker in one breath disqualifies the work from the neoclassical apparatus of learned commentary by linking it to a minor, popular genre, the literature of knight errantry. The attribution of these words to Cervantes, the interpretive stance of many critics from the seventeenth century well into the twentieth, firstly conflates the voice of the author with that of a fictional character and, secondly, fails to recognize the deflation of the text involved in its parodic relationship to a popular rather than learned genre. See below in chap. 1 for further information on this camp of critics.

6 Cervantes, *Don Quixote*, 2:526. As the Spanish reads, "desconsolóle pensar que su autor era moro, según aquel nombre de Cide; y de los moros no se podía esperar verdad alguna, porque todos son embelecadores, falsarios y quimeristas" (2:558).

7 For studies of the problem of narration in *Don Quixote* see Ruth El Saffar, *Distance and Control in Don Quixote*; James A. Paar, *Don Quixote: An Anatomy of Subversive Discourse*; and José Manuel Martín Moran, "La función del narrador múltiple en el *Quijote* de 1615."

8 Cervantes, *Don Quixote*, 2:531. The Spanish states, "los niños la manosean, los mozos la leen, los hombres la entiende y los viejos la celebran; y, finalmente, es tan trillada y tan leída y tan sabida de todo género de gentes, que apenas han visto algún rocín flaco, cuando dicen: 'Allí va Rocinante'" (2:562).

9 Ibid., "hijo seco" (1:19).

10 Walter Benjamin, "The Work of Art in the Age of Mechanical Reproduction," 221.

11 Alvin Kernan, *Samuel Johnson and the Impact of Print*, 54.

12 William Mills Ivins Jr, *Prints and Visual Communication*, 3.

13 Edward Hodnett, *Image and Text*, 7. Original emphasis.

14 Ibid., 7.

15 Ibid., 7–8.

16 Ibid., 14.

17 Stephen C. Behrendt, "The Functions of Illustrations – Intentional and Unintentional," 30; original emphasis.

18 Ibid., 40.

19 Evelyn Goldsmith, *Research into Illustration*, 334.

20 W.J.T. Mitchell, *Iconology*, 41.

21 Hodnett, *Image and Text*, 17.

22 Suzanne K. Langer, "Deceptive Analogies," 85–6.

23 Rudolf Arnheim, *Visual Thinking*, 13.

24 Ernst Gombrich, "The Visual Image," 149–50.

25 Arnheim, *Visual Thinking*, 235.

26 Ibid., 50.

27 Ernst Gombrich, *Art and Illusion*, 313.

28 Ibid., 227.

29 Oscar Mandel, "The Function of the Norm in *Don Quixote*," 154–5.

30 Hans Robert Jauss, *Toward an Aesthetic of Reception*, 19.

31 T.S. Eliot, "Tradition and Individual Talent," 4–5.

32 Ibid., 5.

33 For an insightful critique informed by a reading of Pierre Bourdieu of both the conservatives' call for a return to the "classics" and the liberal pluralists' call for an expansion of the canon, see John Guillory, *Cultural Capital*. According to Guillory, the current canon debate masks the more central problem of the study of literature – its loss of capital, i.e. value, for the new professorial-managerial class which is replacing the old bourgeoisie (x). As will be clear in this study, the

canonization of *Don Quixote* was intimately linked to the social interests and "capital" of the emergent bourgeoisie of eighteenth-century England, if not Spain.

34 Walter Cahn, *Masterpieces*, 121–4.

35 Frank Kermode, *The Classic*, 117.

36 Ibid., 40.

37 Ibid.

38 Ibid., 39.

39 Cornel West, *Keeping Faith*, 34, 42–3.

40 Ibid., 43.

41 John Guillory, "The Ideology of Canon-Formation," 358.

42 Guillory, *Cultural Capital*, 22, 23, 26.

43 Ibid., 27–8, and Jan Gorak, *The Making of the Modern Canon*, 252.

44 Jürgen Habermas, *The Structural Transformation of the Public Sphere*, 27–42.

45 Ibid., 37.

46 Guillory, *Cultural Capital*, 11–13.

47 Among the errors in the text, most notable are the several names of Sancho Panza's wife and the unexplained theft of Sancho's donkey. Cervantes himself includes these criticisms in Book 2, chap. 3, to which Sancho responds in explanation in chap. 4. Of additional concern to early neoclassical readers was the inclusion of the interpolated tales, stories unrelated to the main narrative but told in the inns along the way for the diversion of the novel's characters, which of course broke the unity of action. An important problem for the literary critics who undertook the canonization of *Don Quixote* was its defence from the charges of carelessness and indecorum against its author.

48 In this work I have chosen to refer to the editions not by their actual publishers but by the names of the person or persons most important to the undertaking of the enterprise and the shaping of the interpretive approach to the edition. The 1738 Lord Carteret edition was published in London by the prestigious publisher J.R. Tonson, as the 1780 Real Academia edition was in Madrid by the famous publisher Joaquín Ibarra. The identity of the publishers reveals, in both instances, that the edition was produced by the best publisher available for a presumably elite market. In the case of the edition published by Millar in 1755 containing the illustrations of Francis Hayman and the translation and biography of the author by Tobias Smollett, I will refer to the Smollett edition.

49 Guillory, "The Ideology of Canon-Formation," 339.

50 Arnold Hauser, *The Social History of Art*, 3:46.

51 Ibid., 3:53.

CHAPTER TWO

1 In fact the first known visual representation of Don Quixote occurred in a cartel portraying a parade of carnival characters, including Sancho Panza and Maritornes, executed by A. Bretschneider, advertising a festival in Leipzig in 1613 (Johannes

Hartau, *Don Quijote in der Kunst*, 14–17). For more information on carnival and theatrical representations of the characters, see Esther J. Crooks, *The Influence of Cervantes in France in the Seventeenth Century;* Edwin B. Knowles, "Cervantes and English Literature," 277–303; and Alberto Navarro, *El Quijote español del siglo XVII.*

2 "Grandes libros se han impreso, y dan cada día a la estampa en el mundo, de materias raras, singulares, y sublimes, así divinas, como profanas, de que no es menester hacer alarde a quien tanto ha visto, y leído como V.S. Entre todos este de DON QUIXOTE DE LA MANCHA, aunque menor en la sustancia, por ser una Novela de Caballerías, toda burla de las antiguas, y entretenimiento de las venideras, inventado solo para pasar tiempo en la ociosidad." (Juan Mommarte, Prefacio, in Cervantes, *Vida y hechos del Ingenioso Cavallero Don Quixote de la Mancha* [Brussels: Mommarte 1662], 3). I have chosen to modernize all quotes in Spanish.

3 Knowles, "Cervantes and English Literature," 281.

4 Peter Stallybrass and Allon White, *The Politics and Poetics of Transgression*, 98.

5 "Pero en esta pequeñez ha adquirido tanta grandeza en el mundo, como publica la de su artificio, de todos alabado, y nunca suficientemente encarecido; su disposición en los discursos tan parecidos a la verdad, que supuesta ella, el mismo DON QUIXOTE leyéndolos se engolfara, y engolfado se engañara, y volviera a perder el juicio mejor que con los de Don Belianis de Gaula, Don Rogelio de Grecia, Don Splendian, etcétera" (Mommarte, Prefacio, 3–4).

6 "Y juntamente con tanta propriedad en las palabras, llenas de morales documentos, que a vuelta de estas burlas se han bebido muchos los desengaños, y entre la risa, aprendido a despreciar las presunciones y altiveces; con que su aplauso común, no sólo ha llegado a tener crédito entre la nación española, que como se precia de seria, también de bueno, y sazonado gusto; sino aún en las demás naciones extranjeras, de quienes también ha sido recibido con estimación, leído con aplauso, y celebrado con universal aclamación" (ibid., 4).

7 Jacques Heers, *Carnavales y fiestas de locos*, 14; Stallybrass and White, *The Politics and Poetics of Transgression*, 12–15.

8 Heers, *Carnavales y fiestas de locos*, 16.

9 "Por lo cual sea dilatado tanto, como pueden decir sus repetidas impresiones; pues me parece (y es la verdad) que no se ha visto libro que mas veces haya sudado en la estampa, haya ocupado oficiales, ni haya dado de comer a mas Libreros; bastante prueba de que supo su autor darle el último punto de la sazón para sabios e ignorantes; pequeños y grandes; mozos y viejos; estudiantes y soldados; guisando este plato al sabor del paladar de cada uno, de donde ha aspirado a mayor grandeza." (Mommarte, Prefacio, 4–5).

10 Mikhail Bakhtin, *Rabelais and His World*, 11. Manuel Durán notes that, for the study of *Don Quixote*, "the great merit of Bakhtin consists in having signalled the internal thread that unites the beads in the necklace: the orgy, the contest, disguises, schatology, madness" / "el gran mérito de Bakhtine consiste en haber señalado el hilo interno que une las cuentas del collar: la orgía, el desafío, los disfraces, la escatología, la locura" ("El Quijote a través del prisma de Mikhail Bakhtine," 74).

11 Bakhtin, *Rabelais and His World*, 12.

12 Ibid., 20.

13 Heers, *Carnavales y fiestas de locos*, 210.

14 Ibid., 203.

15 "Pues viéndose entre los vestidos y armas cortadas, y tejidas en los reinos de España de tanto metal y papel, se ha venido a estos estados a buscar nuevas aventuras, para poder decir, que este libro, como caballero andante y soldado aventurero, también ha pasado por los bancos de Flandes" (Mommarte, "Prefacio," 5).

16 Crooks, *The Influence of Cervantes in France in the Seventeenth Century*, 36.

17 Manuel García Martín, *Cervantes y la comedia española en el siglo XVII*, 56. Addison offers an alternative neoclassical analysis of the burlesque: "The two great branches of Ridicule in writing are Comedy and Burlesque. The first ridicules persons by drawing them in their proper characters; the other by drawing them quite unlike themselves. Burlesque is therefore of two kinds; the first represents mean persons in accountrements [sic] of Heroes, the other describes great persons acting and speaking like the basest among the people. *Don Quixote* is an instance of the first, and *Lucian's* gods of the second" (*Spectator*, no. 249, in *Works* [London 1721], 3:245, qtd in Paolo Cherchi, *Capitoli di critica cervantina (1605–1789)*, 23–4). Thus, Addison sees Don Quixote as a mock-hero and the work as mock-heroic.

18 Heers, *Fiestas y carnavales de locos*, 210.

19 According to Chartier, the urban illiterate had access to printed material via the readings aloud that took place in workshops, religious and fraternal organizations, and the carnival into the eighteenth century in France (*The Cultural Uses of Print in Early Modern France*, 152–8).

20 The illustrations to the 1657 Dordrecht edition have been attributed to Jacobus Savery by some bibliographers. Gaspar Bouttats appears to have copied these illustrations and then designed his own for the 1662 Antwerp edition. Because Bouttats' plates were reprinted and disseminated more widely, and because attribution of the 1657 illustrations to Savery is somewhat problematic, I will refer to the series as Bouttats' illustrations. For a list of French editions bearing these illustrations by Bouttats or based on his work, see Crooks, *The Influence of Cervantes*, 20.

21 In his *Lectures on Don Quixote* Vladimir Nabokov expresses the best-known objections to the violence, but he is certainly not alone. For example, Arnold Hauser comments on the cruelty of the novel in the same breath that he cites the cruelty of *Gulliver's Travels* and other books that formulate the basis of civilized behaviour on social conditions (*The Social History of Art*, 3:49). Hauser's understanding of the cruelty helps to contextualize its use in the eighteenth century to express through negative example the bourgeois interest in establishing another code of civility based on manners and sentiment. The sentimental distaste for violence also inverts the reading of *Don Quixote* by swaying sympathy towards the beaten protagonist.

22 García Martín, *Cervantes y la comedia española en el siglo XVII*, 53; Crooks, *The Influence of Cervantes*, 44.

23 Even Jean Mosnier's wall paintings for the Château de Cheverny commissioned by Marie de Medici (1625) depict Don Quixote as a doll thrown about in battles, revealing the popularity of the burlesque reading in the court (see Maurice Bardon, *Don Quichotte en France au XVIIe et au XVIIIe siècle (1618–1815)*, 57–60).

24 Bakhtin, *Rabelais and His World*, 275.

25 Ibid., 198.

26 Heers, *Carnavales y fiestas de locos*, 123–4.

27 Cervantes, *Don Quixote de la Mancha* (Brussels 1662), 2:fp89. The similarities between this episode and Calderon's *Mojiganga de las visiones de la muerte / The Visions of Death* are telling. The short burlesque skit pokes fun at a traveller who mistakes a theatrical troupe, composed of Death, a jester, et al., for the real thing and suffers the consequences of his inability to distinguish fact from fiction. In particular the *mojiganga*, like the illustration, repeatedly breaks the theatrical frame through a metatheatrical parody of the conventions of the *auto sacramental*, the short religious plays celebrating the Eucharist performed by just such troupes. Perhaps, in an epoch distinguished by the increased production of imagery, both in theatre and in books, it was necessary to educate the people concerning the boundary between fiction and fact. Margaret Rich Greer points out that in seventeenth-century theatre, "a frequent source of humor, both on stage and in other literary genres, is laughter at the expense of innocents who do not possess the required competence to separate theatrical performance from lived experience" ("La vida es sueño – ¿o risa?: Calderón Parodies the *Auto*," 3).

28 Heers, *Fiestas y carnavales de locos*, 133.

29 Bakhtin, *Rabelais and His World*, 266.

30 Crooks, *The Influence of Cervantes*, 132.

31 Bakhtin, *Rabelais and His World*, 267.

32 Stallybrass and White, *The Politics and Poetics of Transgression*, 23.

33 Cervantes, *Vida y hechos del ingenioso Cavallero Don Quixote de la Mancha* (Madrid: Andrés García de la Iglesia 1674), 107.

34 Hartau, *Don Quijote in der Kunst*, 210.

35 Cervantes, *Don Kichote de la Mantscha, Das Ist* (Frankfurt am Main: In Verlegung Thomas Matthiae Gotzen 1669), fp 295.

36 Cervantes, *Vida y hechos del ingenioso Cavallero Don Quixote de la Mancha* (Madrid: Antonio Sanz 1735), 105.

37 Bakhtin, *Rabelais and His World*, 173.

38 Ibid., 22.

39 Cervantes, *Don Quixote de la Mancha* (1673), 1:fp518.

40 Alberto Navarro, *El Quijote español del siglo XVII*, 270.

41 Knowles, "Cervantes and English Literature," 280. Concerning the derisive attitude towards Don Quixote's supposed chastity, see the following quote from Ward's play (1711): "The *Don* in this abstemious life, / Without a mistress or a

wife, / Except the keeper of his house, / Supply'd the office of a spouse, / And when she tucked him in at night / Received the nipple of delight" (qtd in Knowles, 286; original emphasis).

42 Cervantes, *Don Quixote de la Mancha* (1673), 2:fp424.

43 Cervantes, *Don Quixote de la Mancha* (Brussels 1662), 1:fp133.

44 Several critics maintain that sixteenth-century readers of the romances of chivalry came largely from the middle and upper classes; see Maxime Chevalier, *Lectura y lectores en la España de los siglos XVI y XVII*, and Daniel Eisenberg, *Romances of Chivalry in the Spanish Golden Age*, 110. None the less, as evidenced in Heer's study, *Fiestas y carnavales de locos*, the lower classes would have been familiar with many of the characters and rituals of chivalric literature through their representation in popular spectacles.

45 Bardon, *Don Quichotte en France*, 496.

46 Cervantes, *The History of the valorous and witty Knight-Errant Don Quixote de la Mancha* (London: Knaplock 1731), 1:fp15.

47 Hauser, *The Social History of Art*, 3:15.

48 I disagree with Hartau's judgment of Coypel that "Love and Sympathy, which the Knight in spite of or because of his laughableness experiences, are the central themes" / "Liebe und Sympathie, die der Ritter trotz oder wegen seiner Lächerlichkeit erfährt, sind das zentrale Thema" (*Don Quijote in der Kunst*, 45). As I will argue in this chapter, Coypel's images illustrate the incorporation of burlesque laughter into a socially superior smirk.

49 For a discussion of Coypel's theater, see I. Jamieson, *Charles Antoine Coypel Premier Peintre de Louis XV et Auteur Dramatique (1694–1752)*.

50 "Tout contribue dans les spectacles à l'instruction du peintre": Antoine Coypel, "Sur l'Esthetique du peintre," in Henry Jouin, ed., *Conférences de l'Académie Royale de Peinture et de Sculpture* (Paris 1883), 350, qtd in Michael Fried, *Absorption and Theatricality: Painting and Beholder in the Age of Diderot*, 79.

51 "Aristotle said that tragedy is an imitation of an action, and subsequently it is principally an imitation of persons who act. What the philosopher said of tragedy applies equally well to painting, which should through action and gestures express everything pertaining to the subject it represents" / "Aristote dit que la tragédie est une imitation d'une action, et par conséquent elle est principalement une imitation de personnes qui agissent. Ce que ce philosophe dit de la tragédie convient également à la peinture, que doit par l'action et par les gestes exprimer tout ce que est du sujet qu'elle représente" (Antoine Coypel, *Conférences*, 351, qtd in Fried, *Absorption and Theatricality*, 76–7).

52 Antoine Schnapper, "A Propos de deux nouvelles acquisitions," 262.

53 Cervantes, *Don Quixote de la Mancha* (1731), 3:fp264.

54 Heers, *Fiestas y carnavales de locos*, 135–6.

55 Cervantes, *Don Quixote de la Mancha* (1731), 3:fp235.

56 Hauser, *The Social History of Art*, 3:3, 31–5.

57 According to Chartier, the chivalric romances enjoyed a new vogue in France during the seventeenth and eighteenth centuries among the readers of Nicholas

Oudet's *livrets bleus*, blue booklets (*The Cultural Uses of Print in Early Modern France*, 170–1).

58 Cervantes, *Den Verstandigen Vroomen Ridder, Don Quichot de la Mancha*, (Dordrecht: Kasteel van Gent 1657).

59 Stallybrass and White, *The Politics and Poetics of Transgression*, 21–2.

60 Cervantes, *Don Quixote de la Mancha* (1731), 1:fp8.

61 For the complete quotation, see chap. 3, n 67.

62 For a discussion of the Platonic mistrust of literature's power to delude through mimesis and its impact on early modern thinkers, particularly those of Spain, see B.W. Ife, *Reading and Fiction in Golden-Age Spain: A Platonist Critique and Some Picaresque Replies*, 24–83.

63 Cervantes, *Don Quixote de la Mancha* (1731), 4:fp253.

64 "Transporté comme j'étois, & plus Don Quichote que Don Quichote même." The rest of the quote reads as follows: "I saw two merchants coming, that I took for two knights. They carried sticks that looked to me like lances, and turned-down hats like those of My Lord Townsend, which passed in my mind for helmets with visors. This equipment, which seemed to me a true apparatus of war, did not let me doubt about combat: and with this thought I cried three times, 'Friend Sancho, saddle Rocinante and ready your ass'" / "[J]e vis venir deux Marchands, que je pris aussi-tôt pour deux Chevaliers. Ils avoient des Bâtons que me parurent des Lances, & des Bonnets rabattus comme celui de Mylord Townsend, que passerent dans mon esprit pour des Casques dont la Visiere étoit abaissée. Cet équipage que me sembloit un vrai appareil du Guerre, ne me laissa pas douter du combat: & dans cette pensée je criai trois fois, 'Ami Sancho, selle Rossinante & accommode le Grison'" (St Evremond, *Œuvres* [London 1709], 2:343–4, qtd in Crooks, *The Influence of Cervantes*, 40).

65 Jürgen Habermas, *The Structural Transformation of the Public Sphere*, 27.

CHAPTER THREE

1 This edition, *Vida y hechos del ingenioso caballero Don Quixote de la Mancha* (London: J.R. Tonson 1738) will be referred to as the 1738 Lord Carteret edition, so called after the English nobleman who commissioned its production. It includes the "Advertencias de D. Juan Oldfield Doctor en Medicina sobre las Estampas desta Historia," the "Vida de Miguel de Cervantes Saavedra por D. Gregorio Mayans i Siscar," and illustrations designed by William Kent and John Vanderbank. Tonson himself was a book publisher renowned for his editions of writers such as Shakespeare and Racine. For more information on Tonson, see T.S.R. Boase, "Illustrators of Shakespeare," and Gary Taylor, *Reinventing Shakespeare*, 52–75.

2 Roger Chartier has charted the development of two distinct reading publics, one elite and the other popular, whose existence was evidenced by and even partially created by two different categories of books. "We can see traces, then, of an opposition, which was to prove lasting, between two sorts of texts: those that provided food for thought for the wealthiest or the best-educated members of

society and those that fed the curiosities of the common people. Even though these two sets of works did not have two radically different publics in the seventeenth century – as we have seen, there were many occasions for shared reading – it nevertheless remains true that they characterize two sorts of material that the printers published, aimed at clienteles, circulations, and uses that were not the same. These contrasting intentions can be read in the material aspect of the book. For one group the book is a noble object, well-made, leatherbound, and to be carefully preserved; for the other, it is an ephemeral and roughly made thing. By its form and by its text, the book became a sign of distinction and a bearer of a cultural identity" (*The Cultural Uses of Print in Early Modern France*, 181).

3 According to Frank Kermode, there are "two ways of maintaining a classic, of establishing its access to a modern mind. The first of these depends on philology and historiography – it asks what the classic *meant* to its author and his best readers, and may still mean to those who have the necessary knowledge and skill. The second is the method of accommodation, by which I mean any method by which the old document may be induced to signify what it cannot be said to have expressly stated. The chief instrument of accommodation is allegory, if we use the word in a sense wide enough to include prophecy" (*The Classic*, 40). The method of accommodation is, of course, the recourse used more often by the persons discussed in this study.

4 The Spanish reads thus: "la fábula más agradable y discreta que se había escrito en el mundo" (Martín Fernández de Navarrete, *Vida de Miguel de Cervantes Saavedra*, 204).

5 For a discussion of Cervantes' own questioning of the precepts of Renaissance classicism, see Alban Forcione, *Cervantes, Aristotle, and Persiles*, 343.

6 The defence of their culture from the ravages of imperial decadence was an overriding concern to almost all Spanish eighteenth-century writers and intellectuals. In the case of Mayans y Siscar, Jesús Pérez Magallón argues that this decadence provided the very basis for his work. "All Mayans' intellectual labor starts from one unquestionable fact: the lamentable state into which Spanish culture has fallen, an inevitable consequence of the general collapse of the society, with all the reservations with which such sweeping assertions must be qualified" / "Toda la labor intelectual de Mayans parte de una evidencia incuestionable: el lamentable estado en que ha caído la cultura española, consecuencia inevitable del hundimiento general de la sociedad, con todas las matizaciones que a dichas afirmaciones pueden señalarse" (*En torno a las ideas literarias de Mayans*, 49). Russell Sebold has argued that the decadence actually took place in the last part of the seventeenth century and that the flurry of activity characterizing Mayans' time is evidence of cultural renewal (*Descubrimiento y fronteras del neoclasicismo español*, 28–31). For historical accounts of the political and economic decay of eighteenth-century Spain, see Jean Sarrailh, *La España ilustrada de la segunda mitad del siglo XVIII*, and Richard Herr, *The Eighteenth-Century Revolution in Spain*.

7 Not only did Cervantes appear a national hero, as will be shown in this chapter, but his eighteenth-century champion Mayans y Siscar has appeared to be a hero of Spanish literature to his own twentieth-century biographers. Antonio Mestre writes, "Mayans' *Life of Cervantes* was more than a simple literary history. It constituted an acerbic censure of the 'Frenchifying' of Spanish culture, of the predominance of the essay and the superficiality of our letters" / "La *Vida de Cervantes* mayansiana era algo más que una simple historia literaria. Constituía una ácida censura del afrancesamiento cultural español, del predominio del ensayo y de la superficialidad de nuestras letras" (*Mayans y la España de la ilustración*, 74).

8 The emergence of a new type of reader, leisurely rather than professional, has been noted by many critics of the eighteenth century. Roger Chartier has observed that in France the majority of these book-owners would have come from "families of robes," the professional classes rather than the families of military titles (*The Cultural Uses of Print in Early Modern France*, 192). Ian Watt characterizes these English readers as urban businessmen and the female members of their families (*The Rise of the Novel: Studies in Defoe, Richardson and Fielding*, 35–49). Jürgen Habermas also views these readers as bourgeois individuals who sought in literature the intimacy of the new private sphere of the bourgeois self and home (*The Structural Transformation of the Public Sphere*, 50–1).

9 For Habermas, the coffee shop, salon, and newspaper provided spaces for public debate between private readers of literature, all meeting as equals (although all sufficiently comfortable to belong to the new middle class), thus contributing to the construction of the new public sphere (ibid., 32–6). Even more public spaces such as public libraries and *chambres de lecture*, which required nothing more than that the reader possess a few *sous*, appeared after 1750 (Chartier, *The Cultural Uses of Print in Early Modern France*, 209–15).

10 Chartier discusses the attempt by various eighteenth-century intellectuals to prescribe an ideal, non-frivolous reader, engaged with the text in an actively critical manner and changed by its instruction (ibid., 224–5). The same exhortations towards salutory reading had appeared already early in the sixteenth century, and seem to represent a fear of the easy availability of texts to "naïve" readers, particularly women and persons of the lower class, made possible by the technology of printing (see B.W. Ife, *Reading and Fiction in Golden Age Spain: A Platonist Critique and Some Picaresque Replies*).

11 "Por la fertilidad de su ingenio produjo (aunque a lo burlesco) los más seriosos, útiles, y saludables efectos, que pudieran imaginarse" (Gregorio Mayans y Siscar, Dedicatory letter to the Countess of Montijo, in Cervantes, *Don Quixote de la Mancha* [1738], 1:iii).

12 The association of "obscure" Moorish ideas with the supposed backwardness of Spanish culture is not unique to Mayans. For example, in 1580 the Sevillian poet Francisco de Herrera referred to the "Dark Ages" of the Moorish epoch to account for Spain's belated adoption of Renaissance literary forms (Antonio Gallego Morell, *Garcilaso de la Vega y sus comentaristas*, 313).

13 "Se puede decir de él, sin tener recurso a su inimitable arte de ironía, que un pobre soldado viejo, manco, y encarcelado, fue el mayor instrumento para la expulsión de los moros de España, sin efusión de sangre, ruina de familias, ni inconveniente alguno, que de tal obra en las dos famosas expulsiones acaeció" (Mayans y Siscar, Dedicatory letter to the Countess de Montijo, 1:iii–iv).

14 "Sólo él fue capaz de desterrar las fantásticas y extravagantes ideas, que habían inficionado la del valor y trato civil; y si con verdad se pudiera decir, que él que encomienda el genio de una nación, y le da tales realces, hace más provecho a un reino que él que extiende sus límites" (ibid., 1:iv).

15 Jean H. Hagstrum, *The Sister Arts*, 191.

16 The English version of Oldfield's essay comes from an English edition of Cervantes' masterpiece, *The Life and Exploits of the ingenious gentleman Don Quixote de la Mancha*, trans. Charles Jarvis, Esq (London: Tonson 1742), 1:xxv–xxxiii. The essay is entitled "Advertencias de D. Juan Oldfield, Doctor en Medicina, Sobre las Estampas desta Historia" in the Lord Carteret edition.

17 Cervantes, *Don Quixote de la Mancha* (1780), 1: frontispiece. Mayans also referred to another seventeenth-century Spanish writer, Diego Saavedra Fajardo, as a "Celtic Hercules" in his defence of good literature in his *Oración en alabanza de las eloqüentíssimas obras de Don Diego Saavedra Fajardo*, 117–18). Hanns Hammelmann argues that an artist named Highmore drew from Vanderbank's image when he designed his own allegorical frontispiece for *Don Quixote* in Samuel Croxall's series *Select Collection of Novels and Histories* (1729), in which Apollo hands a laurel wreath to the triumphant Cervantes at the foot of Mount Parnassus ("Two Eighteenth-Century Frontispieces," 448–9). The figure of the author as Hercules, although so strange to a twentieth-century viewer, was clearly not unknown to an eighteenth-century one.

18 On the use of the satyr with a mask as an emblem for satire in book frontispieces, see Robert Halsband, *The "Rape of the Lock" and Its Illustrations 1714–1896*, 20.

19 Oldfield, "Advertisement concerning the Prints," 1:xxxii. The Spanish reads thus: "los instrumentos a propósito para lograr su fin; que fue ciertamente una graciosidad satírica, simbolizada aquí por la máscara, que es el don que le ofrece" (Oldfield, "Advertencias sobre las estampas," 1:ii).

20 Oldfield, "Advertisement concerning the Prints," 1:xxxi. "Propuso éste como blanco de su pluma, derribar de la común estimación de los españoles todas aquellas máquinas fantásticas de libros de caballerías, cuyos héroes, concebidos en unas imaginaciones fecundas sí, pero delirantes, llegaron a ser la idea del valor y trato civil; y quiso reestablecer al mismo tiempo la antigua, natural y propia manera de tratar los asuntos proporcionados a una decorosa ficción. Para poder representar todo esto por medio del diseño, el Monte Parnaso, asiento de las musas, el cual se ve en la estampa enseñoreado de monstruos y quimeras de libros de caballería, servirá para dar bastante idea del desordenado y extravagante estado del orbe literario en aquellos tiempos, y de la reforma de que tenía necesidad" (Oldfield, "Advertencias sobre las estampas," 1:i).

21 Cervantes, *Don Quixote de la Mancha* (1738), 1:np. Johannes Hartau dates this portrait to 1723, and claims that the Gothic hall through which Don Quixote and Sancho Panza ride is a reference to Queen Caroline's Merlin Grotto, a product of the Gothic revival initiated by William Kent (*Don Quijote in der Kunst*, 64–6). H.S. Ashbee has suggested that it was drawn by William Kent according to Cervantes' self-description (*Don Quixote and British Art*, 8).

22 Although a portrait of Cervantes painted by his contemporary Juan Jáuregui has been alleged to exist, there is no evidence that the painting in question is an original. Juan Givanel Mas and "Gaziel" (Agustín Calvet) even hint that the canvas in question may have been a copy of the Kent portrait (*Historia gráfica de Cervantes y del Quijote*, 28–32).

23 Cervantes' descriptions of the protagonists are scattered throughout the novel. Don Quixote is presented in general as a tall, attenuated type, whereas Sancho is a suitably corpulent and sturdy peasant. Sancho's name is, in fact, a pun, for Panza means "belly." Quixote, on the other hand, may be a form of *quijada*, which means "jaw bone." In both cases one can see how the author has used the names ironically to characterize the protagonists both physically and psychologically.

24 Françoise Etienvre, "De Mayáns a Capmany," 28. Nor did Ignacio de Luzán, the most important Spanish aesthetician of the century, deign to mention Cervantes in his *La poética*. He did mention the author in his *Memorias literarias de París* (1751), an attack on the vogue of French literature, but only once again to accuse Cervantes of having destroyed the literature of knight errantry to the detriment of the Spanish nation and literature (I.L. McClelland, *The Origins of the Romantic Movement in Spain*, 55).

25 The discussion of this debate over the relative literary worth of Cervantes' and Avellaneda's works owes much to Antonio Mestre's *El mundo intelectual de Mayans* and his prologue to the republication of Gregorio Mayans y Siscar's *Vida de Miguel de Cervantes Saavedra*, vii–xciii. For shorter discussions of the Avellaneda debate, see R. Merritt Cox, "Cervantes and Three *Ilustrados*," 12–20; and Vicent Peset, *Gregorio Mayàns i la cultura de la il.lustració*.

26 The French reads: "il en fait un Chevalier errant, qui est toujours grave, & dont toutes les paroles sont magnifiques, pompeuses & fleuries" (Alain-René Lesage, Préface to Alonso Fernández de Avellaneda, *Nouvelles aventures de l'admirable Don Quichotte de la Manche*, np).

27 "C'est un païsan qui a tout le bon sens de l'autre; mais il est encore plus simple" (ibid.).

28 "J'oublie que c'est Sancho qui parle; & je sens, malgré moy, que c'est l'Auteur sous le nom de Sancho" (ibid.).

29 Etienvre, "De Mayáns a Capmany," 28.

30 Mestre, Prólogo, lx.

31 "En el de Cervantes no me parece fácil de conciliar la suma simpleza que descubre algunas veces, con la delicada picardía que usa en otras, y la particular discreción que manifiesta en muchas, a menos que no digamos que habla y obra

Sancho de cuando en cuando como el autor, en lugar de obrar y hablar éste siempre como Sancho" (Agustín Montiano y Luyando, "Aprobación," in Avellaneda, *Vida y hechos del ingenioso hidalgo Don Quixote de la Mancha*, 3:np).

32 "No faltarán hoy parciales de su dictamen, bien que por diferente causa como es, porque anda muy desvalido el buen gusto, y la ignorancia de bando mayor. Deben dar, no obstante, poco cuidado tales contrarios, siquiera por ser gentes que celebran sólo lo que les hace reír y no conocen dónde peca la demasiada graciosidad" (ibid.).

33 Paolo Cherchi writes: "quel particolare modo meccanico e dogmatico d'intendere il concetto di *mimesi*, soddisfatto più un grossolano realismo che da uno sfumato studio de caratteri, e isparato da una tendenza di gusto per il romanzo picaresco, quello stesso gusto che aveva portato Lesage a giustificare la sua preferenza" (*Capitoli di critica cervantina (1605–1789)*, 76).

34 Mestre, *El mundo intelectual de Mayans*, 133–4.

35 Mestre quotes a letter from José Octavio Bostanza, a mutual friend of Mayans and Keene, to the former. "Speaking of the *Life of Cervantes* Keene has told me that he would regret it if your very delicate taste wished to manifest itself in said work by criticizing (as you so eruditely would know how to do) the life of Don Quixote, for Lord Carteret, who values it greatly, would not appreciate the disillusionment, especially since *Don Quixote* is being published there at his expense and for his pleasure" / "Hablando de la *Vida de Cervantes* me ha dicho [Keene] que sentiría que el delicadísimo gusto de Vm. se quisiesse manifestar en dicha obra criticando (como doctamente supiera Vm. hacer) la vida de D. Quijote, y es que My Lord Carteret, que la aprecia infinitamente, no recibiera de buena gana el desengaño, y mas siendo a su costa y por su diversión el Quijote que allá se imprime" (Prólogo, xlii).

36 "In opposition to Montiano's 'no judicious man would sentence in favor of what Cervantes …' appears Mayáns' 'there is no man of good taste who appreciates' Avellaneda" / "Frente a 'ningún hombre juizioso sentenciará a favor de lo que Cervantes alega' de Montiano, aparece el 'no ai hombre de buen gusto que haga aprecio' de Avellaneda, según Mayans" (ibid., lxii).

37 Mayans' at times fiery debates with his Spanish colleagues have interested several critics. A. Morel-Fatio attributes at least part of the controversies to Mayans' extreme self-confidence ("Un erudit espagnol au XVIIIe siècle D. Gregorio Mayans y Siscar,": 177–8). For a description of Mayans' fierce participation in the controversy surrounding his *Orígenes de la lengua española*, see Jesús Castañón, *La crítica literaria en la prensa española del siglo XVIII (1700–1750)*, 69–74. Jesús Pérez Magallón attributes the scholar's isolation to his independence of thought (*En torno a las ideas literarias de Mayans*, 57), and his criticism of what he saw to be the three causes of Spain's decadence: the inadequate and antiquated educational system; the disregard for the nation's great authors from earlier ages; and the general ignorance of the people (ibid., 85–6).

38 "No falta quien crea haber perdido la juventud una enseñanza muy útil en los libros de caballerías (que son ya muy raros) por el heroicismo a que persuadían

la generosidad y valor que representaban con las fábulas bien imaginadas" (Anonymous, review of Avellaneda's and Cervantes' *Don Quixote de la Mancha*, in *El Diario de los Sabios*, 31 Mar. 1704, f 207).

39 For discussions of the conservative attack on Cervantes as a maligner of Spain and a traitor to the nation's military values, see Cherchi, *Capitoli di critica cervantina*, 95–113, and Francisco Aguilar Piñal, "Anverso y reverso del quijotismo en el siglo XVIII español," 30.

40 Etienvre, "De Mayáns a Capmany," 30.

41 Luis López Molina, "Una visión dieciochesca del Quijote," 105.

42 "Y quiso por medio de estas ocho comedias, y entremeses, como por otros tantos Don Quijotes y Sanchos, que desterraron los portentosos, y desatinados libros de caballerías, que trastornaban el juicio de muchos hombres: quiso, digo, con comedias enmendar los errores de la comedia, y purgar del mal gusto, y mala moral el teatro, volviendo a la razón, y a la autoridad, de que se había descartado, por complacer al ínfimo vulgo, sin tener respeto a lo restante, y más sano del pueblo" (Blas Antonio Nasarre, *Comedias y entremeses de Miguel de Cervantes Saavedra* [Madrid 1749], np).

43 For a discussion of the search for biographical details, such as Cervantes' birthplace, see Francisco Aguilar Piñal, "Cervantes en el siglo XVIII," 153–5.

44 The Spanish reads: "para encubrir de alguna manera con tan rico y vistoso ropaje, la pobreza y desnudez de aquella person dignísima de mejor siglo; porque, aunque dicen que la edad en que vivió era de oro; y yo sé, que para él y algunos otros beneméritos fue de hierro" (Gregorio Mayans y Siscar, Dedicatory letter to Lord Carteret, in Cervantes, *Don Quixote de la Mancha* [1738], 1:iv).

45 According to Cherchi, Mayans, like other *ilustrados*, would have counted Cervantes on his side against the conservative aristocracy. "They never identified with the foolish *hidalgo* who, in eighteenth-century Spain, was 'the ridiculously serious man, or deeply involved in what did not concern him,' according to the definition given in that year (1737) in the fifth volume of the *Dictionary of the Authorities*. Mayans and the *ilustrados* did identify with Cervantes!" / "Si identificarono mai con il folle *hidalgo* il quale, per la Spagna del Settecento, era "el hombre ridículamente serio, o empeñado en lo que no le toca," secondo la definizione che si dava quell-anno (1737) nel quinto tomo del Diccionario delle "autoridades": Mayáns e gli "ilustrados" si identificarono con Cervantes!" (*Capitoli di critica cervantina*, 95)

46 "V.E. le tiene tan justo de sus obras, que ha manifestado ser el más liberal mantenedor y propagador de su memoria; y es por quien *Cervantes* y su *Ingenioso Hidalgo* logran hoy el mayor aprecio y estimación. Salga pues nuevamente a la luz del mundo el Gran *Don Quijote de la Mancha*, si hasta hoy caballero desgraciadamente aventurero, en adelante por V.E. felizmente venturoso. Viva la memoria del incomparable *Miguel de Cervantes Saavedra*." (Gregorio Mayans y Siscar, Dedicatory letter to Lord Carteret, 1:v).

47 Mayans' biography of Cervantes became the standard source for other biographies throughout Europe until the end of the eighteenth century (Martín

Fernández de Navarette, *Vida de Miguel de Cervantes Saavedra, escrita e ilustrada con varias noticias y documentos inéditos pertenecientes a la historia y literatura de su tiempo* [Madrid: Real Academia Española 1819], 2–4).

48 Herder echoed this interpretation of the chivalric romances as barbaric in his essay "Romantic Characters" (1801), a judgment upon which he based his declaration that the individual must restrain his own will according to social limits (Lienhard Bergel, "Cervantes in Germany," in *Cervantes across the Centuries,* 324).

49 "El que más podía, más valía. Pudo más la barbarie, y salió vencedora y triunfante; quedaron abatidas las letras, perdido el conocimiento de la antigüedad, y aniquilado el buen gusto. Pero, como donde no se hallan estas cosas, la necesidad las echa menos; sucedieron en su lugar, la falsa doctrina y depravado gusto. Escribieron historias, que fueron fabulosas, porque se perdió, o no sabía buscarse la memoria de los sucesos pasados. Unos hombres que de repente querían ser los maestros de la vida, mal podían enseñar a los lectores lo que nunca habían aprendido. Tal fue Theletino Helio, escritor inglés, que cerca del año seiscientos cuarenta, reinando Artús en Bretaña, escribió los hechos de este rey fabulosamente" (Gregorio Mayans y Siscar, "Vida de Cervantes," in Cervantes, *Don Quixote de la Mancha* [1780], 1:10).

50 The confusion of history with fiction was also a concern to Cervantes' contemporaries. For a discussion of critical responses to the romance of chivalry, see Alban Forcione, *Cervantes, Aristotle, and the* Persiles, especially chap. 1. It is important to keep in mind Mayans' self-conscious appropriation of sixteenth-century Spanish writers as "an antidote against the cultural and linguistic decadence of the baroque writers" / "un antidoto alla decadenza culturale e linguistica degli scrittori barrochi" (Cherchi, *Capitoli di critica cervantina,* 79).

51 "Fuera de las letras divinas no hay qué afirmar, ni qué negar en ninguna de ellas" (Gregorio Mayans y Siscar, "Vida de Cervantes," in Cervantes, *Don Quixote de la Mancha* [1780], 1:13).

52 "Consideraba Cervantes que un clavo saca a otro; y que supuesta la inclinación de la mayor parte de los ociosos a semejantes libros, no era el medio mejor para apartarlos de tal lectura la fuerza de la razón, que sólo suele mover a los ánimos considerados, sino un libro de semejante inventiva y de honesto entretenimiento, que excediendo a todos los demás en lo deleitable de su lectura, atragesse a sí a todo género de gentes, discretos y tontos" (ibid., 1:17).

53 Those twentieth-century critics who have viewed the Canon's words as Cervantes' run the gamut from Américo Castro, in his early work *El pensamiento de Cervantes,* 49, 53, to his harsh critic and espouser of the "*Don Quixote* as funny book" argument, Anthony Close (see his *The Romantic Approach to Don Quixote,* 24). Recent narratological theory has, of course, thrown into question the belief that the words of a character express the author's ideas.

54 For a discussion of Spanish eighteenth-century theatre, see René Andioc, *Teatro y sociedad en el Madrid del siglo XVIII.* The taste for Golden Age plays and for neoclassical works was largely confined to the upper classes (24). The marvellous

appealed much more to the "clases populares" in "comedias de santos," "comedias de magia," and even works based on chivalric romances (94–102).

55 "Fuera de sus manías habla Don Quijote como hombre cuerdo, y son sus discursos muy conformes a razón. Son muy dignos de leerse lo que hizo sobre el Siglo de Oro, la primera edad del mundo, poéticamente descrita; sobre la manera de vivir de los estudiantes y soldados; sobre las distinciones que hay de caballeros y linajes; sobre el uso de la poesía; y las dos instrucciones, una política y otra económica, las cuales dio a Sancho Panza, cuando iba a ser gobernador de la ínsula Barataria, son tales, que se pueden dar a los gobernadores verdaderos; y ciertamente deben ponerlas en práctica" (Gregorio Mayans y Siscar, "Vida de Cervantes," in Cervantes, *Don Quixote de la Mancha* [1780], 1:19–20).

56 "¡Admirable crítica! Uno de los preceptos de la fábula es, o seguir la fama, o fingir las cosas de manera que convengan entre sí. Cervantes había figurado a Don Quijote como caballero andante, valiente, discreto y enamorado; y esa fama tenía cuando el llamado Fernández de Avellaneda se puso a continuar su historia; y en ella le pinta cobarde, necio y desamorado … Cervantes ideó a Sancho Panza simple, gracioso, y no comedor, ni borracho: Fernández de Avellaneda, simple sí, pero no nada gracioso, comedor y borracho. Y así ni siguió la fama, ni fingió con uniformidad" (ibid., 1:49).

57 See especially Peter Russell, "*Don Quijote* as a Funny Book," 312–26.

58 "Las estampas son admirables, ahora se atienda la elección de los asuntos, ahora la egecución del buril. Sólo puede notarse lo que ya V.Ex. con tanto juicio me tiene advertido, que tal vez se falte al decoro de la nación en la alusión a los trages … Pero éstas son cosas que deven dissimularse a vista de tanta perfección en todo lo demás" (qtd in Mestre, Prólogo, XLV).

59 For more information on John Vanderbank (1694–1739), see Hanns Hammelmann's article "John Vanderbank's *Don Quixote*," 3–15. Vanderbank completed his drawings for these illustrations by 1729 at the latest, although the publication of the edition was delayed almost a decade on account of Mayans' tardiness in completing his biography of Cervantes (ibid., 13). According to Hartau, the illustrations may have been begun as early as 1723 (*Don Quijote in der Kunst*, 66).

60 Kenneth Clark, *The Nude: A Study in Ideal Form*, 98–101.

61 Hammelmann, "John Vanderbank's *Don Quixote*," 7.

62 Lawrence Lipking, *The Ordering of the Arts in Eighteenth-Century England*, 113.

63 Ibid., 118.

64 Hartau, *Don Quijote in der Kunst*, 79.

65 Oldfield, "Advertisement concerning the Prints," 1:xxxi.

66 "Uno y otro ejecutó nuestro autor con feliz acierto, pues venció, desbarató y acabó toda la caterva de caballeros andantes y de sus encantadores, procurando vencerlos con sus propias fuerzas, quiero decir, figurando un héroe igualmente fantástico, pero de invención tan decorosa, que desbaratados y deshechos ellos, quedasse como perpetuo triunfo, erigido en memoria de tan gloriosa hazaña" (Oldfield, "Advertencia sobre las estampas," 1:i).

67 Oldfield, "Advertisement concerning the Prints," 1:xxvi. The Spanish reads that the illustration of these episodes "no hace en efecto otra cosa sino señalar a la vista su falsedad, y aplicar aquella misma ridiculez a las acciones de nuestro caballero, la cual intentaba el autor que se aplicasse por medio de aquellas a las acciones de otros antiguos campeones, amplificando y exagerando su extravagancia e imposibilidad" ("Advertencias sobre las estampas," 1:iv).

68 Lipking, *The Ordering of the Arts*, 116.

69 Oldfield, "Advertisement concerning the Prints," 1:xxvi. "Esta solemne acción, o la de conducirla hacia la cama, que es la introducción, o parte de esta acción quizás, da una imagen más entretenida, que otra cualquiera en toda la historia: por cuyo motivo parece que le señaló como tal el mismo autor para este fin, según lo que dice en la cláusula inmediata, donde se halla este gracioso chiste. 'Aquí hace Cide Hamete un paréntesis y dice, que por Mahoma que diera (por ver ir a los dos así asidos, y trabados desde la puerta al lecho) la mejor almalafa de dos que tenía' ("Advertencia sobre las estampas," 1:viii).

70 For a discussion of irony and play on authority in *Don Quixote*, particularly with regard to the establishment and undercutting of authority resulting from print, see chap. 1.

71 Oldfield, "Advertisement concerning the Prints," 1:xxvii. "Acostumbrado pues Don Quixote a semejantes credulidades, se persuadió la ficción, bajó a la cueva, y hallándose impresionado de las exhalaciones de ella; vió y exploró (en su imaginación) todas las particularidades de que deseaba informarse" ("Advertencia sobre las estampas," 1:v).

72 Oldfield, "Advertisement concerning the Prints," 1:xxvii; original emphasis. "Todo el asunto quedará historiado suficientemente, por medio de un dibujo de él (como se ha ejecutado en la estampa) puesto en la concavidad de la cueva, de manera que se vea por la boca de ella. De semejante artificio suelen servirse hartas veces los pintores y abridores de láminas, de cuyos ejemplares vemos uno en cierta estampa de Rembrandt donde él refiere la historia que un astrólogo está contando a un amigo suyo; y para esto se vale de un ligerito dibujo puesto sobre la pared de su aposento. Este mismo método siguió Rafael en una pintura suya, donde representó el sueño de Faraón" ("Advertencia sobre las estampas," 1:v).

73 Hammelmann, "John Vanderbank's *Don Quixote*," 7.

74 In the words of Don Quixote, "Know that here in your presence – you have but to open your eyes and you will see him – is that great knight of whom the wise Merlin prophesied so many things, I mean the famous Don Quixote de la Mancha, who once again and to better advantage than in past ages has undertaken to revive in this present age the long-forgotten profession of knight-errantry. It may be that, thanks to his favor and mediation, we shall be disenchanted; for great exploits are reserved for great men" (Cervantes, *The Ingenious Gentleman Don Quixote de la Mancha*, trans. Samuel Putnam, 2:660) / "Sabed que tenéis aquí en vuestra presencia, y abrid los ojos y veréislo, aquel gran caballero, de quien tantas cosas tiene profetizadas el Sabio Merlín: aquel Don Quijote de la Mancha, digo, que de nuevo, y con mayores ventajas que en los pasados siglos, ha resucitado en

los presentes la ya olvidada andante caballería, por cuyo medio y favor podría ser, que nosotros fuésemos desencantados; que las grandes hazañas para los grandes hombres están guardadas" (Cervantes, *El ingenioso hidalgo Don Quijote de la Mancha*, ed. Martín de Riquer, 2:706–7).

75 Oldfield, "Advertisement concerning the Prints," I:xxvi. The Spanish reads: "las cuales aventuras, aunque son muy deleitosas en las descripciones que el autor hizo de ellas, en cuanto sirven para hacer entender las impresiones que causan los libros de caballerías, en las imaginaciones de los muy dados a su lectura; eso no obstante cuando se exponen a la vista, causan demasiada extrañeza, para que se les dé crédito" ("Advertencias sobre las estampas," I:iii).

76 In his influential work *Laokoon* (1766) Gotthold Ephraim Lessing makes the deceptively self-evident assertion that literature is a temporal art, because narratives take place through time, and that painting is a spatial art, because visual composition arranges objects in space. As Hagstrum notes, Lessing was writing against "a condition in the arts in which painting had become excessively literary and poetry excessively pictorial. The plastic arts, he believed, were intended to express only the beauty of physical form and not the meanings of the mind and the emotions of the heart" (*The Sister Arts*, 155). Lessing's censure of visual narrative and insistence upon the purity of medium has dominated the values of later aestheticians and artists, particularly in the emptying of content from painting by modernists. W.J.T. Mitchell remarks that Lessing "rationalizes a fear of imagery that can be found in every major philosopher from Bacon to Kant to Wittgenstein, a fear not just of the 'idols' of pagan primitives, or of the vulgar marketplace, but of the idols which insinuate themselves into language and thought, the false models which mystify both perception and representation" (*Iconology: Image, Text, Ideology*, 113).

77 Oldfield, "Advertisement concerning the Prints," I:xxvi. "Esto mismo vemos que suele suceder fuera del suceso que tratamos, y particularmente en las representaciones dramáticas, donde muchos asuntos que son muy propios de una muy alta y perfecta narración, no conviene que se manifiesten a los ojos, y que la vista se haga el juez inmediato" ("Advertencia sobre las estampas," I:iii).

78 Oldfield, "Advertisement concerning the Prints," I:xxv. The Spanish reads, "y unicamente sirven de divertimiento a los que se pagan de soltar galanuras" ("Advertencia sobre las estampas," I:ii).

79 Oldfield, "Advertisements concerning the Prints," I:xxv. The Spanish text says, "otro fin mas elevado, representando y dando luz a muchas cosas, las cuales por medio de las palabras no se pueden expresar tan perfectamente" ("Advertencia sobre las estampas," I:ii).

80 Oldfield, "Advertisement concerning the Prints," I:xxv. "Y así, como se hallan particularmente en los autores de esta clase, muchísimos casos, donde la fantasía del lector le guía a idearse el modo con que las pasiones y aficiones del alma se manifiestan a la vista en cierta coyuntura; y a figurarse la apariencia de ellas con los semblantes y ademanes de las personas de que se trata; así en tales circunstancias un perito artista que conoce las impresiones que los internos movimientos

del alma deben causar en el semblante y compostura exterior de la persona; el artista, digo, que se anima a representar estos varios efectos valiéndose de la expresión del buril, podrá fácilmente suministrar lo que necesita la imperfecta imaginación de él que lee, y todo aquello que se podría echar [de] menos en la descripción del autor: la cual en muchos casos no puede dejar de ser fastidiosa, y por eso desagradable" ("Advertencia sobre las estampas," 1:ii–iii).

81 Oldfield, "Advertisement concerning the Prints," 1:xxv. "Por la introducción … de personajes en la escena con la apostura y acciones más apropiadas, puede en cierta manera una escrita narración lograr las ventajas de una representación dramática" (Oldfield, "Advertencia sobre las estampas," 1:iii).

82 Oldfield, "Advertisement concerning the Prints," xxvii. The Spanish text reads, "fijado por el teatro de la acción" ("Advertencia sobre las estampas," 1:v).

83 Chartier, *The Uses of Print in Early Modern France*, 228.

84 The Spanish reads, "capaz de desterrar las fántasticas y extravagantes ideas, que habían inficionado la del valor y trato civil" (Mayans y Siscar, Dedicatory letter to the Countess of Montijo, 1:iii).

85 "Mas si los libros de humor han de ser acompañados para aficionar a los ojos, las advertencias podrán dar algunos indicios para mejorarlos en lo venidero" (ibid., 1:ii).

86 Etienvre, "De Mayáns a Capmany," 30.

87 R.M. Flores, *Sancho Panza through Three Hundred Seventy-Five Years of Continuations, Imitations, and Criticism, 1605–1980*, 47.

88 Oldfield, "Advertisement concerning the Prints," 1:xxvii. "El uno de los oyentes, a quienes hizo Don Quixote una seria y exacta relación de todo lo que le suministró su engañada y engañosa fantasía, creyó cuanto oyó; pero el otro que sabía muy bien, que él mismo era el que había fingido el encanto de Dulcinea, no pudo dejar de concebir algunos escrúpulos poco favorables a la veracidad de su amo: bien que le importaba callar el oculto motivo de ellos" (Oldfield, "Advertencias sobre las estampas," 1:v).

89 Flores, *Sancho Panza through Three Hundred Seventy-Five Years*, 22.

90 Cervantes, *Don Quixote de la Mancha* (1949), 2:950–1. "Y así, [Don Quijote] procuraba y pugnaba por desenlazarle, viendo lo cual Sancho Panza, se puso en pie, y arremetiendo a su amo, se abrazó con él a brazo partido, y echándole una zancadilla, dio con él en el suelo boca arriba; púsole la rodilla derecha sobre el pecho y con las manos le tenía las manos, de modo que ni le dejaba rodear ni alentar. Don Quijote le decía: – ¿Cómo, traidor? ¿Contra tu amo y señor natural te desmandas? ¿Con quién te da su pan te atreves? – Ni quito rey, ni pongo rey – respondió Sancho – , sino ayúdome a mí, que soy mi señor" (Cervantes, *Don Quijote de la Mancha* [1979], 2:973).

91 Cervantes, *Don Quixote de la Mancha* (1949), 2:971. "Acudió don Quijote luego al son de la lastimada voz y del golpe del riguroso azote, y asiendo del torcido cabestro que le servía de corbacho a Sancho, le dijo: – No permita la suerte, Sancho amigo, que por el gusto mío pierdas tú la vida, que ha de servir para sustentar a tu mujer y a tus hijos" (Cervantes, *Don Quijote de la Mancha* [1979], 2:1050).

92 Habermas, *The Structural Transformation of the Public Sphere*, 30.

93 Ibid., 50.

94 Chartier, *The Cultural Uses of Print in Early Modern France*, 253–5.

95 "Es la lectura de los libros malos una de las cosas que corrompen más las costumbres, y de todo punto destruyen las repúblicas. Y, si tanto daño causan los libros, que solamente refieren los malos ejemplos, ¿qué no harán los que se fingen de propósito para introducir en los ánimos incautos el veneno almibarado con la dulzura del estilo?" (Mayans y Siscar, "Vida de Cervantes," in *Don Quixote de la Mancha* [1738], 1:9).

96 "Si en esa mano diestra, fina y ahusada, que descansa sobre el libro abierto, le ponemos nada más que una pluma de ave, como las empleadas en aquellos tiempos, tendremos una imagen perfecta de algún escritor celebérrimo" (Givanel Mas and "Gaziel," *Historia gráfica de Cervantes y del Quijote*, 130).

97 The German reads, "überraschenderweise gewisse Àhnlichkeiten mit der von Kent entworfenen Shakespeare-Statue in Westminster Abbey auf" (Hartau, *Don Quijote in der Kunst*, 66).

98 Hartau considers this edition a turning-point in the reception of *Don Quixote* because it demonstrates the turn away from a caricatured Don Quixote, "against Hogarth" / "gegen Hogarth," and towards a "lovable" hero. "No more is the distorted caricature sought, but rather the reproduction of behaviour that is transferable to every man. Vanderbank's Don Quixote wins through costumes from Rubens, a classical face and heroic gestures a heroic appearance, and can sometimes pass for a true hero" / "Nicht mehr die verzerrende Karikierung wird gesucht, sondern de Wiedergabe eines Verhaltens, das auf jedermann übertragbar ist. Vanderbanks Don Quijote gewinnt durch Rubens-Kostüme, klassische Gebärde und heroische Geste ein heroisches Aussehen und kann zuweilen als wirklicher Held gelten" (ibid., 80). Whereas I agree with his characterization of Vanderbank's sentimental vision of Don Quixote, I disagree strongly with his assertion that the caricatural is overcome. In the following chapters I will discuss the coexistence of an elevated, sentimentalizing vision and a humorous, caricatural one.

99 "Vanderbanks Interpretation der Don Quijote-Figur betonte … die heroische Seite und die >>solemnity<<. In einer Skizze … , die von Horace Walpole als >>ideal study for the portrait of Don Quijote<< bezeichnet wird, ist der >>Hero of La Mancha<< nicht mehr von einem römischen Krieger zu unterscheiden"(ibid., 80).

100 Eric J. Ziolkowski, *The Sanctification of Don Quixote: From Hidalgo to Priest*, 54–61, 84–7.

101 Anthony Ashley Cooper, Third Earl of Shaftesbury, *An Inquiry concerning Virtue, or Merit*, 19; original spelling.

102 Theodor W. Adorno and Max Horkheimer, *Dialectic of Enlightenment*, 57.

CHAPTER FOUR

1 Peter Anthony Motteux, "Translator's Preface," in Cervantes, *The History of the Renoun'd Don Quixote de la Mancha* (London: 1700), np.

2 Paolo Cherchi observes that Motteux freed the interpretation of *Don Quixote* from the anti-Spanish discourse of the day (the Black Legend), set the work within a discourse of universals, and thus "prepared a meditation in psychological terms, disposed to capture the Cervantine *humor*, with a dolorousness unknown in French letters" / "ne preparava una meditazione in termini psicologici, disposta a cogliere l'*humour* cervantino, con una penosità sconosciuta ai lettori francesi" (*Capitoli di critica cervantina*, 23; original emphasis).

3 Jürgen Habermas, *The Structural Transformation of the Public Sphere*, 27.

4 Ibid., 85.

5 Ibid., 83; original emphasis.

6 Theodor W. Adorno and Max Horkheimer, *Dialectic of Enlightenment*, 31.

7 Habermas insists on the free discussion of cultural items produced for consumption as the quality that distinguishes his idealized notion of critical debate in the eighteenth century from the manipulation of public opinion in the twentieth century by the media. "Put bluntly: you had to pay for books, theater, concert, and museum, but not for the conversation about what you had read, heard, and seen and what you might completely absorb only through this conversation. Today the conversation itself is administered. Professional dialogues from the podium, panel discussions, and round table shows – the rational debate of private people becomes one of the production numbers of the stars in radio and television, a salable package ready for the box office; it assumes commodity form even at 'conferences' where anyone can 'participate'" (*The Structural Transformation of the Public Sphere*, 164). In contrast, one of the central assumptions of this study is that the de luxe eighteenth-century editions *do* package interpretation. To obscure this fact is to overlook the ways in which the print medium, in general valued by Habermas over newer technologies, can also be used to shape debate. The extent to which the packaged readings do not control private readings is hard to determine, but the continued changes in interpretation evident in the history of the reception of *Don Quixote* indicate that editorial control is not omnipotent.

8 For any discussion of the development of sentimental literature in eighteenth-century England and its relation to sociological, historical, and intellectual contexts, the followings works are fundamental: Ian Watt, *The Rise of the Novel*; R.F. Brissenden, *Virtue in Distress*; and John Mullan, *Sentiments and Sociability*.

9 Despite the different angle of their approaches, first the art historian Frederick Antal(*Hogarth and His Place in European Art*, 7–9), and then, twenty-five years later, the literary critic Robert Markley ("Sentimentality as Performance)," traced the parallel developments of sentimentalism and satire from Lord Shaftesbury's ideas on taste and virtue via their popularization among the middle-class reading public through Addison and Steele's journalistic essays and the literary and artistic works of Richardson, Fielding, Sterne, and Hogarth.

10 Ronald Paulson, *Book and Painting*, 17.

11 Ronald Paulson, *Hogarth: His Life, Art and Times*, 1:164–5.

12 Hanns Hammelmann, "John Vanderbank's *Don Quixote*," 13.

13 Edward Hodnett, *Image and Text*, 10.

14 Hildegard Omberg, *William Hogarth's Portrait of Captain Coram*, 19.

15 Jack Lindsay, *Hogarth*, 49.

16 Omberg, *William Hogarth's Portrait of Captain Coram*, 23.

17 Ibid., 23–4.

18 Jonathan Richardson, *The Theory of Painting* (1715), 73, qtd in Omberg, *William Hogarth's Portrait of Captain Coram*, 36.

19 Ronald Paulson, *Hogarth: The "Modern Moral Subject" 1697–1732*, 1:106.

20 John Dryden, *De arte graphica* (London 1695), xxviii, qtd in Omberg, *William Hogarth's Portrait of Captain Coram*, 35.

21 See chap. 2 for a discussion of the impact of the carnivalesque culture described by Mikhail Bakhtin (*Rabelais and His World*) on the seventeenth-century reception of *Don Quixote*. Unlike Peter Stallybrass and Allon White (*The Politics and Poetics of Transgression*, 84–7), I believe that the marketplace under attack by Dryden is not so much the old, popular marketplace, which, of course, left the upper class unchallenged, but rather the new capitalist marketplace, which created economic power among the new middle class.

22 Alvin Kernan, *Samuel Johnson and the Impact of Print*, 70.

23 For more information on *Don Quixote* as a literary model in eighteenth-century English authors, particularly for Henry Fielding, see William Leon Coburn's dissertation, "In Imitation of the Manner of Cervantes: Don Quixote and Joseph Andrews."

24 Ibid., 17.

25 Ibid.

26 Lindsay, *Hogarth*, 120.

27 Antal, *Hogarth and His Place in European Art*, 133.

28 Henry Fielding, *The History of the Adventures of Joseph Andrews and His Friend Mr. Abraham Adams*, xx.

29 Ibid., xxi.

30 Ibid.

31 Unlike Fielding, I define the burlesque as a genre existing in the visual arts as well as the literary. As seen in chap. 2, the burlesque arises from a popular interpretation of *Don Quixote*, which emphasizes the violent, physical nature of the humour and devalues characterization and didactic content. Caricature, by contrast, represents a visual genre that heightens and exaggerates characteristic idiosyncrasies, often grotesquely and with a didactic and/or satirical intention.

32 Fielding, *Joseph Andrews*, xxii.

33 The marked subjectivity of eighteenth-century sentimentalism and its influence on literature has been studied from various viewpoints. For its connection to a reading public composed of women, see Watt, *The Rise of the Novel*, 135–207. For its connection to the private bourgeois individual, see Habermas, *The Structural Transformation of the Public Sphere*, 46–51.

34 Fielding, *Joseph Andrews*, xxii–iii.

35 Ibid., xxiii.

36 Ibid., xxiv.

37 Fielding's reading of *Don Quixote* adopted a middle ground between the conservative reading of the work as an attack on Spain and the more progressive reading
of the work as a universal satire. He believed that Cervantes intended to improve
his country through satire (Edwin B. Knowles, "Cervantes and English Literature," 291), but also thought that all readers should sympathize with Don Quixote as a fellow madman. As he wrote in his own play *Don Quixote in England*:

> Since your madness is so plain,
>> Each spectator
>> Of good nature,
> With applause will entertain
> His brother of La Mancha; (ibid., 292)

If, as Eric Ziolkowski argues, Fielding viewed Don Quixote sympathetically as a
"good man" and a model of Christian virtue (*The Sanctification of Don Quixote*,
44), then his reading of the novel as expressed in *Joseph Andrews* differed sub-
stantially from Hogarth's satiric one. His earlier presentation of an overriding
satire that encompassed everyone in *Don Quixote in England* was much closer to
Hogarth's vision.

38 Lindsay, *Hogarth*, 35.

39 Paulson, *Book and Painting*, 16.

40 Lindsay, *Hogarth*, 249.

41 Paulson, *Hogarth: His Life, Art, and Times*, 1:147ff.

42 In his 1991 book *Hogarth: The "Modern Moral Subject" 1697–1732*, 1:107, Paulson
quotes from John Elsum, *The Art of Painting after the Italian Manner* (1703), 66,
138, in order to define history painting as the highest form of art. "As one critic
put it, 'History-Painting is that Concert, comprising all the other Parts of Painting, and the principal end of it is to move the Passions' – 'a Complication of all
other sorts of Painting,' story, figure painting, portraiture, landscape, and therefore obviously greater in the aggregate. It also stood higher on the absolute scale
of value: history painting showed man performing at his most heroic. Every
manual on painting worked up, chapter by chapter, to history. Descending on
this humanistically oriented scale, next came portraits, concerned with human
character; then lower down, landscape, sea pieces, animal pictures, fruit and
flower pieces, still lifes, and inanimate objects; and at the bottom 'drolls' and
grotesques, which showed man as less than he was."

43 Lindsay, *Hogarth*, 31.

44 Paulson, *Hogarth: His Life, Art, and Times*, 1:161–4. Paulson accepts the ultimate
authority of Oldfield's control over Vanderbank's and Hogarth's designs, as indicated in a letter from Carteret to Keene. This, the art historian argues, would
have irritated Hogarth and possibly led to his dismissal or resignation from the
project. According to Hodnett, the publisher's control over the illustrations was
common practice in eighteenth-century England (*Image and Text*, 10).

45 Paulson, *Hogarth: His Life, Art, and Times*, 1:164.

46 Antal, *Hogarth and His Place in European Art*, 150.

47 Paulson, *Hogarth: The "Modern Moral Subject" 1697–1732*, 1:116–18.

48 Hammelmann, "John Vanderbank's *Don Quixote*," 8.

49 Ibid.

50 Paulson, *Book and Painting*, 18.

51 It is debatable which of the above-analysed prints circulated independently and when they would have been released. Juan Givanel Mas and "Gaziel" state that Tonson owned the plates and passed them on to his successors, who did not allow any prints to be made from them until 1791 (*Historia gráfica de Cervantes y del Quijote*, 128). However, Paulson assumes their earlier circulation in his many discussions of their impact in eighteenth-century England.

52 Paulson, *Hogarth: His Life, Art, and Times*, 1:165, and Lindsay, *Hogarth*, 38.

53 Paulson, *Hogarth: His Life, Art, and Times*, 1:165.

54 Antal, *Hogarth and His Place in European Art*, 149.

55 Paulson, *Hogarth: His Life, Art and Times*, 1:165.

56 Lewis Mansfield Knapp, *Tobias Smollett*, 164.

57 Following is the footnote mentioned in the text, a prime example of Smollett's earthy content expressed humorously with mock-intellectual tone: "Gripes and grumblings, in Spanish *Duelos y Quebrantos*: the true meaning of which, the former translators have been at great pains to investigate, as the importance of the subject (no doubt) required. But their labours have, unhappily, ended in nothing else than conjectures, which for the entertainment and instruction of our readers, we beg leave to repeat. One interprets the phrase into collops and eggs, 'being' saith he, 'a very sorry dish.' In this decision, however, he is contradicted by another commentator, who affirms, 'it is a mess too good to mortify withal'; neither can this virtuoso agree with a late editor, who translates the passage in question, into an amlet [sic]; but takes occasion to fall out with Boyer for his description of that dish, which he most sagaciously understands to be a 'bacon froize,' or 'rather fryze, from its being fried, from *frit* in French;' and concludes with this judicious query, 'after all these learned disquisitions, who knows but the author means a dish of nichils [sic]?' If this was his meaning indeed, surely we may venture to conclude, that fasting was very expensive in la Mancha, for the author mentions the *Duelos y Quebrantos*, among those articles that consumed three fourths of the knight's income. Having considered this momentous affair with all the deliberation it deserves, we in our turn present the reader, with cucumbers, greens, and pease-porridge, as the fruit of our industrious researches, being thereunto determined, by the literal signification of the text, which is not 'grumblings and groanings', as the last mentioned ingenious annotator seems to think; but rather pains and breakings; and evidently points at such eatables as generate and expel wind; qualities (as every body knows) eminently inherent in those vegetables we have mentioned as our hero's saturday [sic] repast" (footnote, in Cervantes, *The History and Adventures of the Renowned Don Quixote* [London 1755], 1–2). Of course, the great debate over the meaning of "duelos y quebrantos" was yet to come, initiated by John Bowle, Nicolás de

Benjumea, and other such erudites, to provide fodder for articles well into the twentieth century. For a discussion of Smollett's translation, see Knowles, "Cervantes and English Literature," 288–9. The translation was extremely popular, and enjoyed republication in thirteen editions (ibid., 288).

58 Paulson, *Book and Painting*, 14.

59 Tobias Smollett, "Preface concerning the translation," in Cervantes, *Don Quixote de la Mancha* (1755), xxi.

60 Ibid., xxi.

61 Richard Graves, *The Spiritual Quixote* (1772), ed. Charles Whibley (1926), 3, qtd. in Robert Giddings, *The Tradition of Smollett*, 55.

62 Gabriel Martín del Río y Rico, *Catálogo bibliográfico de la colección de Cervantes de la Biblioteca Nacional*, 190.

63 Smollett, "The Life of Cervantes," in Cervantes, *Don Quixote de la Mancha* (1755), i.

64 This picture of an alienated Cervantes was repeated by Edward Clarke in his *Letters Concerning the Spanish Nation* (1763) and taken up by Sterne and Coleridge, among others (A.P. Burton, "Cervantes the Man Seen through English Eyes in the Seventeenth and Eighteenth Centuries," 13). As Clarke wrote, "Poor MIGUEL CERVANTES ... underwent many severe sufferings in combating those triple monsters, prejudice, ignorance, and superstition" (51, qtd in Burton, 13).

65 Smollett, "The Life of Cervantes," ix.

66 Ibid.

67 William Windham, the author of a pamphlet criticizing Smollett's translation entitled "Remarks on the Proposals lately published for a New Translation of Don Quixote" (1755), wrote of Cervantes' exploits as a captive of the Moors, as related by Haedo, that he was "a man of most undaunted and desperate courage: and there can be no manner of doubt, but that he had all the Spanish *punto,* and high notions of valour and honour as strong in him as any man of the whole nation, and would not have dared to have contradicted or ridiculed any of the most romantick opinions of his countrymen in these affairs; which, to all soldiers, are most particularly tender points" (26, qtd in Burton, "Cervantes the Man Seen through English Eyes," 11). As is clearer here than in Smollett's quote, "romantick" honour was associated with military valour, and thus genetically linked to the chivalric code.

68 For a history of the old belief that Cervantes destroyed Spain's nobility by attacking the concept of chivalric honour, see Burton, "Cervantes the Man Seen through English Eyes," 2–5.

69 Ibid., 12.

70 Paolo Cherchi, *Capitoli di critica cervantina*, 28–9.

71 Habermas, *The Structural Transformation of the Public Sphere*, 30.

72 For a discussion of "romantic poetry" as understood in the literary debates of the seventeenth and eighteenth centuries to refer to Ariosto, Tasso, and the medieval romances, see René Wellek, "The Concept of Romanticism in Literary History," 3–4.

73 Smollett, "The Life of Cervantes," xi.

74 Ibid., iii.

75 Ibid.

76 Johannes Hartau reads this allegory as a straight presentation of an Enlightenment interpretation, thus demonstrating the difficulty of reading irony into a
visual image as well as a literary one (*Don Quijote in der Kunst*, 91). He quotes a
caption that was added to the image in a 1794 edition as support for his interpretation: "Emblematical Representation of Truth, with her Mirror, Dispelling
the Visions of Gothic Superstition and Knight Errantry, while the Enchanted
Castle and its Giant Master, the Dragon, the Distressed Damsel Ghost in the
background etc. describe the wild creations of a distempered brain" (91). That
the caption was added to clarify the allegorical message supports my more ironic
reading of the image. In fact, Angus Fletcher has described irony as "'collapsed
allegories,' or perhaps, 'condensed allegories.' They show no diminishing, only a
confusion, of the semantic and syntactic processes of double or multiple-leveled
polysemy" (*Allegory*, 230). Hayman's allegory provides a fine example of just such
collapsing allegorical figures and edifices.

77 Smollett, "Preface concerning the translation," xxi.

78 Ellis Waterhouse, *Painting in Britain. 1530–1790*, 136; Brian Allen, *Francis Hayman*, 162.

79 Coburn, *In Imitation of the Manner of Cervantes*, 17.

80 For an example of the new sympathy for Don Quixote's physical suffering as the
unjust fruits of his goodness rather than the just deserts of his folly, Burton
quotes Henry Brooke, "How greatly, how gloriously, how divinely superior was
our hero of the Mancha! who went about righting of wrongs, and redressing of
injuries, lifting up the fallen, and pulling down those whom iniquity had exalted.
In this his marvellous undertaking, what buffettings, what bruisings, what tram-
plings did his bones not endure? ... But, toil was his bed of down, and the house
of pain was, to him, a bower of delight, while he consider'd himself as engaged in
giving ease, advantage, and happiness to others" (*Fool of Quality* [1766], 1:153–4,
qtd in Burton, "Cervantes the Man Seen through English Eyes," 12).

81 Allen, *Francis Hayman*, 19–20.

82 As T.S.R. Boase writes of the development of theatrical gesture, "Hayman marks
the meeting-place of two schools, the continental and the English. His achievement required not only the French example, but also that of Hogarth, with his
direct approach to the play itself, his paintings of the actual theatre, with the
gestures and facial expressions of the acting of the time exactly rendered, not
conventionalized by any formulas of elegance" ("Illustrators of Shakespeare in the
Seventeenth and Eighteenth Centuries," 86).

83 Robert Halsband, "The Rococo in England," 876.

84 Cervantes, *Don Quixote de la Mancha* (1755), 3:189. The Spanish text reads:
" – Hermano, si sois juglar – replicó la dueña –, guardad vuestras gracias para
donde lo parezcan y se os paguen; que de mí no podréis llevar sino una higa. –
¡Aun bien – respondió Sancho – que será bien madura, pues no perderá vuesa
merced la quínola de sus años por punto menos! – Hijo de puta – dijo la dueña,

toda ya encendida en cólera –, si soy vieja o no, a Dios daré la cuenta; que no a vos, bellaco, harto de ajos" (Cervantes, *Don Quijote de la Mancha*, ed. Martín de Riquer, 2:762–3).

85 Cervantes, *Don Quixote de la Mancha* (1755), 3:194. This phrase does not seem to correspond directly to Cervantes' text.

86 Ibid., 3:296. The Spanish text reads: "Aquí hace Cide Hamete un paréntesis, y dice que por Mahoma que diera, por ver ir a los dos así asidos y trabados desde la puerta al lecho, la mejor almalafa de dos que tenía" (Cervantes, *Don Quijote de la Mancha* [1979], 2:882).

87 Ziolkowski, *The Sanctification of Don Quixote*, 55–60.

88 John Skinner, "*Don Quixote* in Eighteenth-Century England," 55.

89 Hartau, *Don Quijote in der Kunst*, 93–4.

90 Paulson, *Hogarth: His Life, Art, and Times*, 1:165.

91 Samuel Johnson, *Rambler* 2 (1750), qtd in Knowles, "Cervantes and English Literature," 291.

CHAPTER FIVE

1 "En esta nación hay un libro muy aplaudido por todas las demás. Lo he leído, y me ha gustado sin duda; pero no deja de mortificarme la sospecha de que el sentido literal es uno, y el verdadero es otro muy diferente" (José Cadalso, *Cartas marruecas*, 224).

2 With reference to this comment on the deeper meaning of *Don Quixote*, Anthony Close assumes that Cadalso must be referring to a hidden satirical meaning (*The Romantic Approach to Don Quixote*, 246). Francisco Aguilar Piñal mentions Cadalso's oblique statement but fails to analyse it ("Anverso y reverso del 'quijotismo,'" 215).

3 Lest the word "national" call up visions of protest on the street, it is important to note that this debate was limited to the intelligentsia, a few short-lived literary journals, and certain figures in the court of Charles III. In this sense, the nation of Spain was still perceived as the body of the monarch. In 1780, when this edition appeared, the debate occasioned by Morviller's acerbic *Encyclopédie méthodique* article on Spain was in full rage. Morvillier had asked the rhetorical question, "What does Europe owe Spain?" to which he answered: "Nothing!" Many Spaniards throughout Europe took up the pen to defend their national honour against the French offence. Literary pride, as part of the concept of national honour, was also at stake. Thus, Cervantes' literary repute was drawn into the fray. The general effect was to rescue Cervantes from the earlier accusations of being anti-Spanish, since the *ilustrados* involved considered it necessary to praise the one Spanish work widely translated and praised outside Spain. For a concise discussion of this debate and Cervantes' place in it, see Paolo Cherchi, *Capitoli di critica cervantina (1605–1789)*, 146–155.

4 Eduardo Subirats claims that the Spanish Enlightenment itself largely fails on account of its lack of critical independence from Spanish institutions such as the

court and the Catholic church: "The philosophical and scientific thought of the Enlightenment offers thus a double perspective; on the one hand, with a sovereign gesture it encompasses the problems of its time with the sign of its transformations and domination; on the other hand, it inaugurates the historical compromise of the scientific spirit with new coactive powers" / "El pensamiento filosófico y científico de la Ilustración brinda así una doble perspectiva; por una parte, abarca con un gesto de soberanía los problemas de su tiempo bajo el signo de su transformación y dominio; por otra, inaugura el compromiso histórico del espíritu científico con nuevos poderes coactivos" (*La ilustración insuficiente*, 34).

5 According to Jürgen Habermas, the public sphere of letters and politics developed in eighteenth-century England, France, and Germany as a realm independent of state control and initiative in which the participants were viewed as private persons working for their own interests and seeking their own minds (*The Structural Transformations of the Public Sphere*, 30). By contrast, the reform activity of the latter part of the century in Spain depended on the financial support and political backing of the crown, and at times even on the crown's initiative. Thus, a traditional two-tiered society, based on a simple division between the state and private realms with no mediating public sphere, continued to operate in Spain.

6 Montesquieu himself had contributed earlier to Spain's loss of honour within the realm of European letters when he stated that *Don Quixote*, a work that attacked other Spanish works, was the only one of that nation worth reading. Cherchi comments, "For the whole century Cervantes was considered a 'friend of reason,' and his work was always seen as a miracle, like a luminous torch held over a nation still wandering lost in the dense Medieval night" / "Per tutto il secolo Cervantes fu considerato un "ami de la raison," e la sua opera fu sempre vista come un miracolo, come una folgore luminosa abbattutasi su una nazione dove ancora era densa la notte medievale" (*Capitoli di critica cervantina*, 19).

7 See Book 1, chap. 9, and Book 2, chap. 3 of *Don Quixote* for a reference to the Spanish topos of the lying Moor.

8 According to Russell Sebold, the structure of the play negates any external reality, so that "in the microcosm of this work nothing exists except the I of Tediato and the other I that could be the reflection of his own self" / "en el microcosmo de esta obra no existe nada sino el yo de Tediato y aquello que puede ser reflejo de su yo" (*Cadalso: el primer romántico "europeo" de España*, 186). Sebold has consistently argued that, in general, Spanish Romanticism was genetically linked to Enlightenment ideologies, such as the cult of sentiment (see, for example, *Trayectoria del romanticismo español*, 75–108).

9 "Ninguna obra necesita más que ésta el diccionario de Nuño: Lo que se lee es una serie de extravagancias de un loco, que cree que hay gigantes, encantadores, etcétera; algunas sentencias en boca de un necio, y muchas escenas de la vida bien criticada; pero lo que hay debajo de esta apariencia es, en mi concepto, un conjunto de materias profundas e importantes" (Cadalso, *Cartas marruecas*, 224).

10 Paul Ilie, "Cadalso and the Epistemology of Madness," 182–3.

11 Habermas, *The Structural Transformation of the Public Sphere*, 83; original emphasis.

12 Subirats, *La ilustración insuficiente*, 34.

13 For the most complete discussion of Cervantes' theatre, see Jean Canavaggio, *Cervantès dramaturge: un théâtre à naître*. Although *Don Quixote* does not reflect the use of neo-Aristotelian norms, Cervantes' earlier play *La Numancia* (ca 1585) follows certain neoclassical rules.

14 For a discussion of those critics who continued to attack Cervantes as anti-Spanish around 1750, see Cherchi, *Capitoli di critica cervantina*, 103. As one anonymous wag wrote, "But, with all this, there is no Spanish book that they value so much, because there is no other one that flatters so much their taste with its dullness and its outlandish picture of the spirit and genius of the Span-ish Nation. This was the great Work of the applauded Spaniard Cervantes: this was the glory that his fatherland received from him, and the perseverant nobil-ity that enlightens it, of whom he boasts of being the stepfather, in the name of Don Quixote, as he says in his prologue, and results from the effects" / "Mas, con todo esso, no hay libro Español, que tanto aprecien porque no hay otro, que tanto lisongee su gusto con el deslucimiento, y estrafalaria pintura del espíritu y genio de la Nación Española. Esta fué la magna Obra del aplaudido Español Cervantes: esta fué la gloria que de él recibió su Patria, y la constante Hidalguía que la ilustra, de quien se ostenta padrastro, en nombre de Don Quixote, según dice en su Prólogo, y resulta de los efectos" (qtd in Cherchi, *Capitoli di critica cervantina*, 103). This quote expresses well the conservative belief that Cervantes had attacked and weakened the Spanish upper classes through his attack on the concept of chivalric honour. Lord Byron continued this tradition when he quipped in his *Don Juan* that "Cervantes smiled Spain's chivalry away."

15 Ignacio Henares Cuéllar, *La teoría de las artes plásticas en España en la segunda mitad del siglo XVIII*, 86.

16 "La historia es concebida como un movimiento progresivo y cíclico dentro del marco de la propia nación. La historia nacionalista se orienta tanto hacia dentro como hacia otros países en el sentido de Europa. Y hacia dentro, la idea de deca-dencia forma parte – por reacción – de la conciencia de atraso que sienten los ilustrados al comparar la realidad nacional con la europea. La "restauración" a su vez implica la recuperación del sentido racional de la cultura, concebida como un todo unitario y cíclico: florecimiento de las artes en la antigüedad, su deca-dencia en la Eda [sic] Media; restauración en el Renacimiento, y nueva decaden-cia en el Barroco" (ibid., 86).

17 Antonio Mestre has characterized the cultural debate at the time of Mayans as centring around the dialectic of tradition/novelty, praise/disapproval (*Mayans y la España de la ilustración*, 85). By contrasting this dialectic to that signalled by Henares Cuéllar for the end of the century, decadence/restoration, we can see how the balance of power, at least at the level of the court, had shifted to favour the reformers.

18 For more information on the gathering of biographical material concerning Cervantes, see "Pruebas y Documentos que justifican la vida de Cervantes" in

Cervantes, *El ingenioso hidalgo Don Quixote de la Mancha* (Madrid: Ibarra 1780), clxvi-clxxii, and Francisco Aguilar Piñal, "Cervantes en el siglo XVIII," 156.

19 "Cervantes, ridiculiza, pisa, anhiquila, deshace quanto es manía caballeresca, ufanía y ridículo punto de honor, que era su fin" (qtd in Francisco Aguilar Piñal, "Un comentario inédito del Quijote," 315).

20 Ibid., 319.

21 Paolo Cherchi, *Capitoli di critica cervantina*, 113.

22 Joaquín Ibarra y Marín enjoyed world renown as a printer, in part because he developed the technique used to satin the paper after an engraving had been made to remove the mark of the impression (Inocencio Ruiz Lasala, *Joaquín Ibarra y Marín (1725–1785)*, 60–1).

23 Juan de Contreras, *Historia del arte hispánico*, 4:520.

24 For a discussion of the lower body, see chap. 2.

25 In his *Analysis of Beauty* (1753) Hogarth actually cited Coypel's presentation of the figure of Sancho Panza in the illustration of Maese Pedro's puppet play as an example of the S-curve, the perfect form in art (Frederick Antal, *Hogarth and His Place in European Art*, 72).

26 For example, Rejón de Silva, in an eighteenth-century poem dedicated to the aesthetics of painting, reflected the widespread belief that landscape and the sociological condition of the subject should reflect his/her sentiments as well as the face and gestures (Francisco José León Tello and María Virginia Sanz Sanz, *Tratados neoclásicos españoles de pintura y escultura*, 23).

27 "Por vengar a Rocinante de los injustos palos de que le veías lleno, os molieron con estacas los desalmados yangueses. Por resistir la superchería amorosa de Maritornes, un asturiano os llenó de cachetes; y de aceite y mocos de candil un cuadrillero. Por defender los diestros y retumbantes rebuznos de Sancho, visteis descargar sobre vuestras costillas un nublado de pedradas" (Anonymous, "Dedicatorio al valiente y andante Don Quixote, alias el Caballero de la Triste Figura y de los Leones," in Cervantes, *Don Quixote de la Mancha* [1771], 1:5).

28 Cervantes, *Don Quixote de la Mancha* (1949), 1:26. The Spanish reads: "La razón de la sinrazón que a mi razón se hace, de tal manera que mi razón enflaquece, que con razón me quejo de la vuestra fermosura" (Cervantes, *Don Quixote de la Mancha* [1979], 1:37).

29 "Pues si se busca en vos entendimiento claro, amor a los libros, y noticias de las principales artes, todo se halla con perfección: porque fuisteis dotado de un entendimiento, no sólo claro, sino *lúcido*: teníais en la uña cuantos libros caballerescos hubo, hay, y havrá; y fuisteis, y sois tan leído, cuanto ninguno otro hombre en el mundo. Entendíais de música como un cuervo: hablabais de política como un tordo: discurríais en matemática como una marica: disputábais como un papagayo" (Anonymous, "Dedicatorio a Don Quixote" [1771], 1:6; original emphasis).

30 The Royal Academy of the Language decided against listing the place names from chivalric romances to which Cervantes alluded because they believed the genre to have been almost extinguished by then (Armando Cotarelo Valledor,

El Quijote académico, 14–15). This burlesque dedication indicates, however, that something of the genre was still known to the eighteenth-century Spanish reading public.

31 "La nobleza heredada es tan rancia en vuestra QUIXOTESCA prosapia, que ya en tiempo de Adán andaba por los montes orientales, en huesos, de puro vieja: y así sabemos que se halló un QUIXADA en compañía de Caín en el primer sangriento destrozo que vio el mundo. Y porque a un origen tan claro se siguiese la gloria de la mas fecunda extensión, ha permitido la Providencia que haya habido siempre, y haya de haber para siempre QUIXOTES, como llovidos; y así se ven hoy, con gran complacencia mía, un QUIXOTE en cada esquina, y ciento en cada lugar; pero con tanta felicidad suya, que lo mismo es darse a conocer por hijos de vuestra casa, que ponerlos en posesión de todos los privilegios de vuestra QUIXOTERIA" (Anonymous, "Dedicatorio a Don Quixote" [1771], 1:3–4).

32 "Verdaderamente (celebérrimo Don Quijote) fuisteis sin par en las hazañas, y en los trabajos; y dijo muy bien Orlando cuando dijo:

> Si no eres Par, tampoco le has tenido,
> Que Par pudieras ser entre mil Pares:
> No puede haberle donde tú te hallares,
> Invicto vencedor, jamás vencido."   (Ibid., 1:6)

33 "Sería abusar de la paciencia de los lectores, y perder el tiempo inútilmente, detenerse en este prólogo en recomendar una obra, que por el largo espacio de cerca de dos siglos ha corrido siempre con el mayor aplauso y estimación entre las naciones cultas, habiendo merecido a todas ellas muy grandes elogios" ("Prólogo de la academia," in Cervantes, *El ingenioso hidalgo Don Quixote de la Mancha* [Madrid: Ibarra 1780], 1:i).

34 "Limpia, fija, y da esplendor" (ibid., i). Luiz Costa Lima sees this institutionalization of *Don Quixote* as an outgrowth of Friedrich Schlegel's insistence on national literature, of which Cervantes' novel was Spain's masterpiece ("The Space of Fiction and the Reception of Don Quijote in Nineteenth-Century Spain," in *The Crisis of Institutionalized Literature in Spain*, 102–4). I would argue that this institutionalization of the work as a national masterpiece had already taken place by the nineteenth century, and grew out of both the seventeenth-century conflicts between European states (from which arose the *leyenda negra*) and the eighteenth-century philosophies of sense and sentiment. Herder, in particular, offered a glimpse of some of nationalism's roots in sentimental thought in his early works, "Von der Veränderung des Geschmacks" and "Ueber die neuere deutsche Literatur" (1767), in which he played with the idea of a difference in taste between nations based on physiological and environmental differences. In addition, as in the example of the 1780 Real Academia edition, the academies that fostered the canonization of certain works of literature and art as "Spanish" masterpieces were devoted to the exaltation of the nation in the person of the monarch (Francisco José León Tello and María M. Sanz Sanz,

La estética académica española en el siglo XVIII, 57). For a discussion of the manner in which elites establish a national literary canon through different functions of literary criticism, such as the writing of literary history and the establishment of authoritative critical editions, see Vassilis Lambropoulos, *Literature as National Institution*.

35 Robert E. Pellisier notes that the Spanish *ilustrados* were highly intelligent men who sought radical reform in the intellectual institutions of their country (*The Neo-Classic Movement in Spain during the XVIII Century,* 176). Since some of them were also ministers in the court of Charles III, it is known that they also saw need of radical change in social and economic policy.

36 "Los que conozcan el mérito de esta obra, y sepan apreciar la pureza, elegancia y cultura de su lenguaje, no extrañarán, que un cuerpo, cuyo principal instituto es cultivar y promover el estudio de la lengua castellana, haya resuelto publicar uno de los mejores textos y modelos de ella: particularmente cuando entre tantas ediciones como se han hecho del Quijote dentro y fuera del reino, puede con verdad decirse, que ninguna hay que no tenga defectos substanciales, hasta haberse llegado a alterar y corromper el mismo título de la obra, pues habiéndola intitulado Cervantes con mucha propriedad y conocimiento: EL INGENIOSO HIDALGO DON QUIXOTE DE LA MANCHA, en casi todas las ediciones posteriores a las primeras se ha puesto: *Vida y hechos del Ingenioso Hidalgo Don Quixote de la Mancha*: título tan impropio y tan ajeno a esta fábula, como sí a la Odisea de Homero se pusiese: *Vida y hechos* del prudente Ulíses" ("Prólogo de la academia," 1:i-ii).

37 Cotarelo Vallador characterizes the academy's approach to the text as almost "fetishistic" in their attempt to restore it to its original state. Lexical changes that the same body had itself introduced in earlier editions were omitted; the title was restored to Cervantes' original one; and the order of certain passages was changed to reflect the first editions. The body used as standards for the author's original text the Madrid 1605 Cuesta edition of the first part and the Valencia 1615/1616 Patricio May edition of the second part, along with the 1738 Lord Carteret edition and its republication in 1744 in the Hague (*El Quijote académico*, 16).

38 The Kent portrait was reproduced by various engravers in the eighteenth century and was published in editions of *Don Quixote* and the *Exemplary Novels* throughout Europe (ibid., 23). The extent to which the Spanish portraits of Cervantes fit into the British portraiture tradition of representing authors and poets is surprising unless one takes into account the importance of engraved copies of paintings in the training of artists. This particular illustration, for example, bears a strong resemblance to the series of portraits of Dryden, which present the poet as a sensitive soul with large, pathetic, almond-shaped eyes. In particular, this image is similar to J. Maubert's portrait of the English author, in which he appears with a dog at his feet and a pile of books beside him on the table (David Piper, *The Image of the Poet*, 48).

39 Piper, *The Image of the Poet*, 52.

40 Ibid., 50.

41 Richard Herr, *The Eighteenth-Century Revolution in Spain*, 63–6, and Joan Lynn Pataky Kosove, *The "Comedia lacrimosa" and Spanish Romantic Drama (1773–1865)*, 42.

42 Kosove writes of the article, which was published in *Cartas eruditas y curiosas* (Madrid 1781) and probably written between 1750 and 1753: "This essay is Feijoo's declaration of belief in a sense other than the ones of sight, smell, touch, taste and hearing: 'He discurrido ò pensado, que hay en nosotros una Potencia Sensitiva, ò llámese meramente Perceptiva, distinta de todas las demás ... '" / "I have argued or thought, that there is in us a Sensitive Power, or call it merely a Perceptive one, different from all the rest" (*The "Comedia lacrimosa,"* 42).

43 R.F. Brissenden, *Virtue in Distress: Studies in the Novel of Sentiment from Richardson to Sade*, 77.

44 Close, *The Romantic Approach to Don Quixote*, 14.

45 "Esta situación capaz de postrar y rendir a cualquier hombre de espíritu, hizo un efecto contrario en Cervantes. Su ánimo heroico encorvado bajo el yugo de una esclavitud tan violenta, pugnó con mayor vigor y con doblado esfuerzo para escaparse de su opresión. Cuesta dificultad persuadirse que un esclavo fuese capaz de intentar tan extraordinarias y arriesgadas empresas a vista de un dueño bárbaro y sanguinario; pero el éxito acreditó que Cervantes debió su conservación a la firmeza y osadía con que porfió siempre, aunque en vano, por evadirse del cautiverio" (Vicente de los Ríos, "Vida de Cervantes," in Cervantes, *Don Quixote de la Mancha* [1780], 1:vii).

46 John Mullan, *Sentiments and Sociability: The Language of Feeling in the Eighteenth Century*, 146.

47 "Parecerá sin duda cosa maravillosa que Cervantes escapase sin castigo alguno en medio de estos atentados, y que pudiese salir ileso entre dueños tan tiranos y enemigos de la humanidad; pero el valor sólido y el ánimo heroico y extraordinario son prendas recomendables y respetadas hasta de los mismos bárbaros" (Ríos, "Vida de Cervantes," 1:x).

48 "Había vivido en ella [La Mancha] y observado puntualmente sus particularidades, como las lagunas de Ruidera y cueva de Montesinos, la situación de los batanes, puerto Lápice y demás partes que hizo después teatro de las aventuras de Don Quijote, cuando de resulta de una comisión que tenía, le capitularon, maltrataron y pusieron en la cárcel los vecinos del lugar donde estaba comisionado. En medio del abandono e incomodidad de esta triste situación, compuso sin otro auxilio que el de su maravilloso ingenio esta discreta fábula, cuya difícil ejecución, que pide mucho espacio, madura reflección y continuado trabajo, manifiesta que permaneció largo tiempo en la prisión" (ibid., 1:xv).

49 Henares Cuéllar, *La teoría de las artes plásticas en España en la segunda mitad del siglo XVIII*, 102–3.

50 The Spanish reads, "la paradoja, la limitación del Espíritu de las Luces aparece desde el momento en que la *élite* iluminista asume su aislamiento en el seno de una sociedad donde la idea misma de reforma carece de sentido y hace cuestión

de honor el no esperar nada que no se vincule a su propio desarrollo" (ibid., 103; original emphasis).

51 Cotarelo Valledor, *El Quijote académico*, 12, 17.

52 Ríos was not alone in his characterization of Cervantes as a would-be reformer of his own society. Linda Ann Friedman Salgado observes that Pedro Gatell, in his *Historia del más famoso escudero, Sancho Panza, desde la gloriosa muerte de Don Quixote de la Mancha hasta el último día y postrera hora de su vida* (Madrid 1793), followed his contemporaries' model of the enlightened Cervantes by putting words of reason and reform into the mouth of his Sancho ("Imitaciones del Quijote en la España del siglo XVIII," 198).

53 "Aquí se ve que Cervantes estaba libre de las preocupaciones de su siglo, y que supo conocerlas, publicarlas, y reprehenderlas con el tiento y circunspección que pedían aquellos tiempos: por lo cual merece más gloria que algunos escritores de nuestro siglo, porque mucho antes, y sin tener igual libertad que ellos, corrigió los mismos abusos" (Ríos, "Vida de Cervantes," 1:cxxvi).

54 "La poca afición de los poderosos a las ciencias, y la ignorancia del vulgo hizo que los hombres capaces de ilustrar la nación con su literatura, la abandonasen, y se dedicasen a lo que siendo del gusto del pueblo podía darles de comer. Por eso Lope de Vega se dedicó a componer malas comedias, sabiendo hacerlas buenas. Así lo da a entender Cervantes en el citado discurso del Canónigo de Toledo, y así lo confesó también el mismo Lope" (ibid., 1:cxxxiii).

55 "Restituido Don Quijote a su antiguo ser de Alonso Quijano el Bueno, conoció sus desvaríos, detestó su locura y los libros que la habían causado, y murió en el seno de la paz y tranquilidad cristiana …, terminando este personaje con toda la felicidad imaginable, y concluyendo la fábula con la instrucción más oportuna y propia del fin para qué se compuso" (ibid., 1:lxxxvi).

56 Françoise Etienvre, "De Mayáns a Capmany: Lecturas españolas del Quijote," *Actas del Coloquio Cervantino Würzburg 1983*, 40. One of the most important schools of twentieth-century Cervantine criticism, perspectivism, considers the novel a discourse on the problems of perception and epistemology. The best-known spokesman for this point of view was Leo Spitzer. See especially his article "Linguistic Perspectivism in the *Don Quijote*," 41–85.

57 "El lector siente un secreto placer en ver primero estos objetos como son en sí, y contemplar después el extraordinario modo con que los aprehende Don Quijote, y los graciosos disfraces con qué los viste su fantasía" (Ríos, "Vida de Cervantes," 1:lv).

58 "Encontramos dos gustos, él de ver lo ridículo de los vicios, y él de verlo aplicado a otro sujeto distinto" (ibid., 1:lv).

59 Ibid., 1:lxvii.

60 "Este es el mérito principal de Cervantes: aquellos hechos que vistos como son en sí hacen ridículo y digno de risa a Don Quijote, aquellos mismos mirados con el lente de la locura de este héroe, le representan como un caballero valiente y afortunado. Sola la discreción de este autor podía haber descubierto un medio tan ingenioso para que las aventuras de Don Quijote ridiculizasen su acción en la realidad, y la hiciesen plausible en su imaginación" (ibid., 1:lvii).

61 William Leon Coburn, "In Imitation of the Manner of Cervantes: Don Quixote and Joseph Andrews," 17.

62 "Lo que más debe admirar en este asunto, es que muchas gentes, que son naturalmente tiernas y compasivas, suelen sin embargo gustar de tan bárbaro recreo, lo cual procede sin duda de no consider a los locos como enfermos, y creer que porque ríen, comen, y nada les duele, no son acreedores a nuestra lástima: error que nace, como otros muchos, de las falsas ideas que se reciben en la crianza" (Ríos, "Vida de Cervantes," 1:cxxiv).

63 George Rosen, *Madness in Society: Chapters in the Historical Sociology of Mental Illness*, 170.

64 "As civilization developed and spread through the inexorable march of progress, irrationality and insanity were conceived as due to a separation of man from nature, to a deranged sensibility arising from a loss of immediacy in his relations with nature" (ibid., 170). This concept of madness as a separation of man from nature certainly came into play in the Romantic opposition of Don Quixote as a representative of the ideal world and Sancho Panza as a representative of the material world.

65 Coburn, *In Imitation of the Manner of Cervantes*, 17.

66 Anthony Ashley Cooper, Third Earl of Shaftesbury, *An Inquiry concerning Virtue, or Merit*, 56.

67 "Don Quijote es un hidalgo naturalmente discreto, racional, e instruido, y que obra y habla como tal; menos cuando se trata de la caballería andante. Sancho es un labrador interesado, pero ladino por naturaleza, y sencillo por su crianza y su condición. De suerte que estos dos personajes tienen un carácter duplicado, el cual varía el diálogo y la fábula, y entretiene gustosamente al lector, representándole a Don Quijote unas veces discreto, otras loco, y manifestando sucesivamente a Sancho como ingenuo y como malicioso. Estos carácteres jamás se desmienten. Don Quixote dentro de su misma locura conserva las vislumbres de su discreción, y en los asuntos indiferentes siempre toma el hilo del discurso desde su manía, o va al fin a parar en ella" (Ríos, "Vida de Cervantes," 1:lxvi).

68 The Spanish reads, "conforme a su ridículo carácter" (ibid., 1:lxxiii).

69 Cotarelo Valledor, *El Quijote académico*, 12.

70 The Spanish text reads, "correcta y magnífica …, añadiendo el trabajo del Sr. Ríos, porque servirá para descubrir las perfecciones de esta obra y para ilustrar varios pasajes de la vida de su autor" (ibid.).

71 Ibid., 14.

72 "Pudieran haberse omitido las estampas, cabeceras y remates, sin que por eso faltase ninguna cosa esencial a la obra. Pero la Academia, sin detenerse en los crecidos gastos que era necesario hacer, ha querido, que no le faltasen tampoco estos adornos, en obsequio del público, y con el objeto de contribuir al mismo tiempo por su parte a dar ocupación a los profesores de las artes" ("Prólogo de la academia," 1:vii).

73 José Caveda notes that prints were published in books in general as an ornament and improvement upon the book, often in order to improve instruction,

be it religious or scientific, or to show respect to great men through reproducing their images (*Memoria para la Historia de la Real Academia de San Fernando y de las Bellas Artes en España desde el advenimiento al trono de Felipe V hasta nuestros días*, 227).

74 Leopoldo Rius y de Llosellas, *Bibliografía crítica de las obras de Miguel de Cervantes Saavedra*, 1:42–4.

75 Cotarelo Valledor, *El Quijote académico*, 27.

76 Ibid., and Angel González Palencia, *Las ediciones académicas del Quijote*, 18.

77 Cotarelo Valledor, *El Quijote académico*, 26–7.

78 The Spanish text reads, "podría ser causa de que recayese sobre la misma Academia toda la crítica del público, y que si se encontraban defectos en las Estampas, se atribuirían á impericia del Cuerpo, lo que sería injusto" (Rius, *Bibliografía crítica de las obras de Miguel de Cervantes Saavedra*, 1:43).

79 For copies of the letters themselves, see González Palencia, *Las ediciones académicas del Quijote*, 38–44, and Cotarelo Valledor, *El Quijote académico*, 35–6.

80 The Spanish text reads, "para los asuntos de las láminas se han escogido las aventuras más principales, cuidando de representarlas en aquel punto, o acción, que las distingue y caracteriza más" ("Prólogo de la academia," 1:viii).

81 Juan Antonio Pellicer, "Vida de Miguel de Cervantes Saavedra," in Cervantes, *El ingenioso Don Quixote de la Mancha* (Madrid: Sancha 1797), 1:xx.

82 Cotarelo Valledor, *El Quijote académico*, 30.

83 Valentín de Sambricio, *José del Castillo*, 10, 17.

84 For a brief summary of Antonio Carnicero's career, which involved continued book illustration, especially for the 1799 Sancha edition of *Don Quixote*, see González Palencia, *Las ediciones académicas del Quijote*, 48.

85 The academy first chose Fernando Selma to design the illustrations for the edition, although he never actually drew any of the full-page prints. Francisco Calvo Serraller attributes this to the institution's lack of faith in the artist's capability (*Ilustraciones al Quijote de la Academia*, 10). Castillo followed Selma, only to be replaced by Carnicero as chief designer after he delayed producing more images and demanded more money.

86 Cervantes, *Don Quixote de la Mancha* (1949), 2:506. " – ¿Pensarán vuestras mercedes ahora que es poco trabajo hinchar un perro? – ¿Pensará vuestra merced ahora que es poco trabajo hacer un libro?" (Cervantes, *Don Quixote de la Mancha* [1979], 2:537).

87 A visual precedent for this image exists in a little-noted print by William Hogarth entitled "The First Stage of Cruelty" (see Fig. 48), an image that illustrates Robert Darnton's *The Great Cat Massacre and Other Episodes in French Cultural History*, fp 73. Darnton notes that the torture of animals was widespread in early modern Europe and that it had its roots in Bakhtinian carnivalesque culture (90). Hogarth's placement of this image as the first in a cautionary series would indicate a bourgeois distaste for the practice as inhumane.

88 Indeed, Darnton suggests that the incident of the cat massacre he investigates, in which journeymen working for a master printer killed his wife's cat, "served as an oblique attack on the master and his wife" (ibid., 78). The cat was a sign of

the wealth and leisure of the bourgeois master as well as a figure of carnivalesque ritual and witchcraft: "The workers pushed their symbolic horseplay to the brink of reification, the point at which the killing of cats would turn into an open rebellion. They played on ambiguities, using symbols that would hide their full meaning while letting enough of it show through to make a fool of the bourgeois without giving him a pretext to fire them" (101). It is very possible that the young artists involved in the creation of these illustrations for the 1780 Real Academia edition were involved in a similarly rebellious play with representations, instead of the creatures themselves.

89 Janis A. Tomlinson, *Francisco Goya*, 53.

90 Ibid., 64.

91 Ibid., 61.

92 Caveda, *Memorias para la Historia de la Real Academia de San Fernando*, 267.

93 Real Academia de Bellas Artes de Madrid, *La Real Calcografía de Madrid*, 96–7.

94 The reversal of the direction of recession can be attributed to the reversal of the image that takes place in printing.

95 Real Academia de Bellas Artes de Madrid, *La Real Calcografía de Madrid*, 97.

96 Angus Fletcher maintains that ambivalence is an outgrowth of the dualism of "Good" and "Bad" central to much allegory (in the case of *Don Quixote*, the "goodness" of rationality, the "badness" of delusion). As he writes, "we should not assume the polar opposites are really separated by any distance. This above all is a case where the expression 'extremes meet' is not a metaphor. It is a psychological fact … In a word, allegorical literature always displays toward its polar antagonisms a certain ambivalence" (*Allegory*, 224).

97 James Hall, *Dictionary of Subjects and Symbols in Art*, 55.

98 Rius, *Bibliografía crítica de las obras de Miguel de Cervantes Saavedra*, 1:42.

99 The text in Spanish reads, "de este objeto escogido con tanto acierto dedujo Cervantes la acción de su fábula, que es la locura de Don Quijote" (Ríos, "Vida de Cervantes," 1:xlix).

100 The text in Spanish reads, "el carácter de Sancho no es ser simple, ni agudo, animoso, o cobarde, sino ser interesado, y serlo de modo que el interés le hace parecer bajo distintas formas, según el conato que necesita emplear para conseguirle" (ibid., 1:lxvii).

101 Sambricio, *José del Castillo*, 19; Tomlinson, *Francisco Goya*, 9–10.

102 Tomlinson, *Francisco Goya*, 9–10.

103 Rudolf Arnheim, *The Power of the Center*, 91.

104 León Tello and Sanz Sanz, *Tratados neoclásicos españoles*, 15.

105 Roger Chartier, *The Cultural Uses of Print in Early Modern France*, 220–1.

106 The scene is in fact a quite faithful rendition of the details from the novel (1: chap. 1), all of which point towards Alonso Quijano's social status as a penniless gentleman, a fact not to be lost on a Spanish reader.

107 Spanish neoclassical theorists such as Mayans saw the imitation of gesture as the means to represent interior feelings and motivations mimetically (León Tello and Sanz Sanz, *Tratados neoclásicos españoles*, 10).

108 Antonio Palomino de Castro y Velasco, *El museo pictórico y escala óptica*, 113, 116.

109 Robert Rosenblum, *Transformations in Late Eighteenth-Century Art*, 28.

110 Ibid., 29.

111 Fletcher, *Allegory*, 7.

112 Edith Helman, *Jovellanos y Goya*, 139–42; Guillermo Carnero, *La cara oscura del siglo de las luces*, 93–4, 117–18.

113 Emilio Cotarelo y Morí, *Iriarte y su época*, 124.

CHAPTER SIX

1 Anthony Close, following the impetus of Oscar Mandel and Peter Russell, considers any reading of the novel as other than satirical or parodic to be anachronistic. Unfortunately, his description of the seventeenth- and eighteenth-century reception of the text fails to analyse the multiplicity of interpretations at the time, and, in so doing, minimizes early reception to the poles of either popular joke literature or neoclassical satire. See Close, *The Romantic Approach to Don Quixote*; Mandel, "The Function of the Norm in *Don Quixote*," 154–5; and Russell, "*Don Quijote* as a Funny Book," 312–36. At the same time, twentieth-century readers and critics who have read *Don Quixote* as a serious work of literature on any level generally acknowledge a debt to the German Romantics for their approach to the text as an almost philosophical work. Among the best-known of these readers would be Georg Lukács in his early work *The Theory of the Novel*, where he describes the work as the first modern novel, expressing the alienation of the individual from society, or Miguel de Unamuno in his adaptation of the novel, *Vida de Don Quijote y Sancho, según Miguel de Cervantes Saavedra, explicada y comentada*, where he carries the ennoblement of the protagonist to its extreme.

2 Anthony Close has shaped the current history of the reception of *Don Quixote* through his definition of the "Romantic approach" as: "a) the idealisation of the hero and the denial of the novel's satiric purpose; b) the belief that the novel is symbolical and that through this symbolism it expresses ideas about the human spirit's relation to reality or about the nature of Spain's history; c) the interpretation of its symbolism, and more generally, of its whole spirit and style, in a way which reflects the ideology, aesthetics, and sensibility of the modern era" (*The Romantic Approach to Don Quixote*, 1). Close clearly states that he considers this tradition "misguided in each of its basic tendencies," largely because it ignores Cervantes' presumed intention to satirize the chivalric romances.

3 For further discussion of the interpretive traditions informing the Romantic illustration of *Don Quixote*, see the author's article "The Romancing of *Don Quixote*."

4 "Sí, señores, el Censor es, y lo tiene a mucha honra, muy semejante a un Don Quijote del mundo filosófico, que corre por todos sus países en demanda de las aventuras, procurando desfacer errores de todo género, y enderezar tuertos y sinrazones de toda especie, pertenezcan unos y otros a la materia que pertenecieren. He aquí su manía" (*El Censor (1781–1787)*, 132).

5 The Spanish reads, "enamorado de su castísima Dulcinea, a quien llama la *Verdad*" (ibid., 133).

6 The Spanish reads, "alguna satirilla tan débil como una caña" (ibid.).

7 The Spanish reads, "el valor jamás ... se vió descaecer ni en un punto" (ibid., 135).

8 Joseph de Serna anticipated Cañuelo's identification of himself with Don Quixote in the first issue of *El bufón de la corte* (Madrid: Imprenta de D. Gabriel Ramírez 1767). As he wrote, "Here there is no more prologue than to say that, seeing so many stupid writers, I want to be one of many ... Finally, I am going to be a writer of enthusiasm ..., or a new Don Quixote of good taste" / "Aquí no hay más Prólogo, que decir, que a vista de tantos Escritores tontos, quiero yo ser uno de tantos ... Finalmente, yo voy a ser un Escritor de entusiasmo ..., ó un nuevo Don Quixote del buen gusto" (7–8, qtd in Jesús Castañón, *La crítica literaria en la prensa española del siglo XVIII (1700–1750)*, 40). None the less, it is obvious that he understood the epithet of Don Quixote in negative terms, as a *Schwärmer*, a man of excessively passionate and ill-founded beliefs.

9 "A pesar de todo cuanto expone el señor [Vicente de los] Ríos en su excelente *Análisis del Don Quijote*, jamás he podido yo perdonar a Cervantes el que hubiese hecho asunto de su inmortal obra burlarse de una locura como la de este héroe fabuloso" (*El Censor*, 129).

10 The Spanish text reads, "un loco, pero al fin un hombre veraz, íntegro, lleno de probidad y de honradez, incapaz de decir ni hacer cosa que en su concepto fuese una vileza: amante de la gloria, sobrio en la abundancia, liberal en la pobreza, valiente en todas ocasiones, compasivo, misericordioso, agradecido con todos; en una palabra, un hombre cabal y perfecto, a excepción de aquel trastorno que su imaginación padecía" (ibid., 129–30).

11 The Spanish text reads, "arrinconado por desgracia nuestra; acaba de morir con la muerte más dolorosa y funesta, turbados sus sentidos, creyendo que no le restaba más que mendigar para tener el preciso sustento" (ibid., 21).

12 Ibid., 63.

13 For a discussion of the power interests beneath the apparent universality of rational debate in the public sphere, see Jürgen Habermas, *The Structural Transformation of the Public Sphere*, 57–88.

14 "Para la sensibilidad de Goya, el mundo es un caos en el que cada bestialidad puede intentar su aventura en la seguridad de encontrar víctimas sin tasa. Pero esta despiadada visión de la realidad no supone, como en Hoggarth [sic], una intención moralizadora, ni como en Gross una subversión social. Goya no califica. Consigna en breve síntesis las anormalidades y los demonios que palpitan en la rabia de los hombres y en las insinuaciones de la mujer, eludiendo a veces hasta su simpatía por los sacrificados" (José Camón Aznar, "Estética de Goya," 477).

15 André Malraux, *Saturn: An Essay on Goya*, 154.

16 Ibid., 91.

17 Eleanor A. Sayre, *The Changing Image*, 100.

18 Reva Wolf, *Goya and the Satirical Print in England and on the Continent, 1730–1850*, 2.

19 "Lo más significativo del "capricho de algún pintor demente," de Cadalso, lo que más afectó a Goya, es que de un precepto puramente estético hizo una doctrina moral y social con la que podía censurar una teoría tan absurda como lo de la nobleza hereditaria" (Edith Helman, *Jovellanos y Goya*, 136).

20 Paul Ilie, "Cadalso and the Epistemology of Madness," 186.

21 Juan Givanel Mas and "Gaziel," *Historia gráfica de Cervantes y del Quijote*, 164–8.

22 Francisco José León Tello and María M. Sanz Sanz, *Tratados neoclásicos españoles de pintura y escultura*, 262.

23 Edith Helman, *Trasmundo de Goya*, 63.

24 The Spanish text reads, "la única voz posible para un conato de opinión pública en libertad de expresar un juicio moral sin compromisos" (Teresa Lorenzo de Márquez, in *Goya y el espíritu de la ilustración*, 109).

25 The Spanish text reads, "triunfo del desorden" (ibid., 397).

26 The Spanish text reads, "Al vulgo supersticioso lo había representado tal como lo concebían Moratín o Jovellanos, como masa idiotizada por el miedo y la ignorancia y, sobre todo, despersonalizada masa; en fin, mucho antes de que se empleara la palabra "masa" en castellano en este sentido" (Helman, *Jovellanos y Goya*, 246).

27 Pierre Gassier, *The Drawings of Goya: The Complete Albums*, 432.

28 Pierre Gassier and Juliet Wilson, *Vie et œuvre de Francisco Goya*, 376.

29 William Mills Ivins, Jr, *Prints and Visual Communication*, 70.

30 The Spanish text reads, "como si del cráneo enfermo brotase una corriente eléctrica" (Givanel Mas and "Gaziel," *Historia gráfica de Cervantes y del Quijote*, 168).

31 Ibid.

32 In reference to the satyr in frontispieces to Pope's *The Rape of the Lock*, Robert Halsband points to anecdotal evidence that the erotic implications of the satyr as well as the allusion to literary satire were evident to eighteenth-century readers (*The Rape of the Lock and Its Illustrations 1714–1896*, 20).

33 Erwin Walter Palm, "Zu Goyas Capricho 56," *Aachener Kunstblätter* 41 (1971): 20–7, qtd by Eleanor Sayre in *Goya y el espíritu de la ilustración*, 237.

34 Ibid., 244. The Ayala and Prado manuscripts consist of handwritten interpretations of the images and their subtitles, usually as allegorical illustrations of various vices, superstitions, and follies. These commentaries have proved to be very useful to art historians, both because they give indication of Goya's reception by his contemporaries and because they assist in the deciphering of the often very ambiguous and baffling imagery. They also serve to show that prints were objects of interpretation and were read in a manner that combined the text and the image to communicate an often didactic message.

35 Enrique Lafuente Ferrari, *Los caprichos de Goya*, 176.

36 Gassier, *The Drawings of Goya*, 361.

37 Gassier and Wilson, *Vie et œuvre de Francisco Goya*, 376.

38 The French text reads, "les deux compositions en effet montrent l'auteur assailli par les créatures de ses rêves et de ses visions" (ibid., translation mine).

39 Gassier, *The Drawings of Goya*, 362.

40 Eric J. Ziolkowski, *The Sanctification of Don Quixote*, 122.

41 "El artista compartía sin duda las opiniones filantrópicas de sus amigos ilustrados sobre la locura o el tratamiento que merecían los locos, pero en sus imágenes parece avanzar intuitivamente hacia los descubrimientos de la moderna psicología y con ello denunciar las arraigadas ideas tradicionales y populares sobre las enfermedades de la mente" (Manuela Mena in *Goya y el espíritu de la ilustración*, 461).

Bibliography

PRIMARY SOURCES

I. Illustrated editions of Don Quixote referred to in text

Cervantes Saavedra, Miguel de. *The History of Don Quixote*. London: Blount [1620?]. Illustrator anonymous.

– *Den Verstandigen Vroomen Ridder, Don Quichot de la Mancha*. Dordrecht: Kasteel van Gent 1657. Illustrated by Jacobus Savery (attributed).

– *Vida y hechos del Ingenioso Cavallero Don Quixote de la Mancha*. Brussels: Juan Mommarte 1662. Illustrated by Gaspar Bouttats.

– *Don Kichote de la Mantscha, Das Ist*. Frankfurt am Main: In Verlegung Thomas Matthiae Gotzen 1669. Illustrator anonymous.

– *Vida y hechos del ingenioso Cavallero Don Quixote de la Mancha*. New edition. Amberes: Geronymo y Juanbautista Verdussen 1673. Illustrated by Gaspar Bouttats.

– *Vida y hechos del ingenioso Cavallero Don Quixote de la Mancha*. Madrid: Andrés García de la Iglesia 1674. Illustrated by Diego Obregón.

– *The History of the Most Renowned Don Quixote of Mancha and his Trusty Squire Sancho Pancha*. London: Thomas Hodgkin 1687. Illustrated by J.P.

– *The History of the Valorous and Witty Knight-Errant Don Quixote of the Mancha*. London: Knaplock 1731. Illustrated by Charles Antoine Coypel.

– *Vida y hechos del ingenioso Cavallero Don Quixote de la Mancha*. Madrid: Antonio Sanz 1735. Illustrator anonymous.

– *Vida y hechos del ingenioso caballero Don Quixote de la Mancha*. London: J. and R. Tonson 1738. Includes "Advertencias de D. Juan Oldfield Doctor en Medicina sobre las Estampas desta Historia" and "Vida de Miguel de Cervantes Saavedra por D. Gregorio Mayáns i Siscár." Illustrations designed by William Kent and John Vanderbank, engraved by John Vandergucht.

– *The History and Adventures of the renowned Don Quixote*. London: Millar 1755. Translation and "Life of Cervantes" by Tobias Smollett. Illustrated by Francis Hayman.
– *Vida, y hechos del ingenioso caballero Don Quixote de la Mancha*. Madrid: Ibarra 1771. Illustated by Juan Camarón.
– *The History of the renowned Don Quixote de la Mancha*. London: Cooke 1774. Illustrated by Robert Wale.
– *El ingenioso hidalgo Don Quixote de la Mancha*. Madrid: Ibarra 1780. Includes "Vida de Cervantes" and "Análisis del Quixote" by D. Vicente de los Ríos. Illustrated by Pedro Arnal, Antonio Carnicero, Isidro Carnicero, José del Castillo, Bernardo Barranco, José Brunete, Jerónimo Gil, and Gregorio Ferro.
– *Leben und Thaten des weisen Junkers Don Quixote von Mancha*. Leipzig: Bertuch, Weimar, Fritsch 1775–81. Illustrated by Daniel Chodowiecki.
– *El ingenioso hidalgo Don Quixote de la Mancha*. Madrid: Sancha 1797–98. "Vida de Miguel de Cervantes Saavedra" and "Discurso preliminar" by Juan Antonio Pellicer. Illustrated by Ximeno, Navarro, Monnet, Camarón, and Paret.
– *Don Quixote de la Mancha*. London: Bulmerand 1818. Illustrated by Robert Smirke.
– *The History and Adventures of the Renowned Don Quixote*. London: Wilson 1833. Illustrated by George Cruikshank.
– *L'ingénieux Hidalgo Don Quichotte de la Manche*. Paris: Dubochet et Cie. 1836. Illustrated by Tony Johannot.
– *L'ingénieux hidalgo Don Quichotte de la Manche*. Paris: L. Hachette 1863. Illustrated by Gustave Doré.

II. Other illustrated editions (1620–1800) consulted

– *Histoire de l'admirable Don Quichotte de la Manche*. Paris: Compagnie des Librairies 1732. Illustrated by Bonard and Charles Antoine Coypel.
– *Vida y hechos del ingenioso hidalgo Don Quixote de la Mancha*. Barcelona: Juan Jolis 1755. Illustrator anonymous.
– *El ingenioso hidalgo Don Quixote de la Mancha*. Madrid: Ibarra 1782. Illustrated by Isidro and Antonio Carnicero.
– *The History and Adventures of the renowned Don Quixote*. London: F. and C. Rivington 1792. Illustrator anonymous.
– *The History and Adventures of the renowned Don Quixote de la Mancha*. London: A. Hogg 1794. Illustrator Riley.
– *El ingenioso hidalgo Don Quixote de la Mancha*. Madrid: Imprenta Real 1797–8. Illustrator Antonio Rodríguez.
– *El ingenioso hidalgo Don Quixote de la Mancha*. Madrid: Sancha 1798–1800. Illustrated by Paret and Alcántara.
– *Don Quichotte de la Manche*. Paris: P. Didot 1799. Illustrated by Robert Lefebvre and Jean Jacques Lebarbier.

- *The History and Adventures of the renowned Don Quixote.* London: Cooke 1799. Illustrated by Francis Hayman, R. Corbould, and T. Kirk.

III. Other primary sources

Anonymous. Review of Lesage's translation of Cervantes' and Avellaneda's *Don Quixotes.* In *El Diario de los Sabios,* 31 Mar. 1704, folio 207.

Avellaneda, Alonso Fernández de. *El ingenioso hidalgo Don Quijote de la Mancha que contiene su tercera salida y es la quinta parte de sus aventuras.* Ed. F. García Salinero. Madrid: Castalia 1971.

Cadalso, José. *Cartas marruecas y noches lúgubres.* Ed. Joaquín Arce. Madrid: Cátedra 1978

Castro, Guillen de. *Don Quijote de la Mancha.* Ed. Luciano García Lorenzo. Madrid: Anaya 1971.

El Censor (1781–1787). Ed. E. García-Pandavenes. Prologue by José F. Montesinos. Barcelona: Labor 1972.

Cervantes Saavedra, Miguel de. *El ingenioso hidalgo Don Quijote de la Mancha.* Ed. Martín de Riquer. 2 vols. 9th ed. Barcelona: Editorial Juventud 1979.

- *The Ingenious Gentleman Don Quixote de la Mancha.* Trans. Samuel Putnam. 2 vols. New York: Viking 1949.

Fielding, Henry. *The History of the Adventures of Joseph Andrews and His Friend Mr. Abraham Adams.* New York: W.W. Norton 1958.

Forner, Juan Pablo. *Oración apologética por la España y su mérito literario.* Badajoz: Imprenta de la Excma. Diputación 1945.

Gatell, Pedro. *La Moral de Don Quixote deducida de la historia que de sus gloriosas hazañas escribió Cide-Hamete Benengeli.* Madrid: Josef Herrera 1789.

Lesage, Alain-René. Préface. In *Nouvelles aventures de l'admirable Don Quichotte* by Alonso Fernández de Avellaneda. Paris: 1704.

Luzán, Ignacio de. *La Poética: o Reglas de la poesía en general y de sus principales especies: ediciones de 1737 y 1789.* Ed. Isabel M. Cid de Sirgado. Madrid: Cátedra 1974.

Mayans y Siscar, Gregorio. *Oración en alabanza de las eloqüentíssimas obras de Don Diego Saavedra Fajardo.* 1725. In *Dieciocho* 5, no. 2 (Fall 1982): 113–48.

Mayans y Siscar, Juan Antonio, and Juan Antonio Pellicer y Saforcada. *Cartas sacadas a luz por Francisco Martínez y Martínez.* Valencia: Hijos de F. Vives Mora 1917.

Motteux, Peter Anthony. Translator's Preface. In *The History of the Renoun'd Don Quixote de la Mancha,* by Miguel de Cervantes Saavedra. London 1700.

Nasarre, Blas Antonio. *Comedias y entremeses de Miguel de Cervantes Saavedra.* Madrid 1749.

Navarette, Martín Fernández de. *Vida de Miguel de Cervantes Saavedra, escrita e ilustrada con varias noticias y documentos inéditos pertenecientes a la historia y literatura de su tiempo.* Madrid: Real Academia Española 1819.

Palomino de Castro y Velasco, Antonio. *El museo pictórico y escala óptica.* 1715. Reprint. Madrid: M. Aguilar 1947.

Pellicer, D. Juan Antonio. "Vida de Miguel de Cervantes Saavedra." In Cervantes, *El ingenioso hidalgo Don Quixote de la Mancha.* Vol. 1. Madrid: Sancha 1797.

SECONDARY SOURCES

Adorno, Theodor W., and Max Horkheimer. *Dialectic of Enlightenment.* Trans. John Cumming. New York: Continuum 1993.

Aguilar Piñal, Francisco. "Un comentario inédito del *Quijote* en el siglo XVIII." *Anales cervantinos* 8 (1959–60): 307–19.

– "Anverso y reverso del quijotismo en el siglo XVIII español." *Anales de literatura española* 1 (1982): 207–16.

– "Cervantes en el siglo XVIII." *Anales cervantinos* 21 (1983): 153–64.

Allen, Brian. *Francis Hayman.* New Haven: Yale University Press 1987.

Allen, John J. *Don Quixote, Hero or Fool? A Study in Narrative Technique.* Humanities Monograph no. 29. Gainesville: University of Florida Press 1969.

Andioc, René. *Teatro y sociedad en el Madrid del siglo XVIII.* 2d ed. Madrid: Castalia 1988.

Antal, Frederick. *Hogarth and His Place in European Art.* London: Routledge and Kegan Paul 1962.

– *Classicism and Romanticism, with Other Studies in Art.* London: Routledge and Kegan Paul 1966.

Armas, José de. *Cervantes en la literatura inglesa.* Madrid: Imprenta Renacimiento 1916.

Arnheim, Rudolf. *Toward a Psychology of Art: Collected Essays.* Berkeley: University of California Press 1966.

– *Visual Thinking.* Berkeley: University of California Press 1969.

– *Art and Visual Perception: A Psychology of the Creative Eye.* Rev. ed. Berkeley: University of California Press 1974.

– "The Unity of the Arts: Time, Space, and Distance." *Yearbook of Comparative and General Literature* 25 (1976): 7–13.

– *The Power of the Center: A Study of Composition in the Visual Arts: The New Version.* Berkeley: University of California Press 1988.

Arte Español. 23 Apr. 1916. Número extraordinario. Madrid: Bernardo Rodríguez.

Ashbee, H.S. *An Iconography of Don Quixote, 1605–1895.* London and Aberdeen: University Press 1895.

– *Don Quixote and British Art.* London: Blades, East and Blades 1900.

Avalle-Arce, Juan Bautista. *Don Quijote como forma de vida.* Madrid: Castalia 1976.

Aznar, José Camón. "Estética de Goya." *Revista de ideas estéticas* 4, nos. 15–16 (1946): 473–500.

Bakhtin, Mikhail Mikhailovich. *The Dialogic Imagination: Four Essays.* Trans. Caryl Emerson and Michael Holquist. Austin: University of Texas Press 1981.

– *Rabelais and His World.* Trans. Hélène Iswolsky. Bloomington: Indiana University Press 1984.

Bardon, Maurice. *Don Quichotte en France au XVIIe et au XVIIIe siècle (1618–1815)*. Paris: Honoré Champion 1931.

Behrendt, Stephen C. "The Functions of Illustrations – Intentional and Unintentional." In *Imagination on a Long Rein: English Literature Illustrated*, ed. Joachin Möller, 29–44. Marburg: Jonas Verlag 1988.

Benjamin, Walter. "The Work of Art in the Age of Mechanical Reproduction." In *Illuminations*, ed. Hannah Arendt, trans. Harry Zohn, 217–51. New York: Schocken 1969.

Bergel, Lienhard. "Cervantes in Germany." In *Cervantes across the Centuries*, ed. Angel Flores and M.J. Bernardete, 315–52. New York: Gordian Press 1969.

Berger, John. *The Sense of Sight*. New York: Pantheon 1985.

Bertrand, J.J.A. *Cervantès et le romantisme allemand*. Paris: Librairie Félix Alcan 1914.

– *Cervantes en el país de Fausto*. Madrid: Ediciones Cultura Hispánica 1950.

– "Génesis de la concepción romántica de Don Quijote en Francia." *Anales cervantinos* 3 (1953): 1–41.

Beruete y Moret, A. de. *Goya*. Madrid: Blass 1928.

Bland, David. *A History of Book Illustration*. 2nd ed. London: Faber and Faber Ltd. 1969.

Boase, T.S.R. "Illustrators of Shakespeare in the Seventeenth and Eighteenth Centuries." *Journal of the Warburg and Courtauld Institute* 10 (1947): 83–108.

Bologna, Ferdinand. *Francesco Solimena*. Naples: L'Arte Tipografica 1957.

Bredvold, Louis I. *The Natural History of Sensibility*. Detroit: Wayne State University Press 1962.

Brissenden, R.F. *Virtue in Distress: Studies in the Novel of Sentiment from Richardson to Sade*. London: Macmillan 1974.

Brüggemann, Werner. *Cervantes und die Figur des Don Quijote in Kunstanschaaung und der deutschen Romantik*. Munster/Westfalen: Aschendorffesche Verlagsbuchhandlung 1958.

Bryan's Dictionary of Painters and Engravers. New York: MacMillan 1905.

Burton, A.P. "Cervantes the Man Seen through English Eyes in the Seventeenth and Eighteenth Centuries." *Bulletin of Hispanic Studies* 45 (1968): 1–15.

Cahn, Walter. *Masterpieces: Chapters on the History of an Idea*. Princeton: Princeton University Press 1979.

Calvo Serraller, Francisco. *Ilustraciones al Quijote de la Academia*. Madrid: Turner 1978.

Canavaggio, Jean. *Cervantès dramaturge: un théâtre à naître*. Presses Universitaires de France 1977.

Carnero, Guillermo. *La cara oscura del siglo de las luces*. Madrid: Cátedra 1983.

Carrete Parrondo, Juan. *El arte de la estampa en la Ilustración: Las Bellas Artes*. Valencia: Murta 1988.

Casalduero, Joaquín. *Sentido y forma del Quijote, 1605–1615*. Madrid: Ediciones Insula 1975.

Castañón, Jesús. *La crítica literaria en la prensa española del siglo XVIII (1700–1750)*. Madrid: Taurus 1973.

Castro, Américo. *Hacia Cervantes*. Madrid: Taurus 1973.

– *El pensamiento de Cervantes*. 2nd ed. Barcelona: Editorial Crítica 1987.

Caveda, José. *Memorias para la Historia de la Real Academia de San Fernando y de las Bellas Artes en España desde el advenimiento al trono de Felipe V hasta nuestros días*. Madrid: Manuel Tello 1967.

Chaffee, Diane. "Pictures and Portraits in Literature: Cervantes as the Painter of *Don Quijote*." *Anales cervantinos* 19 (1981): 50–6.

Chartier, Roger. *The Cultural Uses of Print in Early Modern France*. Trans. Lydia G. Cochrane. Princeton: Princeton University Press 1987.

Cherchi, Paolo. *Capitoli di critica cervantina*. Rome: Bulzoni Editores 1977.

Chevalier, Maxime. *Lectura y lectores en la España de los siglo XVI y XVII*. Madrid: Turner 1976.

Clair, Colin. *A History of European Printing*. London: Academic Press 1976.

Clark, Kenneth. *The Nude: A Study in Ideal Form*. Bollingen Series 35, no. 2. Princeton: Princeton University Press 1984,

Close, Anthony J. *The Romantic Approach to Don Quixote: A Critical History of the Romantic Tradition in Quixote Criticism*. Cambridge: Cambridge University Press 1978.

Coburn, William Leon. "In Imitation of the Manner of Cervantes: Don Quixote and Joseph Andrews." PhD. Ann Arbor: University Microfilms International 1969.

Contreras, Juan de. *Historia del arte hispánico*. 4 vols. Barcelona: Salvat 1945.

Costa Lima, Luiz. "The Space of Fiction and the Reception of Don Quijote in Nineteenth-Century Spain." In *The Crisis of Institutionalized Literature in Spain*, ed. Wlad Godzich and Nicholas Spadaccini, 99–122. Minneapolis: Prisma Institute 1988.

Cotarelo Valledor, Armando. *El Quijote académico*. Madrid: Magisterio Español 1948.

Cotarelo y Mori, Emilio. *Iriarte y su época*. Madrid: Sucesores de Rivadeneyra 1897.

Cox, R. Merritt. *The Rev. John Bowle: The Genesis of Cervantean Criticism*. University of North Carolina Studies in Romance Languages and Literatures, no. 99. Chapel Hill: University of North Carolina Press 1971.

– "Cervantes and Three *Ilustrados*: Mayans, Sarmiento, and Bowle." In *Studies in the Spanish Golden Age: Cervantes and Lope de Vega*, ed. Dana B. Drake and José A. Madrigal, 12–20. Miami: Ediciones Universal 1978.

Crooks, Esther J. *The Influence of Cervantes in France in the Seventeenth Century*. Johns Hopkins Studies in Romance Literatures and Languages, extra vol. 4. Baltimore: Johns Hopkins Press 1931.

– "Translations of Cervantes into French." In *Cervantes across the Centuries*, ed. Angel Flores and M.J. Bernadete, 304–14. New York: Gordian Press 1969.

Darnton, Robert. *The Great Cat Massacre and Other Episodes in French Cultural History*. New York: Basic Books 1984.

Díaz-Plaja, Guillermo. *En torno a Cervantes*. Pamplona: Universidad de Navarra 1977.

Drake, Dana B., and Dominick L. Finello. *An Analytical and Bibliographical Guide to Criticism on Don Quijote (1790–1893)*. Newark, Del.: Juan de la Cuesta – Hispanic Monographs 1987.

Durán, Manuel. "El *Quijote* a través del prisma de Mikhail Bakhtine: carnaval, disfraces, escatología y locura." In *Cervantes and the Renaissance*, papers of the Pomona College Cervantes Symposium, 16–18 Nov. 1978, ed. Michael D. McGaha, 71–86. Easton, Penn.: Juan de la Cuesta – Hispanic Monographs 1980.

Eichner, Hans. "The Genesis of German Romanticism." *Queen's Quarterly* 72, no. 2 (Summer 1965): 213–31.

Eisenberg, Daniel. *Romances of Chivalry in the Spanish Golden Age.* Newark, Del.: Juan de la Cuesta – Hispanic Monographs 1982.

Eisenstein, Elizabeth L. *The Printing Press as an Agent of Change: Communications and Cultural Transformations in Early-Modern Europe.* Cambridge: Cambridge University Press 1979.

Eliot, T.S. "Tradition and the Individual Talent." In *Selected Essays 1917–1932*, 3–11. New York: Harcourt, Brace and Co. 1932.

El Saffar, Ruth. *Distance and Control in Don Quixote: A Study in Narrative Technique.* North Carolina Studies in the Romance Languages and Literatures, no. 147. Chapel Hill: University of North Carolina Press 1975.

Etienvre, Françoise. "De Mayáns a Capmany: Lecturas españolas del Quijote." In *Actas del Coloquio Cervantino Würzburg 1983*, ed. Theodor Benchem and Hugo Laitenberger, 27–47. Munster/Westfalen: Aschendorffsche Verlagsbuchhandlung 1983.

Ferrán Salvador, Vicente. "Ilustradores valencianos del *Quijote*." *Revista bibliográfica y documental* 2, nos. 1–2 (enero–junio 1948): 91–105.

Ferreras, Juan Ignacio. *La estructura paródica del Quijote.* Madrid: Taurus 1982.

Fletcher, Angus. *Allegory: The Theory of a Symbolic Mode.* Ithaca: Cornell University Press 1964.

Flores, R.M. *Sancho Panza through Three Hundred Seventy-Five Years of Continuations, Imitations, and Criticism, 1605–1980.* Newark, Del.: Juan de la Cuesta – Hispanic Monographs 1982.

Forcione, Alban K. *Cervantes, Aristotle, and the Persiles.* Princeton: Princeton University Press 1970.

Fried, Michael. *Absorption and Theatricality: Painting and Beholder in the Age of Diderot.* Berkeley: University of California Press 1980.

Gallego, Antonio. *Historia del grabado en España.* Madrid: Cátedra 1979.

Gallego Morell, Antonio. *Garcilaso de la Vega y sus comentaristas.* Madrid: Gredos 1972.

García Martín, Manuel. *Cervantes y la comedia española en el siglo XVII.* Salamanca: Ediciones Universidad de Salamanca 1980.

Garnier, Nicole. *Antoine Coypel (1661–1722).* Paris: Athena 1989.

Gassier, Pierre. *The Drawings of Goya: The Complete Albums.* London: Thames and Hudson 1973.

– and Juliet Wilson. *Vie et œuvre de Francisco Goya. L'Œuvre complet et illustré: peintures, dessins, gravures.* Fribourg: Office du livre 1970.

Gay, Peter. *The Enlightenment: An Interpretation.* New York: Vintage 1968.

Gerhard, Sandra Forbes. *Don Quixote and the Shelton Translation: A Stylistic Analysis.* Madrid: Studia Humanitatis 1982.

Giddings, Robert. *The Tradition of Smollett.* London: Methuen 1967.

Givanel Mas, Juan. *Catálogo de la exposición de iconografía cervantina.* Barcelona: Diputado de la Provincia Biblioteca Central 1944.

– and "Gaziel" (Agustín Calvet). *Historia gráfica de Cervantes y del Quijote.* Madrid: Editorial Plus-Ultra 1946.

Godzich, Wlad and Nicholas Spadaccini. *The Crisis of Institutionalized Literature in Spain.* Minneapolis: Prisma Institute 1988.

Goldsmith, Evelyn. *Research into Illustration: An Approach and a Review.* Cambridge: Cambridge University Press 1984.

Gombrich, E.H. *Art and Illusion: A Study in the Psychology of Pictorial Representation.* 2nd ed., rev. Princeton: Princeton University Press 1972.

– "The Visual Image: Its Place in Communication." In *The Image and the Eye: Further Studies in the Psychology of Pictorial Representation,* 137–61. Ithaca: Cornell University Press 1982.

González Palencia, Angel. *Las ediciones académicas del* Quijote. Madrid: Revista de Archivos, Bibliotecas y Museos 1947.

Gorak, Jan. *The Making of the Modern Canon: Genesis and Crisis of a Literary Idea.* London and Atlantic Highlands, NJ: Athlone 1991.

Goya y el espíritu de la ilustración. Madrid: Museo del Prado 1988.

Greer, Margaret Rich. "La vida es sueño – ¿o risa?: Calderón Parodies the *Auto.*" Paper read at the Twelfth Annual Golden Age Spanish Drama Symposium, El Paso, Texas, Mar. 1992.

Guiffrey, J.J. "Charles Coypel et l'Histoire de Don Quichotte." *Nouvelles Archives de l'Art Français* 3, no. 3 (1887): 249.

Guillory, John. "The Ideology of Canon-Formation: T.S. Eliot and Cleanth Brooks." In *Canons,* ed. Robert von Hallberg, 337–62. Chicago: University of Chicago Press 1984.

– *Cultural Capital: The Problem of Literary Canon Formation.* Chicago: University of Chicago Press 1993.

Gutiérrez, Jesús. "Mayans y su actualidad: retórica e historia literaria." *Dieciocho* 10, no. 2 (1987): 97–106.

Habermas, Jürgen. *The Structural Transformation of the Public Sphere: An Inquiry into a Category of Bourgeois Society.* Trans. Thomas Burger with Frederick Lawrence. Cambridge: MIT Press 1991.

Hagstrum, Jean H. *The Sister Arts: The Tradition of Literary Pictorialism and English Poetry from Dryden to Gray.* Chicago: University of Chicago Press 1987.

Hall, James. *Dictionary of Subjects and Symbols in Art.* New York: Harper and Row 1974.

Halsband, Robert. *The "Rape of the Lock" and Its Illustrations 1714–1896.* Oxford: Clarendon Press 1980.

– "The Rococo in England: Book Illustrators, Mainly Gravelot and Bentley." *Burlington Magazine* 127, no. 993 (Dec. 1985): 870–80.

Hammelmann, Hanns. "Two Eighteenth-Century Frontispieces." *Journal of the Warburg and Courtauld Institutes* 31 (1968): 448–9.

- "John Vanderbank's *Don Quixote.*" *Master Drawings* 7, no. 1 (1969): 3–15.
- and T.S.R. Boase. *Book Illustrators in the Eighteenth Century.* New Haven and London: Yale University Press 1975.

Hartau, Johannes. *Don Quijote in der Kunst: Wandlungen einer Symbolfigur.* Berlin: Gebr. Mann Verlag 1987.

Harthan, John. *The History of the Illustrated Book: The Western Tradition.* London: Thames and Hudson 1981.

Hauser, Arnold. *Rococo, Classicism, Romanticism.* Vol. 3 of *The Social History of Art.* Trans. Stanley Godman. New York: Vintage 1958.

Heers, Jacques. *Carnavales y fiestas de locos.* Trans. Xavier Riu i Camps. Barcelona: Ediciones Península 1988.

Helman, Edith. *Trasmundo de Goya.* Madrid: Revista de Occidente 1963.
- *Jovellanos y Goya.* Madrid: Taurus 1970.

Henares Cuéllar, Ignacio. *La teoría de las artes plásticas en España en la segunda mitad del siglo XVIII.* Granada: Universidad de Granada 1977.

Herr, Richard. *The Eighteenth-Century Revolution in Spain.* Princeton: Princeton University Press 1958.

Herrero-García, Miguel. *Estimaciones literarias del siglo XVII.* Madrid: Edición Voluntad 1980.

Hodnett, Edward. *Image and Text: Studies in the Illustration of English Literature.* London: Scolar Press 1982.

Hofer, Philip. "*Don Quixote* and the Illustrators." *Dolphin* 4, no. 2 (Winter 1941): 135–43.

Hollstein, F.W.H. *Dutch and Flemish Etchings, Engravings, Woodcuts, ca. 1450–1700.* Ed. K.G. Boon. Vol. 23. Amsterdam: Van Gendt 1980.

Houfe, Simon. *The Dictionary of British Book Illustrations and Caricaturists 1800–1914.* Suffolk: Baron Publishing 1978.

Icaza, Francisco A. de. *El Quijote durante tres siglos.* Madrid: Imprenta de Fortanet 1918.

Ife, B.W. *Reading and Fiction in Golden-Age Spain: A Platonist Critique and Some Picaresque Replies.* Cambridge: Cambridge University Press 1985.

Ilie, Paul. "Cadalso and the Epistemology of Madness." *Dieciocho* 9 (1986): 174–87.

Ivins, William Mills Jr. *Prints and Visual Communication.* New York: DaCapo Press 1969.

Jamieson, I. *Charles-Antoine Coypel: premier peintre de Louis XV et auteur dramatique (1694–1752).* Paris: Librairie Hachette 1930.

Jauss, Hans Robert. *Toward an Aesthetic of Reception.* Trans. Timothy Bahti. Minneapolis: University of Minnesota Press 1982.

Jestin, Loftus. *The Answer to the Lyre: Richard Bentley's Illustrations for Thomas Gray's Poems.* Philadelphia: University of Pennsylvania Press 1990.

Kermode, Frank. *The Classic: Literary Images of Permanence and Change.* New York: Viking 1975.

Kernan, Alvin. *Samuel Johnson and the Impact of Print.* Princeton: Princeton University Press 1989.

Knapp, Lewis Mansfield. *Tobias Smollett: Doctor of Men and Manners.* New York: Russell and Russell 1963.

Knowles, Edwin B. "Cervantes and English Literature." In *Cervantes across the Centuries,* ed. Angel Flores and M.J. Bernadete, 277–303. New York: Gordian Press 1969.

Kosove, Joan Lynn Pataky. *The "Comedia lacrimosa" and Spanish Romantic Drama (1773–1865).* London: Tamesis 1977.

Krauss, Werner. *Miguel de Cervantes: Leben und Werk.* Neuwied and West Berlin: Hermann Luchterhand Verlag GmbH 1966.

Lafuente Ferrari, Enrique. *Los caprichos de Goya.* Barcelona: Gustavo Gili 1978.

Lambropoulos, Vassilis. *Literature as National Institution: Studies in the Politics of Modern Greek Criticism.* Princeton: Princeton University Press 1988.

Langer, Suzanne K. "Deceptive Analogies: Species and Real Relationships among the Arts." In *Problems of Art: Ten Philosophical Lectures,* 75–89. New York: Charles Scribner's 1957.

Lee, Rensselaer W. *Ut Pictura Poesis: The Humanistic Theory of Painting.* New York: W.W. Norton 1967.

León Tello, Francisco José, and María M. Virginia Sanz Sanz. *La estética académica española en el siglo XVIII: Real Academia de Bellas Artes de San Carlos de Valencia.* Valencia: Diputación Provincial 1979.

– *Tratados neoclásicos españoles de pintura y escultura.* Valencia: C. Nácher 1980.

Lessing, Gotthold Ephraim. *Laokoon, oder über die Grenzen der Malerei und Poesie.* Stuttgart: Philipp Reclam 1980.

Lindsay, Jack. *Hogarth: His Art and His World.* London: Hart-Davis, Macgibbon 1977.

Lipking, Lawrence. *The Ordering of the Arts in Eighteenth-Century England.* Princeton: Princeton University Press 1970.

López Estrada, Francisco. "Las ilustraciones de la *Galatea,* edición de Sancha, Madrid, 1784." *Revista bibliográfica y documental* 2, nos. 1–2 (enero–julio 1948): 171–4.

López Molina, Luis. "Una visión dieciochesca del *Quijote.*" *Anales cervantinos* 16 (1977): 97–107.

Lo Ré, A.G. "More on the Sadness of Don Quixote: The First Known Quixote Illustration, Paris, 1618." *Cervantes* 9 (Spring 1989): 75–83.

– "A New First: An Illustration of Don Quixote as 'Le Capitaine de Carnaval,' Leipzig, 1614." *Cervantes* 10 (Fall 1990): 95–100.

– "The Second Edition of Thomas Shelton's *Don Quixote,* Part I: A Reassessment of the Dating Problem." *Cervantes* 11 (1991): 99–116.

Lukács, Georg. *The Theory of the Novel.* Trans. Anna Bostock. Cambridge: MIT Press 1971.

McClelland, I.L. *The Origins of the Romantic Movement in Spain.* Liverpool: Institute of Hispanic Studies 1937.

Madariaga, Salvador. *Guía del lector del Quijote: ensayo psicológico sobre el Quijote.* Madrid: Espasa Calpe 1976.

Malraux, André. *Saturn: An Essay on Goya.* Trans. C.W. Chilton. London: Phaidon Press 1957.

Mandel, Oscar. "The Function of the Norm in *Don Quixote*." *Modern Philology* 55 (Feb. 1958): 154–5.

Marías, Julián. *La España posible en tiempo de Carlos III*. Madrid: Sociedad de Estudios y Publicaciones 1963.

Markley, Robert. "Sentimentality as Performance: Shaftesbury, Sterne and the Theatrics of Virtue." In *The New Eighteenth Century*, ed. Felicity Nussbaum and Laura Brown, 210–30. New York: Methuen 1987.

Martín Moran, José Manuel. "La función del narrador múltiple en el *Quijote* de 1615." *Anales cervantinos* 30 (1992): 9–65.

Mayer, August L. *Francisco de Goya*. Trans. Robert West. London: J.M. Dent and Sons 1924.

Mayor, A. Hyatt. *Prints and People: A Social History of Printed Pictures*. Princeton: Princeton University Press 1980.

Meist, Michel. *The Art of Illustration*. New York: Rizzoli 1984.

Mestre, Antonio. Prólogo. In *Vida de Miguel de Cervantes Saavedra* by Gregorio Mayans y Siscar, vii–xciii. Madrid: Espasa Calpe 1972.

– *El mundo intelectual de Mayans*. Valencia: Publicaciones del Ayuntamiento de Oliva 1978.

– *Mayans y la España de la ilustración*. Madrid: Espasa Calpe 1990.

Mitchell, W.J.T. *Iconology: Image, Text, Ideology*. Chicago: University of Chicago Press 1986.

Morel-Fatio, A. "Un érudit espagnol au XVIIIᵉ siècle D. Gregorio Mayans y Siscar." *Bulletin Hispanique* 17, no. 3 (July–Sept. 1915): 157–226.

Morón Arroyo, Ciriaco. "La retórica de Mayans: para un contexto." *Dieciocho* 10, no. 2 (1987): 151–8.

Mullan, John. *Sentiments and Sociability: The Language of Feeling in the Eighteenth Century*. Oxford: Clarendon Press 1988.

Munro, Thomas. *The Arts and Their Interrelations*. Cleveland: Press of Western Reserve University 1967.

Nabokov, Vladimir. *Lectures on* Don Quixote. Ed. Fredson Bowers. New York: Harcourt Brace Jovanovich 1983.

Navarro, Alberto. *El Quijote español del siglo XVII*. Madrid: Ediciones Rialp 1964.

Nelson, Lowry Jr. "Chaos and Parody: Reflections on Anthony Close's *The Romantic Approach to Don Quixote*." *Cervantes* 2, no. 1 (Spring 1982): 89–95.

Nördstrom, Folke. *Goya, Saturn and Melancholy: Studies in the Art of Goya*. Stockholm: Alquist and Wiksell 1962.

Omberg, Hildegard. *William Hogarth's Portrait of Captain Coram: Studies on Hogarth's Outlook around 1740*. Acta Universitatis Upsaliensis, no. 12. Uppsala 1974.

Páez Ríos, Elena. *Antología del grabado español: 500 años de su arte en España*. Madrid 1952.

Parr, James A. *Don Quixote: An Anatomy of Subversive Discourse*. Newark, Del.: Juan de la Cuesta – Hispanic Monographs 1988.

Paulson, Ronald. *Hogarth: His Life, Art, and Times*. Vol. 1. New Haven: Yale University Press 1971.

– "The Tradition of Comic Illustration from Hogarth to Cruikshank." *Princeton University Library Chronicle* 35, nos. 1–2 (1973–74): 61–92.

– *Book and Painting: Shakespeare, Milton and the Bible.* Knoxville: University of Tennessee Press 1982.

– *Hogarth: The "Modern Moral Subject" (1697–1732).* Vol. 1. New Brunswick, NJ: Rutgers University Press 1991.

Pellicer, J.L. "Las ilustraciones del *Quijote.*" *La Ilustración artística* 14, no. 680 (enero 1895): 21–7.

Pellissier, Robert E. *The Neo-Classic Movement in Spain during the Eighteenth Century.* Leland Stanford Junior University Publications University Series, no. 30. Stanford: Stanford University Press 1918.

Percas de Ponseti, Helena. *Cervantes the Writer and Painter of Don Quijote.* Columbia: University of Missouri Press 1988.

Pérez Magallón, Jesús. *En torno a las ideas literarias de Mayans.* Alicante: Instituto de Cultura "Juan Gil-Albert" 1991.

Peset, Vicent. *Gregorio Mayàns i la cultura de la il.lustració.* Barcelona: Curial 1975.

Piper, David. *The Image of the Poet: British Poets and Their Portraits.* Oxford: Clarendon Press 1982.

Plaza Escudero, Luis María. *Catálogo de la colección cervantina Sedó.* 3 vols. Barcelona: José Porter 1953.

Praz, Mario. *Mnemosyne: el paralelismo entre la literatura y las artes visuales.* Trans. Ricardo Pochtar. Madrid: Taurus 1979.

Predmore, Richard. *El mundo del* Quijote. Madrid: Insula 1958.

Ray, Gordon N. *The Illustrator and the Book in England from 1790–1914.* Oxford and New York: Oxford University Press 1976.

Real Academia de Bellas Artes de Madrid. *La Real Calcografía de Madrid: Goya y sus contemporáneos.* Madrid: Calcografía Nacional 1984.

Real de la Riva, César. "Historia de la crítica e interpretación de la obra de Cervantes." *Revista de filología española* 32 (1948): 107–50.

Riley, E.C. *Cervantes's Theory of the Novel.* Oxford: Clarendon Press 1962.

Río y Rico, Gabriel Martín del. *Catálogo bibliográfico de la sección de Cervantes de la Biblioteca Nacional.* Madrid: Tipografía de la "Revista de Archivos, Bibliotecas y Museos" 1930.

Ríus y de Llosellas, Leopoldo. *Bibliografía crítica de las obras de Miguel de Cervantes Saavedra.* 3 vols. Madrid: M. Murillo 1895–1905.

Romera-Navarro, Miguel. *Interpretación pictórica del Quijote por Doré.* Madrid: Consejo Superior de Investigaciones Científicas 1946.

Rosen, George. *Madness in Society: Chapters in the Historical Sociology of Mental Illness.* Chicago: University of Chicago Press 1968.

Rosenblum, Robert. *Transformations in Late Eighteenth-Century Art.* Princeton: Princeton University Press 1967.

Ruiz Lasala, Inocencio. *Joaquín Ibarra y Marín (1725–1785).* Zaragoza: San Francisco 1968.

Russell, Peter. "*Don Quijote* as a Funny Book." *Modern Language Review* 64 (1969): 312–26.

Saff, Donald, and Deli Sacilotto. *Printmaking: History and Process.* New York: Holt, Rinehart and Winston 1978.

Said, Edward W. *Orientalism.* New York: Vintage 1979.

– *The World, the Text, and the Critic.* Cambridge: Harvard University Press 1983.

Salgado, Linda Ann Friedman. "Imitaciones del Quijote en la España del siglo XVIII." PhD. Ann Arbor: University Microfilms International 1981.

Sambricio, Valentín de. *José del Castillo.* Madrid: Consejo Superior de Investigaciones Científicas 1957.

Sánchez Cantón, F.J. "El libro ilustrado bajo Carlos III y Carlos IV." In *Catálogo de la exposición del libro español en Lisboa,* xi–xxxi. Madrid: Instituto Nacional del Libro Español 1946.

Sarrailh, Jean. *La España ilustrada de la segunda mitad del siglo XVIII.* Mexico City: Fondo de Cultura Económica 1981.

Sayre, Eleanor A. *The Changing Image: Prints by Francisco Goya.* Boston: Museum of Fine Arts 1974.

Schapiro, Meyer. *Words and Pictures: On the Literal and Symbolic in the Illustration of a Text.* The Hague: Mouton 1973.

Schevill, Rudolph. "On the Influence of Spanish Literature upon England in the Early Seventeenth Century." *Romanische Forschungen* 20 (1907): 604–34.

Schmidt, Rachel. "Visions of Don Quijote: The Pictorial Canonization of the Text through Illustrated Editions (1657–1863)." PhD. Ann Arbor: University Microfilms International 1992.

– "The Romancing of *Don Quixote:* Spatial Innovation and Visual Interpretation in the Imagery of Johannot, Doré and Daumier," *Word and Image* 13, no. 1 (Apr.–June 1997).

Schnapper, Antoine. "A Propos de deux nouvelles acquisitions: 'Le Chef-d'œuvre d'un muet' ou la tentative de Charles Coypel." *La Revue du Louvre et des Musées de France* 18, nos. 4–5 (1968): 253–64.

Schottenloher, Karl. *Books and the Western World: A Cultural History.* Trans. Wiliam D. Boyd and Irmgard H. Wolff. Jefferson, NC: McFarland 1989.

Sebold, Russell P. *Cadalso: el primer romántico "europeo" de España.* Madrid: Gredos 1974.

– *Trayectoria del romanticismo español.* Barcelona: Crítica 1983.

– *Descubrimiento y fronteras del neoclasicismo español.* Madrid: Cátedra 1985.

– *El rapto de la mente: poética y poesía dieciochescas.* Barcelona: Anthropos 1989.

Shaftesbury, Third Earl of (Anthony Ashley Cooper). *An Inquiry concerning Virtue, or Merit.* Ed. David Walford. Manchester: Manchester University Press 1977.

Skinner, John. "*Don Quixote* in Eighteenth-Century England: A Study in Reader Response." *Cervantes* 7, no. 1 (Spring 1987): 45–57.

Slythe, R. Margaret. *The Art of Illustration 1750–1900.* London: Library Association 1970.

Smith, Gilbert. "El cervantismo en las polémicas literarias del siglo XVIII." In *Cervantes: su obra y su mundo. Actas del I Congreso Internacional sobre Cervantes*, 1031–5. Madrid 1981.

Spitzer, Leo. "Linguistic Perspectivism in the *Don Quijote*." In *Linguistics and Literary History*, 41–85. Princeton: Princeton University Press 1967.

Stallybrass, Peter, and Allon White. *The Politics and Poetics of Transgression*. Ithaca: Cornell University Press 1986.

Steiner, Wendy. *The Colors of Rhetoric: Problems in the Relation between Modern Literature and Painting*. Chicago: University of Chicago Press 1982.

– *Pictures of Romance: Form against Context in Painting and Literature*. Chicago: University of Chicago Press 1988.

Subirats, Eduardo. *La ilustración insuficiente*. Madrid: Taurus 1981.

Sutherland, Madeline. *Mass Culture in the Age of the Enlightenment: The Blindman's Ballads of Eighteenth-Century Spain*. New York: Peter Lang 1991.

Taylor, Gary. *Reinventing Shakespeare: A Cultural History from the Restoration to the Present*. New York: Oxford University Press 1989.

Tomlinson, Janis A. *Francisco Goya: The Tapestry Cartoons and Early Career at the Court of Madrid*. Cambridge: Cambridge University Press 1989.

Torrente Ballester, Gonzalo. *El Quijote como juego y otros trabajos críticos*. Barcelona: Ediciones Destino 1984.

Trusler, John. *The Works of William Hogarth*. 2 vols. London: E.T. Brain, nd.

Unamuno, Miguel de. "El Caballero de la Triste Figura – ensayo iconológico." *Obras completas*, 1:911–25. Madrid: Escelicer 1966.

Vidart, Luis. *Los biógrafos de Cervantes en el siglo XVIII*. Madrid 1886.

Waterhouse, Ellis. *Painting in Britain. 1530–1790*. Pelican History of Art. Baltimore: Penguin 1953.

Watt, Ian. *The Rise of the Novel: Studies in Defoe, Richardson and Fielding*. Berkeley and Los Angeles: University of California Press 1957.

Weitenkampf, Frank. *The Illustrated Book*. Cambridge: Harvard University Press 1938.

Wellek, René. "The Concept of Romanticism in Literary History." *Comparative Literature* 1 (1949): 1–23, 147–72.

West, Cornel. *Keeping Faith: Philosophy and Race in America*. New York: Routledge 1993.

Wolf, Reva. *Goya and the Satirical Print in England and on the Continent, 1730–1850*. Boston: Boston College Museum of Art 1991.

Ziolkowski, Eric J. *The Sanctification of Don Quixote: From Hidalgo to Priest*. University Park: Pennsylvania State University Press 1991.

Index